I0560273

1862

1862

The Bartender's Guide

BEN HAMMER

1862: The Bartender's Guide

By Ben Hammer

This edition includes a modern adaptation of two original works: *How to Mix Drinks* by Jerry Thomas and *A Manual for the Manufacture of Cordials, Liquors, Fancy Syrups, etc., etc.* by Christian Shultz, originally published in 1862 by Dick & Fitzgerald, Publishers, New York.

ISBN 979-8-9994501-0-4

This print edition © 2025, Ben Hammer. All rights reserved

Cover design by Solomon Augusteyn

Special thanks to Bobby Green of the 1933 Group for allowing photography at Oldfield's Liquor Room, Los Angeles, CA.

Table of Contents

INTRODUCTION

ABOUT THE AUTHOR OF THIS PUBLICATION

When I first decided to learn the craft of bartending, my first step, like many others have done, was to enroll in a bartending school. I had recently lost my job due to my employer shutting down their company, and I needed something fast and flexible. At that time, I knew virtually nothing about beer, wine or cocktails. My knowledge was limited to the drinks I had tried in bars, which was not much: Rum and Coke, Jack and Coke, Midori Sours, beer and Mai Tais.

For someone such as myself, bartending school was the perfect option. I learned what the different types of alcoholic spirits were, along with a little bit of background history and a primer on the various laws relating to alcohol service. I learned the basics of how a bar is setup, the tools and how to use them. I learned how to speed pour, how to take an order and upsell. Last, but not least, I had to learn and pass a test in preparing a whole stack of "standard" drink recipes. In the bartending school I attended, we didn't learn the use of any fresh ingredients. Fruits and herbs (plastic ones in school) were garnishes and nothing more. We used bottles of water that were colored to resemble the spirits they represented. This meant we never got to taste the concoctions we were learning, but that was no big deal. They were just recipe formulas, and the primary job skill we were learning was how to make drinks quickly. I was set!

Immediately after getting my certificate for bartending, proud and cocky, I volunteered to bartend at a friend's party. As I handed out drink after drink, I started to notice that I wasn't getting the enthusiasm from my friends that I had expected. At least they were polite, which is more than could be expected from real customers. I started tasting my drinks and was very disappointed to find that my drinks sucked!

Now I don't want to talk down about bartending schools. The school I attended provided me with a solid foundation for the job. The problem with many bartending schools is that they prepare new bartenders for quick employment at typical bartending jobs. Unfortunately, the drinks at your average restaurant, bar or nightclub venues are also typically average. Making great cocktails is a secondary consideration compared to organization, speed mixing and sales techniques.

By now, you're probably wondering why someone like me would even try to be a bartender. Trust me, I was thinking the same thing at the time. I had no knowledge, no personal history or love for the craft. I was simply looking for a new, portable job to replace the one I had lost. I even tried juggling (non-breakable) items around the house, wondering if I could get one of those good paying "flair bartender" jobs. I finally came to the realization that if I ever hoped to get a decent bartending job, I needed to learn how to make better cocktails. I started searching on the web for different recipes. As I browsed thousands of different recipes from all sorts of web sites, I also came to the conclusion that I had no idea how to tell a good cocktail from a bad one. I was basically picking blindly, hoping that I would strike gold. It was then that I decided I needed to give up on memorizing new recipes and learn what it is that makes a good cocktail good. After scouring the internet for reviews, I decided to buy some books by Dale DeGroff, Gary "Gaz" Regan and Tony Abou-Ganim. These books changed everything for me! I learned about the history of cocktails. I learned mindfulness behind the bar. I learned how to make quality cocktails from scratch and how to adapt cocktails for use behind a busy bar without sacrificing too much speed. For the first time in my life, I realized that cocktails can actually be amazing and delicious! To finish off my personal story, I went on to find work as a bartender. I was very fortunate to be working in Los Angeles, where there are many amazing bartenders to watch, learn and sample from. I worked my way up from being the new guy fresh out of bartending school to a lead bartender in a couple of restaurants and even a teacher for new bartenders. I was even fortunate enough to have one of my recipe's selected to be published in an edition of Gary "Gaz" Regan's "101 Best New Cocktails" annual book series. Even more amazing to me was to walk into a random restaurant a few years later while traveling out of state to find my cocktail featured on the restaurant's cocktail menu. Much more than pride, I experienced a great sense of awe and appreciation towards this restaurant, along with a great sense of accomplishment coming from zero knowledge to having other people honor my work by offering it to their customers. What better compliment could any bartender ever hope for?

Today, I am no longer bartending, as I have moved back into my chosen profession, but I still share a great love for the craft of creating cocktails. I often tell my friends and wife that after I retire, I hope I can find a cozy little bar somewhere where I can spend my retirement being a crazy old bartender making drinks for my customers from seasonal ingredients at my own pace.

ABOUT THIS BOOK

In learning about cocktails, I heard over and over about "the father of American mixology", Jerry Thomas and his famous landmark book from 1862: "How to Mix Drinks or The Bon-Vivant's Companion". Published originally with its companion book "A Manual for the Manufacture of Cordials, Liquors, Fancy Syrups, etc. etc.", this book was a first due to its inclusion of the cocktail. This book has been quoted as an inspiration to some of the best and most influential creators of cocktails of our time.

Oddly enough, as much as this book is talked about, I found it difficult to find a good copy of it. Online availability seemed to be limited to scanned pages and/or scans that had been put together with poor quality character recognition. When I finally got an e-book copy of the book, I also discovered that I didn't understand the measurements! Gills, wine-glasses and such were completely unfamiliar to me. I decided to transcribe the book and adapt it to more conventional terms that I could understand.

I do not consider myself a hardcore cocktail or history buff… I simply like to know how things work. As I got further and further into the process, I realized that this was a considerable amount of work just to satisfy my curiosity about a book that I have seen mentioned so many times. I also realized that there are probably many others who have experienced the same desire and frustration of trying to find, read and understand this book. And so, I transitioned from making massive notes for my personal use, to trying to put this book in an easy-to-read format for those whom, like myself, wish to read and learn from this historical work.

There were subsequent editions published after this 1862 edition, but I have chosen to limit my work to this original edition and its companion manual.

You can find many resources online and elsewhere that have individual recipes that have been adapted, but I am glad to have read through the original. As much as I have seen others mention the lack of information on specifics of preparing each drink, I still feel there is a lot of information to be learned by reading the whole work, rather than individual recipes or "opinioned" adaptations found elsewhere. In David Wondrich's fantastic book "Imbibe!" he describes a little of his creative process and decision making for his book. When describing his decision to not include all of the recipes and rather to go the extra mile with research, adaptation and opinion, he mentions that he decided not to be "like some electronic-age Bartleby, narrowly copying another's work and keeping his thoughts on the matter mostly to himself" *(Wondrich, David. Imbibe! Updated and Revised Edition (pp. 3-4). Penguin Publishing Group. Kindle Edition)*. The resulting book that Mr. Wondrich published is excellent and highly worth reading. I, on the other hand, still desired to have a copy of Jerry Thomas' original book which included ALL of the original recipes, as true to the original work as possible, and so I take up the role of Bartleby, and have attempted to write this transcription in a way that preserves the original feel of the material, while adapting it to a more useable format. It will obviously not be an exact word for word copy, and I recommend getting a copy for the original for the historically curious. This re-work of Jerry Thomas' book contains as little as possible of my own opinions and/or interpretation of drinks, whether it be on amounts or preparation.

ON INGREDIENTS AND TECHNIQUES

This adaptation includes every recipe included in the original 1862 edition (236 recipes in the Jerry Thomas' book and 463 in Christian Shultz's). This includes recipes that have ingredients that are no longer available, unknown (by me), or not considered safe for human consumption. I feel that last phrase should be repeated: *Some of the ingredients in this book have been determined to be unsafe for human consumption, either in their raw form, or through improper preparation.* Please do not make any recipes in which you have not thoroughly familiarized yourself with the ingredients and preparation techniques!

In addition, I must mention that many of the recipes in the second half of this book require a license to produce in the United States and are illegal to make otherwise. Please familiarize yourself with the laws on producing and rectifying spirits in your area. For convenience, I have annotated every recipe title that requires distilling with **[D]**.

Many details of these drinks and their preparation are lacking. I can make an educated guess, but I would often be wrong. I did, in fact, start out by inserting my own interpretation on how to prepare each drink, until I read some other books, such as "Imbibe!" by David Wondrich, which does an excellent job of researching, testing and reconstructing both the history and likely preparation of many of these drinks, in addition to adding suggestions for combining these drinks with modern sensibilities and techniques. Much better authors, historians and bartenders than I have already produced much in the way of both determining how these drinks were originally prepared, and adapting them for modern use. I highly recommend that you do not stop at this book, and continue on your journey by reading from some of the masters. "The Craft of the Cocktail" and "The Essential Cocktail" by Dale DeGroff remain my favorite books on cocktails, by which our current revival of quality and creative craft cocktails should be ever-grateful to. Gary "Gaz" Regan has also published excellent materials on how to be a better bartender, not only in crafting beverages, but also in customer service and professional behavior. Compared to the aforementioned authors and many other great ones out there, I am merely a hobbyist, and you would be much better served to learn from masters of the trade.

There is much debate on just about every aspect of the drinks contained in this book. From ingredients, to techniques, origins and even measurements (the reason I started this project was because I couldn't understand the typography and many of the quantities). I have chosen to list the quantities as close to as written as I could determine. There are sure to be inaccuracies (when is a quart not a quart? You'd be surprised). However, the absence of exact quantities and preparation instruction leaves room for one area of bartending that I feel is very important, and that is taste and experimentation. Pre-mixed drinks and even newer technologies such as robotic bartending are not going away. Making a fantastic individual cocktail, however, still requires some personalized care and attention. Your fresh fruits and herbs are always going to have a little bit of variation from one batch to the next, and this variation needs to be accounted for when preparing a drink, and the drink should be tailored for the individual tastes of the person who will consume it. Even if we did know and possess every single spirit and ingredient used in 1862 when this book was originally published, there still may be something newer on the market that makes that recipe pop in a way that couldn't have been achieved 150 years ago. I hope that readers will use this book as not only a historical reference, but as inspiration for creating wonderful drinks, whether new or classic concoctions.

I hope you enjoy my adaptation and wish you many fantastic cocktails!

Ben Hammer

MEASUREMENTS OF THE 1800'S

The original text of this book contained references to measurements that are no longer in common use. I have converted them to modern equivalents to make this book more practical. Of course, along with the lack of information on many other aspects of this book, there are different opinions on the types of measurements used here. I refer you back to my earlier comment on the value of experimentation and tasting when creating these drinks. However, for the historically curious, here are the original measurements and their modern equivalents as best as I can determine:

SPIRITS

Proof Spirit = 50% ABV (100 Proof)

BAR MEASUREMENTS

1 barspoon = ½ teaspoon

1 teaspoon = approximately 25 drops of liquid

1 Tablespoon - ½ ounce (3 teaspoons)

4 tablespoons = ½ gill (1 Wine Glass)

Pony = 1 ounce

Jigger = 2 ounces

Wine Glass = 2 ounces

Gill = 4 ounces

Pint = 16 ounces

Quart Black Bottle = approx. 1.5 pints

Quart = 2 pints

Gallon = 4 quarts

DRY MEASUREMENTS

1 pound Sugar = approximately:

    2 cups of granulated Sugar

    2 ¼ - 2 ⅓ cups of Brown Sugar

    2 ¾ cups un-sifted Powdered Sugar or Confectioners' Sugar

FROM THE LATTER HALF OF THIS BOOK

VOLUME MEASURES OF THE UNITED STATES (DISTILLED WATER)

1 gallon = 8 lbs. = 2 halves

½ gallon = 4 lbs. = 2 quarts

1 quart = 2 lbs. = 2 pints

1 pint = 1 lb. = 4 gills = 16 fl oz

½ pint = ½ lb. = 2 gills = 8 fl oz

1 ounce = 8 fl drams

WEIGHT MEASURES

1 pound = 16 ounces = 453.6g

½ pound = 8 ounces = 226.8g

¼ pound = 4 ounces = 113.4g

1 ounce = 8 drachms = 28.35g

1 drachm = 60 grains = 3.54 grams

1 scruple = 20 grains = 1.18 grams

1 grain = .06g

HOW TO MIX DRINKS

OR

THE BON-VIVANT'S COMPANION

Modern Adaptation by Ben Hammer.
Original 1862 edition by "Professor" Jerry Thomas

PREFACE

In all ages of the world and in all countries, men have indulged in "social drinks." They have always possessed themselves of some popular beverage apart from water and those of the breakfast and Tea table. Whether it is judicious that mankind should continue to indulge in such things, or whether it would be wiser to abstain from all enjoyments of that character, it is not our province to decide. We leave that question to the moral philosopher. We simply contend that a relish for "social drinks" is universal; that those drinks exist in greater variety in the United States than in any other country in the world; and that he, therefore, who proposes to impart to these drinks not only the most palatable but the most wholesome characteristics of which they may be made susceptible, is a genuine public benefactor. That is exactly our object in introducing this little volume to the public. We do not propose to persuade any man to drink, for instance, a punch or a julep, or a cocktail, who has never happened to make the acquaintance of those refreshing articles under circumstances calculated to induce more intimate relation; but we do propose to instruct those whose "intimate relations" in question render them somewhat fastidious, in the daintiest fashions thereunto pertaining.

We very well remember seeing one day in London, in the rear of the Bank of England, a small drinking saloon that had been set up by a peripatetic American, at the door of which was placed a board covered with the unique titles of the American mixed drinks supposed to be prepared within that limited establishment. The "Connecticut Eye-Openers" and "Alabama Fog-Cutters" together with the "lightning-smashes" and the "thunderbolt-cocktails," created profound sensation in the crowd assembled to peruse the Nectarian bill of fare, if they did not produce custom. It struck us, then, that a list of all the social drinks -- the composite beverages, if we may call them so -- of America, would really be one of the curiosities of jovial literature; and that if it was combined with a catalog of the mixtures common to other nations, and made practically useful by the addition of a concise description of the various processes for "brewing" each, it would be a "blessing to mankind." There would be no excuse for imbibing, with such a book at hand, the "villainous compounds" of bar-keeping Gotha and Vandala, who know no more of the amenities of bon vivant existence than a Hottentot can know of the bouquet of champagne.

"There's philosophy," says Father Tom in the drama, "even in a jug of punch." We claim the credit of "philosophy teaching by example," then to no ordinary extent in the composition of this volume; for our index exhibits the title of eighty-six different kinds of punches, together with a universe of cobblers, juleps, bitters, cups, slings, shrubs, etc., each and all of which the reader is carefully educated how to concoct in the choicest manner. For the perfection of this education, the name, alone, of *Jerry Thomas* is a sufficient guarantee. He has traveled Europe and America in search of all that is recondite in this branch of the spirit art. He has been the Jupiter Olympus of the bar at the Metropolitan Hotel in this city. He was the presiding deity at the Planter's House, St. Louis. He has been the proprietor of one of the most *recherche* saloons in New Orleans as well as in New York. His very name is synonymous in the lexicon of mixed drinks, with all that is rare and original. To the "Wine Press," edited by F.S. Cozzens, Esq., we are indebted for the composition of several valuable punches, and among them we may particularize the celebrated "Nuremberg," and the equally famous "Philadelphia Fish House" punch. The rest we owe to the inspiration of *Jerry Thomas* himself, and as he is as inexorable as the Medes and Persians in his principle that no excellent drink can be made out of anything but excellent materials, we conceive that we are safe in asserting that whatever may be prepared after his instructions will be able to speak eloquently for itself. "Good wine needs no bush," Shakespeare tells us and over one of Jerry's mixtures eulogy is quite as redundant.

PUNCHES

Punch Jelly • *BRANDY PUNCHES* • *WHISKEY PUNCHES* • *GIN PUNCHES*
WINE PUNCHES • *FANCY PUNCHES* • *MILK PUNCHES AND NOGGS*
ARRACK PUNCHES

"To make a punch of any sort in perfection, the ambrosial essence of the Lemon must be extracted by rubbing lumps of Sugar on the rind, which breaks the delicate little vessels that contain the essence, and at the same time absorbs it. This, and making the mixture sweet and strong, using Tea instead of water, and thoroughly amalgamating all the compounds, so that the taste of neither the bitter, the sweet, the spirit, nor the element, shall be perceptible one over the other, is the grand secret, only to be acquired by practice.

In making hot toddy, or hot punch, you must put in the spirits before the water, while in cold punch, grog, etc., it should be the other way around.

The precise portions of spirit and water, or even of the acidity and sweetness, can have no general rule, as scarcely two persons make punch alike." – Jerry Thomas

PUNCH JELLY

- 1.5 oz Isinglass (Gelatin)
- 4 oz water
- 1 pint Hot Punch

Make a good bowl of punch, such as Punch a la Ford (on page 29). To every pint of punch, add 1 ½ ounces of Isinglass gelatin that has been dissolved in 4 ounces of water. Add this gelatin mixture to the punch while still hot, and then fill your molds. Let stand and do not disturb until the jelly is completely set.

Orange, Lemon, Lime, and other flavors may be converted into punch jelly for the evening, taking care to reduce the portion of the acid prescribed in making the sherbet.

NOTE: THE TERM SHERBET IN THIS BOOK REFERS TO A SYRUP MADE FROM COMBINING FRUIT OR HERBS WITH SUGAR AND WATER.

Jerry Thomas: "This preparation is a very agreeable refreshment on a cold night but should be used in moderation. The strength of the punch is so artfully concealed by its admixture with the gelatin, that many persons, particularly of the softer sex, have been tempted to partake so plentifully of it as to render them somewhat unfit for waltzing or quadrilling after supper."

BRANDY PUNCHES

Brandy Punch, Single Serving • Variation: Barbadoes Punch
Variation: West Indian Punch • Brandy Punch • Bimbo Punch • Orgeat Punch
Vanilla Punch

BRANDY PUNCH, SINGLE SERVING

- ½ ounce Raspberry Syrup (on page 309)
- 2 Tablespoons White Sugar
- 2 ounces water
- 3 ounces Brandy
- ½ small Lemon
- 2 slices of Orange
- 1 piece of Pineapple

Add ingredients to a tumbler and fill with shaved ice. Shake well and garnish with seasonal berries. Sip through a straw.

VARIATION: BARBADOES PUNCH

This is made the same as Brandy punch, but to each glass add a Tablespoon of Guava Jelly.

VARIATION: WEST INDIAN PUNCH

This is made the same as Brandy punch, but to each glass add a clove or two of Preserved Ginger, and a little bit of Ginger Syrup (on page 305).

BRANDY PUNCH
Serves 20

- 1 gallon of water
- 3 quarts of Brandy
- 8 ounces of Jamaican Rum
- 2 pounds Sugar
- Juice of 6 Lemons
- 3 Oranges, sliced
- 1 Pineapple, pared and cut up
- 4 ounces of Curaçao (on page 226)
- 8 ounces of Raspberry Syrup (on page 309)
- Seasonal Berries

Mix the materials together well in a large punch bowl with ice, and you have a splendid punch.

BIMBO PUNCH

- 1 quart Cognac Brandy
- 6 Lemons, cut into thin slices
- 1 lb. Sugar
- 1 quart boiling water

Let the Lemons steep in the Cognac for 6 hours. Remove the Lemons without squeezing. Dissolve the Sugar into the boiling water and add the hot solution to the Cognac. Let it stand to cool.

ORGEAT PUNCH

- ¾ ounce Orgeat Syrup (on page 307)
- 3 ounces Brandy
- Juice of ½ Lemon
- dash Port Wine

Add all ingredients except port wine to a large bar glass. Fill with shaved ice, then shake well. Float the port wine on top and garnish with seasonal berries. Place straw as shown in illustration for Mint julep.

VANILLA PUNCH

- 1 Tablespoon Sugar
- 2 ounces Brandy
- Juice of ¼ Lemon
- Vanilla Extract to taste
- 1-2 slices of Lemon

Add ingredients to a large bar glass. Fill with shaved ice, then shake well. Garnish with the Lemon slices and flavor with a few drops of Vanilla extract. This is a delicious drink and should be imbibed through a glass tube or a straw.

WHISKEY PUNCHES

Whiskey Punch, Single Serving • Irish Whiskey Punch • Cold Whiskey Punch
Scotch Whisky Punch • The Spread Eagle Punch • 69th Regiment Punch

WHISKEY PUNCH, SINGLE SERVING

- 2 ounces Irish Whiskey (or Scotch Whisky)
- 4 ounces boiling water
- Sugar to taste

In a small bar glass, dissolve the Sugar well with 2 ounces of the water. Pour in the whiskey and then add the rest of the water. Sweeten to taste, and garnish with a small piece of Lemon rind or a thin slice of Lemon when serving.

IRISH WHISKEY PUNCH

- Whiskey (pure)
- Water (boiling)
- Sugar
- Lemon Juice

This is the genuine Irish beverage. It is generally made with ⅓ pure whiskey, ⅔ boiling water, in which Sugar has been dissolved. If Lemon punch, the rind is rubbed on the Sugar, and a small portion of Lemon Juice is added before the whiskey is poured in.

Jerry Thomas: "Irish whiskey is not fit to drink until it is three years old. The best whiskey for this purpose is Kenshan's LL Whiskey."

COLD WHISKEY PUNCH

Jerry Thomas: "This beverage should always be made with boiling water and allowed to blend and cool for a day or two before it is put on the table. In this way, the materials get more intensely amalgamated than cold water and cold whiskey ever get. As to the beautiful mutual adaptation of cold rum and cold water, that is beyond all praise, being one of Nature's most exquisite achievements." (See Glasgow Punch on page 23)

SCOTCH WHISKY PUNCH

Steep the thin yellow shavings of Lemon Peel in the whisky, which should be Glenlivet Whisky or Islay Whisky, of the best quality. The Sugar should be dissolved in boiling water.

Jerry Thomas: "As it requires genius to make whisky punch, it would be impertinent to give proportions." (See The Spread Eagle Punch on page 11)

THE SPREAD EAGLE PUNCH

- 1 bottle Islay Whisky
- 1 bottle Monongahela Whiskey/Pennsylvania Rye Whiskey
- Lemon Peel to taste
- Sugar to taste
- Boiling water to taste

Combine the spirits, then balance out with the remaining ingredients at your discretion.

69TH REGIMENT PUNCH

- 1 oz Irish Whiskey
- 1 oz Scotch Whisky
- 1 teaspoon Sugar
- 1 piece of Lemon
- 4 oz of hot water

Combine all ingredients into an earthen mug.

Jerry Thomas: "This is a capital punch for a cold night."

GIN PUNCHES

GIN PUNCH, SINGLE SERVING

- ½ ounce of Raspberry Syrup (on page 309)
- 2 Tablespoons of White Sugar
- 2 ounces of water
- 3 ounces Gin
- ½ of a small Lemon
- 2 slices of Orange
- 1 piece of Pineapple
- Seasonal Berries for garnish

Add all ingredients to a large bar glass and fill with shaved ice. Shake well and serve garnished with seasonal berries. This drink should be sipped through a glass tube or straw.

SOYER GIN PUNCH
Credit: From a recipe by Soyer

- 8 ounces of Old Gin
- 4 ounces Maraschino Liqueur (on page 235)
- 2 Lemons
- 4 ounces of Plain White Syrup (on page 136)
- 1 quart of German Seltzer Water

Peel the rind from ½ of a Lemon, then juice both Lemons. Combine the Lemon Peel and juice with the remaining ingredients and ice well.

GIN PUNCH (FOR BOTTLING)

- 36 Lemons with smooth, not-too-thin skins
- 2 lbs. Sugar
- Boiling water
- good Gin

This Gin punch follows the same recipe as Punch a la Ford (on page on page 29), substituting a good Gin for the rum and Brandy.

Peel the Lemons, taking care to include none of the white pith. Combine with the Sugar and stir together with an oar shaped paddle for approximately 30 minutes to extract as much essential oil as possible. Pour boiling water over the sherbet (Lemon mixture) and mix well until the Sugar is completely dissolved. Cut and squeeze the Lemons, separating the juice from the seeds. Put the seeds in a separate container, pour boiling water over them and let sit until the flavorful transparent coating is removed from the seeds.

Add half the Lemon Juice to the sherbet and strain the seed liquids into the mixture as well. Taste the mixture and add either more Sugar or Lemon Juice as needed. You don't want a watery lemonade, but rather a rich fruity taste that is plenty sweet.

Now measure the Lemon mixture, and to every 3 parts of the mixture, add 1 part of Gin, stirring well. Bottle immediately and store in a cold dark place until used. At least 6 months aging in a cool atmosphere seems to improve it much.

Jerry Thomas: "This is an excellent and economical summer drink."

WINE PUNCHES

Apple Punch • Champagne Punch • Claret Punch • Sauterne Punch
Port Wine Punch • Gothic Punch • Imperial Punch • Rochester Punch
Sherry Punch • Tip-Top Punch

APPLE PUNCH

- Apples
- Lemons
- Powdered Sugar
- 1 bottle Claret Wine

In a large non-reactive bowl, place alternate layers of Apple and Lemon slices, thickly strewing Powdered Sugar over each layer, until the bowl is half filled. Pour in the wine. Cover and let stand for 6 hours. Pour through a muslin bag and send it up immediately.

CHAMPAGNE PUNCH

- 1 bottle Wine
- ½ lb. Sugar
- 1 Orange, Sliced
- 1 Lemon, juiced
- 3 slices Pineapple
- 2 ounces Raspberry Syrup (on page 309) or Strawberry Syrup (on page 310)

Combine ingredients and serve in champagne goblets. Garnish with seasonal fruits.

This can be made in any quantity by observing the proportions of the ingredients as given. Four bottles of wine is generally sufficient to make a punch for 15 people in a mixed party. For a good champagne punch, see Rocky Mountain Punch (on page 32)

CLARET PUNCH

- 1 ½ Tablespoon Sugar
- 1 slice Lemon
- 2 or 3 slices Orange
- Claret Wine

Using a large bar glass, add Sugar, Lemon and Orange. Fill with shaved ice and then pour in Claret. Shake well. Garnish with seasonal berries and place a straw in the glass. To make a larger quantity of Claret Punch, see Imperial Punch (on page 17).

SAUTERNE PUNCH
Same as Claret Punch, using Sauterne Wine instead of Claret.

PORT WINE PUNCH
Same as Claret Punch, using Port Wine instead of Claret.

GOTHIC PUNCH

Credit: From a recipe in the possession of Bayard Taylor, Esq.

Serves a party of 10

- 4 bottles (non-sparkling) Catawba Wine or Madeira Wine
- 1 bottle Claret Wine
- 3 Oranges OR 1 Pineapple
- 10 Tablespoons Sugar
- 1 bottle Champagne

Combine the wines, Sugar, and your choice of either the oranges or the Pineapple. Let this stand in a very cold place or in ice for at least one hour. Add the champagne.

IMPERIAL PUNCH

- 1 bottle Claret Wine
- 1 bottle Soda Water (on page 300)
- 4 Tablespoons Powdered White Sugar
- ¼ teaspoon grated Nutmeg
- 1 ounce Maraschino Liqueur (on page 235)
- About ½ pound of ice
- 3 or 4 slices of Cucumber rind

Put all ingredients into a bowl or pitcher and mix well.

ROCHESTER PUNCH

Credit: From a recipe in the possession of Roswell Hart, Esq.

Serves 20

- 2 bottles sparkling Catawba Wine (or Madeira Wine)
- 2 bottles Isabella Wine
- 1 bottle Sauternes Wine
- 4 ounces Maraschino Liqueur (on page 235)
- 4 ounces Curaçao (on page 226)
- Strawberries (ripe)

Fill the tranquil bowl with Strawberries. If Strawberries are not in season, you can use a few drops of Peach Extract or Vanilla Extract.

SHERRY PUNCH

- 4 ounces Sherry
- 1 Tablespoon Sugar
- 2 or 3 slices of Orange
- 2 or 3 slices of Lemon

Add ingredients to a large bar glass. Fill with shaved ice, then shake well. Garnish with seasonal berries. Sip through straw.

TIP-TOP PUNCH
Serves a party of five

- 1 bottle Champagne
- 2 bottles Soda Water (on page 300)
- 1 ounce of Curaçao (on page 226)
- 2 Tablespoons Powdered Sugar
- 1 slice of Pineapple, cut up

Put all the ingredients together in a small punch bowl. Mix well and serve in champagne goblets.

FANCY PUNCHES

Ale Punch • Hot Brandy and Rum Punch • Canadian Punch
Century Club Punch • Cider Punch • Curacao Punch • D'Orsay Punch
Dry Punch • Duke of Norfolk Punch • Duke of Norfolk Punch (Alternate)
Glasgow Punch • Grassot Punch • Imperial Raspberry Whiskey Punch
Kirschwasser Punch • La Patria Punch • Light Guard Punch
Louisiana Sugar-House Punch • Mississippi Punch
National Guard 7th Regiment Punch • Non-Such Punch • Orange Punch
Oxford Punch • Philadelphia Fish-House Punch • Pineapple Punch
Punch a la Ford • Punch a la Romaine • Queen Punch • Raspberry Punch
Regent's Punch • Regent's Punch (another recipe) • Rocky Mountain Punch
Roman Punch • Saint Charles' Punch • Tea Punch
Uncle Toby Punch (English) • Yorkshire Punch • 32nd Regiment or Victoria Punch

ALE PUNCH

- 2 pints mild Ale
- 2 ounces White Wine
- 2 ounces Brandy
- 2 ounces Capillaire (on page 94)
- Juice of 1 Lemon
- Thinly pared Lemon Peel
- Fresh Nutmeg for grating
- Toasted Bread

Thinly peel then juice the Lemon. Combine Ale, Wine, Brandy, Capillaire, Lemon juice and peel. Garnish with grated Nutmeg and a bit of toasted Bread.

*NOTE: IT IS NOT CLEAR WHAT IS INTENDED WITH THE TOASTED BREAD. MY GUESS WOULD BE THAT THE BREAD IS EITHER CRUMBLED LIGHTLY OVER THE TOP WITH THE NUTMEG OR SERVED ON THE SIDE AS A GARNISH. THAT IS, OF COURSE, JUST MY GUESS.

HOT BRANDY AND RUM PUNCH
Serves 15

- 1 quart Jamaican Rum
- 1 quart Cognac
- 1 pound White Loaf Sugar
- 4 Lemons
- 3 quarts boiling water
- 1 teaspoon Nutmeg

Rub the Sugar over the Lemons until it has absorbed all of the yellow part of the skin, then put the Sugar in a punch bowl, along with the Lemons and mix well. Add the boiling water and stir well. Add the rum, Cognac and Nutmeg and mix thoroughly. The punch is now ready to serve. (*Editor's note: these instructions run counter to the general instructions for punch which state that in hot punches, the spirits should be added before the hot water. You decide which method to use.*)

Jerry Thomas: As has been previously mentioned, it is very important in making a good punch, that all the ingredients are thoroughly incorporated. To ensure success, the process of mixing must be diligently attended to. Allow a quart for 4 people, but take this advice with a grain of salt, as individual capacities for this kind of beverage are generally supposed to vary considerably.

CANADIAN PUNCH

- 2 quarts Rye Whiskey
- 1 pint Jamaican Rum
- 6 Lemons, sliced
- 1 Pineapple, sliced
- 4 quarts water
- Sweetener to taste

Mix ingredients and chill with ice.

CENTURY CLUB PUNCH

- 2 parts Santa Cruz Rum
- 1 part Old Jamaican Rum
- 5 parts water
- Lemons to taste
- Sugar to taste

Jerry Thomas: "This is a nice punch."

CIDER PUNCH

- 1 bottle Cider
- 1 Lemon (½ of the rind reserved)
- 8 oz Sherry
- .25 lb. Sugar
- Grated Nutmeg
- Brandy
- Cucumber rinds for garnish

Combine all ingredients except for Brandy and Cucumber. Mix well and if possible, place it in ice. When serving, pour a shot of Brandy into each glass, add the Cider mixture and garnish with the Cucumber rinds.

CURACAO PUNCH

- 1 Tablespoon Sugar
- 2 oz Brandy
- 1 oz Jamaican Rum
- 2 oz water
- ½ oz Curaçao (on page 226)
- .5 Lemon, juiced

Add ingredients to a large bar glass. Fill with shaved ice and shake well. Garnish with seasonal fruits and sip the nectar through a straw.

D'ORSAY PUNCH (10-GALLONS)

To make this recipe, see D'Orsay Punch (on page 271) in "The Manual for the Manufacture of Cordials, etc." in the latter part of this book. This recipe is for 10 gallons.

DRY PUNCH

Credit: From a recipe by Santina, the celebrated Spanish caterer.

- 2 gallons Brandy
- 1 gallon water
- ½ gallon Tea
- 1 pint Jamaican Rum
- 8 ounces Curaçao (on page 226)
- 6 Lemons
- 1.5 pounds White Sugar

For the Sherbet: Peel the Lemons, taking care to include none of the white pith. Combine with the Sugar, then stir together with an oar shaped paddle for approximately 30 minutes to extract as much essential oil as possible. Bring the water and Tea to a boil, then pour over the sherbet and mix well until the Sugar is completely dissolved.

Cut and squeeze the Lemons, separating the juice from the seeds. Put the seeds in a separate container, pour boiling water over them and let sit until the flavorful transparent coating is removed from the seeds.

Add the Lemon Juice to the sherbet and strain the seed liquids into the mixture as well. Taste the mixture and add either more Sugar or Lemon Juice as needed.

Add the Brandy, rum and Curaçao, stirring well. Bottle and keep on ice for three or four days, and the punch will be ready for use, but the longer it stands, the better it gets.

DUKE OF NORFOLK PUNCH

- 20 quarts (5 gallons) French Brandy
- Peel of 30 Lemons (thin with no pith)
- Peel of 30 Oranges (thin with no pith)
- Juice of 30 Oranges
- Juice of 24 Lemons
- 30 quarts (7.5 gallons) boiling water
- 15 pounds Double-Refined Sugar
- 8 cups fresh Milk
- 1 Barrel that has held spirits

Combine the Brandy with the Lemon and Orange peels and let infuse for 12 hours. Dissolve the Sugar into the boiling water. Add the water-Sugar mixture to the Brandy infusion, along with the Orange and Lemon juices. Mix well and then strain through a very fine sieve into the barrel. Add the Milk to the barrel and stir well. Bung the barrel closed and let it stand six weeks in a warm cellar. Bottle the liquor for use, observing great care that the bottles are perfectly clean and dry, and the corks of the best quality and well put in. This liquor will keep many years and improve by age.

DUKE OF NORFOLK PUNCH (ALTERNATE)

- 3 Oranges
- 6 Lemons
- 2 quarts Brandy
- 1 quart White Wine
- 1 quart Milk
- 1.25 lbs. Sugar

Thinly peel then juice the oranges and Lemons. Put the juice and peels into a large pot along with the rest of the ingredients. Mix and cover for 24 hours. Strain through a jelly-bag until clear, then bottle it.

GLASGOW PUNCH

Credit: From a recipe in the possession of Dr. Shelton Mackenzie.

- Lump Sugar
- Cold water
- 2 Lemons
- Old Jamaican Rum
- 2 Limes

Melt Lump Sugar in cold water, with the juice of a couple of Lemons that have been strained through a fine strainer. This is sherbet and must be well mingled. Measure the sherbet and add 1 part of Old Jamaican Rum for every five-parts of sherbet. Halve a couple of Limes and run each section rapidly around the edge of the jug or bowl while gently squeezing in some of the acid.

GRASSOT PUNCH

Credit: This recipe was given by M. GRASSOT, the eminent French comedian of the Palais Royal, to Mr. Howard Paul, the celebrated "Entertainer" when performing in Paris.

- 2 ounces Brandy
- 5 drops Curaçao (on page 226)
- 1 drop Acetic Acid (substitute 1 teaspoon Vinegar)
- 2 teaspoons Plain White Syrup (on page 136)
- 1 teaspoon Strawberry Syrup (on page 310)
- 4 ounces water
- Peel of small Lemon, sliced
- Peach or Apricot slice for garnish

Mix ingredients. If serving cold, serve up with ice in a large goblet. In cold weather, this punch is admirable served hot. Garnish with a slice of Peach or Apricot.

IMPERIAL RASPBERRY WHISKEY PUNCH

To make this recipe, see Imperial Raspberry Whiskey Punch (on page 269) in "The Manual for the Manufacture of Cordials, etc." in the latter part of this book. This recipe is for 10 gallons.

KIRSCHWASSER PUNCH

To make this recipe see Kirschwasser Punch (on page 270) in "The Manual for the Manufacture of Cordials, etc." in the latter part of this book. This recipe is for 10 gallons.

LA PATRIA PUNCH

Credit: From a recipe in the possession of H.P. Leland, Esq.

Serves 20

- 3 bottles Champagne, iced
- 1 bottle Cognac
- 6 Oranges
- 1 Pineapple

Slice the oranges and Pineapple in a bowl. Pour the Cognac over them and let steep for a couple of hours. Add the champagne and serve immediately.

LIGHT GUARD PUNCH
Serves a party of 20

- 3 bottles Champagne
- 1 bottle pale Sherry
- 1 bottle Cognac
- 1 bottle Sauternes Wine
- 1 Pineapple, sliced
- 4 Lemons, sliced
- Sugar to taste

Mix in a punch bowl. Sweeten to taste. Cool with a large lump of ice and serve immediately.

LOUISIANA SUGAR-HOUSE PUNCH
Credit: From a recipe in the possession of Colonel T. B. Thorpe

- 1 quart boiling Syrup (on page 135)
- Whiskey or Brandy to suit the "patient"
- Sour Orange Juice to taste

Add liquor and juice to the syrup, just taken from the heat.

MISSISSIPPI PUNCH

- 2 ounces Brandy
- 1 ounce Jamaican Rum
- 1 ounce Bourbon Whiskey
- 1 ounce water
- 1 ½ Tablespoon Powdered Sugar
- ½ large Lemon
- Small Orange pieces for garnish
- Seasonal Berries for garnish

Add ingredients to a large bar glass, then fill with shaved ice. Shake well, then garnish with small pieces of Orange and seasonal berries.

Jerry Thomas: "To those who like their draughts 'like linked sweetness long drawn out', let them use a glass tube or straw to sip the nectar through"

NATIONAL GUARD 7ᵀᴴ REGIMENT PUNCH

- 1 Tablespoon Sugar
- Juice of ¼ Lemon
- 2 ounces Brandy
- 2 ounces Catawba Wine (or Madeira Wine)
- Raspberry Syrup (on page 309) to taste
- 1 dash Jamaican Rum
- Orange slices to garnish

Add the ingredients, minus the rum and Orange slices, to a large bar glass. Fill with shaved ice, then shake well. Garnish with slices of Orange and a dash of Jamaican Rum.

Jerry Thomas: "This delicious beverage should be imbibed through a straw."

NON-SUCH PUNCH

- 6 bottles Claret Wine
- 6 bottles Soda Water (on page 300)
- 1 bottle Brandy
- 1 bottle Sherry
- 8 ounces Green Tea
- Juice of 3 Lemons
- ½ Pineapple, cut into small pieces
- White Sugar to taste

Mix and sweeten to taste. Strain into a bottle immediately. Keep for one month before using. Chill before serving.

Jerry Thomas: "This is a delicious and safe drink for a mixed evening party."

ORANGE PUNCH
Credit: From a recipe in the 'Bordeaux Wine and Liquor Guide'

- 3 - 4 Oranges
- ¾ lb. Sugar
- 7 cups boiling water
- 8 ounces Porter (on page 143)
- 12-16 ounces each, Rum and Brandy (or either alone 3 to 4 cups)
- 1 ounce Curaçao (on page 226), Noyau (on page 194), or Maraschino (on page 235) (optional)

Peel 1 or 2 of the oranges. Take the Orange peels and infuse with the Orange Juice, Sugar and boiling water for 30 minutes. Strain. Add Porter, Rum and/or Brandy. You can add more Sugar or warm water to adjust taste or strength. Add the Curaçao or other liqueur if you wish to improve the punch. A good Lemon punch may be made by substituting Lemons instead of oranges.

OXFORD PUNCH

Credit: We have been favored by an English gentleman with the following recipe for the concoction of punch as drunk by the students of the University of Oxford.

- 6 Lemons
- 4 sweet Oranges
- 12 ounces Calf's Foot Jelly
- Loaf Sugar (unspecified amount)
- 4 pints boiling water
- 1 bottle Capillaire (on page 94)
- 1 cup Sherry
- 1 pint Cognac
- 1 pint Old Jamaican Rum
- 2 pints Orange Shrub*

Rub the rinds of three Lemons on the Loaf Sugar until you begin to extract the juice. Add the peel of 2 more Lemons, and 2 sweet oranges. Add the juice of 6 Lemons and 4 oranges. Add the Calf's Foot Jelly. Put everything into a large sauce pan and stir well. Add the boiling water and set the pan on the heat for twenty minutes. Strain the liquor through a fine sieve into a large bowl. Pour in the Capillaire, sherry, Cognac, rum and Orange shrub, stirring well as you add it. If you find it requires more sweetness, add Sugar to taste.

*ALTHOUGH THERE IS NO RECIPE FOR ORANGE SHRUB IN THIS BOOK, THERE ARE A FEW SHRUB RECIPES (ON PAGE 289) THAT, PERHAPS, COULD BE USED FOR INSPIRATION IN THE LATTER HALF OF THIS WORK "A MANUAL FOR THE MANUFACTURE OF CORDIALS, LIQUEURS, FANCY SYRUPS, ETC., ETC."

PHILADELPHIA FISH-HOUSE PUNCH

Credit: From a recipe in the possession of Chales G. Leland, Esq.

- 2/3 cup Lemon Juice
- .75 lbs. White Sugar
- 5 cups cold water
- 4 oz Peach Brandy (on page 181)
- 8 oz Cognac
- 4 oz Jamaican Rum

NOTE: THE ORIGINAL TEXT STATES THAT THIS RECIPE IS "GENERALLY SUFFICIENT FOR ONE PERSON", HOWEVER, BY COMPARING IT TO OTHER RECIPES AND USING COMMON SENSE, I BELIEVE THE RECIPE IS INTENDED TO BE 7-8 SERVINGS.

PINEAPPLE PUNCH
Serves a party of 10

- 4 bottles Champagne
- 16 ounces Jamaican Rum
- 16 ounces Brandy
- 4 ounces Curaçao (on page 226)
- Juice of 4 Lemons
- 4 Pineapples, sliced
- 1 lb. superfine or powdered White Sugar

Put the Pineapple and Sugar in a glass bowl and let them stand until the Sugar is well soaked into the Pineapple. Add all the other ingredients, except the champagne. Let this mixture stand in ice for about an hour, then add the champagne. Place a large block of ice in the center of the bowl, and ornament it with Loaf Sugar, sliced oranges and other fruits in season. Serve in champagne glasses.

Jerry Thomas: "Pineapple punch is sometimes made by adding sliced Pineapple to Brandy punch."

PUNCH A LA FORD

Credit: From Benson E. Hill, Esq., author of "The Epicure's Almanac"

Jerry Thomas: "The late General Ford, who for many years was the commanding engineer at Dover, kept a most hospitable board, and used to make punch on a large scale, after the following method:"

- 36 Lemons with smooth, not-too-thin skins
- 2 lbs. Sugar
- Boiling water
- Cognac Brandy
- Old Jamaican Rum

For the Sherbet: Peel the Lemons, taking care to include none of the white pith. Combine with the Sugar and stir together with an oar shaped paddle for approximately 30 minutes to extract as much essential oil as possible. Pour boiling water over the sherbet and mix well until the Sugar is completely dissolved.

Cut and squeeze the Lemons, separating the juice from the seeds. Put the seeds in a separate container, pour boiling water over them and let sit until the flavorful transparent coating is removed from the seeds.

Add half the Lemon Juice to the sherbet and strain the seed liquids into the mixture as well. Taste the mixture and add either more Sugar or Lemon Juice as needed. You don't want a watery lemonade, but rather a rich fruity taste that is plenty sweet.

Now measure the Lemon mixture, and to every 3 quarts (96 oz) of the mixture, add 16 ounces of Cognac and 16 ounces of rum, stirring well. Bottle immediately and store in a cold dark place until used. At least 6 months aging in a cool atmosphere seems to improve it much.

PUNCH A LA ROMAINE
Serves a party of fifteen

- 10 Lemons
- 2 sweet Oranges
- 2 pounds Powdered Sugar
- 10 Egg whites
- 1 bottle Wine
- 1 bottle Rum

Peel the rind thinly from one of the oranges. Combine the rind with the juice from the Lemons and oranges. Dissolve the Powdered Sugar into it and then run through a sieve. Beat the Egg whites into a froth, then stir in by degrees. Put the mixture into an ice pail and let it freeze a little. Stir the wine and rum in briskly.

For another method of making this punch, see Roman Punch (on page 271)in "The Manual for the Manufacture of Cordials, etc." in the latter part of this work.

QUEEN PUNCH
Serves a party of 10

- 2 ounces Cream of Tartar
- 2 Lemons
- 7 quarts boiling water
- Sugar to taste
- 8 ounces Rum

In a stone jar, add the Cream of Tartar, juice, and peels of the two Lemons. Add the boiling water, stir, and cover close. When cold, sweeten with Sugar. Strain the mixture and add the rum. Bottle it and cork it tight.

Jerry Thomas: "This is a very pleasant liquor, and very wholesome… but from the latter consideration was at one time drunk in such quantities as to become injurious."

RASPBERRY PUNCH
Credit: From a recipe in the Bordeaux Wine and Liquor Guide

- 6 ounces Raspberry Juice, or Raspberry Vinegar (on page 300).
- ¾ lb. Sugar
- 7 cups boiling water
- 8 ounces Porter (on page 143)
- 1.5 – 2 pints of either Rum or Brandy, or both in equal proportions depending on strength and flavor balance desired.
- 1 shot of Curaçao (on page 226), Noyau (on page 194), or Maraschino Liqueur (on page 235) (optional)

Infuse the Raspberry, Sugar and boiling water for 30 minutes, then strain. Add the Porter and Rum/Brandy and liqueur (if using). If needed, add more warm water or Sugar to taste.

REGENT'S PUNCH
Serves a party of 20

- 3 bottles Champagne
- 1 bottle Hockheimer Wine
- 1 bottle Curaçao (on page 226)
- 1 bottle Cognac
- ½ bottle Jamaican Rum
- 2 bottles Madeira Wine
- 2 bottles Seltzer Water or Soda Water (on page 300)
- 4 pounds Bloom Raisins (Sun Raisins)
- Oranges (to taste)
- Lemons (to taste)
- Rock Candy (to taste)
- Green Tea (to taste)

Combine all ingredients along with oranges, Lemons, Rock Candy and Green Tea (instead of water) to taste. Refrigerate with all the icy power of the Arctic.

REGENT'S PUNCH (ANOTHER RECIPE)
Credit: From the Bordeaux Wine and Liquor Guide

- 24 ounces hot strong Green Tea
- 24 ounces Lemon Juice
- 24 ounces Capillaire (on page 94)
- 16 ounces Rum
- 16 ounces Brandy
- 16 ounces Arrack
- 16 ounces Curaçao (on page 226)
- 1 bottle Champagne
- 1 Pineapple, sliced

Mix all liquid ingredients, then add the sliced Pineapple.

For still another method of compounding this celebrated punch, see Regent Punch (on page 271) in "A Manual for the Manufacture of Cordials, etc.," in the latter part of this book.

ROCKY MOUNTAIN PUNCH

Credit: From a recipe in possession of Major James Foster

Serves a party 20

- 5 bottles of Champagne
- 4 cups Jamaican Rum
- 2 cups Maraschino Liqueur (on page 235)
- 6 Lemons, sliced
- Sugar to taste
- Block Ice (large)
- Rock Candy to garnish
- Sliced Lemons and/or Oranges to garnish
- Seasonal Fruits to garnish
- Sugar Cubes to garnish

Mix champagne, rum, maraschino, Lemons and Sugar in a large punch bowl, then place a large block of ice in the center of the bowl. Place the garnishes on top of the ice.

Jerry Thomas: "This is a splendid punch for New Year's Day."

ROMAN PUNCH

- 1 Tablespoon Sugar
- Juice of ½ a Lemon
- ½ ounce Raspberry Syrup (on page 309)
- 2 barspoons of Curaçao (on page 226)
- 2 ounces Jamaican Rum
- 1 ounce Brandy
- Dash of Port Wine

Add all ingredients except port wine to a large bar glass and fill with shaved ice. Shake well and float port wine on top. Garnish with seasonal fruits and serve with a straw.

SAINT CHARLES' PUNCH

- 1 Tablespoon Sugar
- 2 ounces Port Wine
- 1 ounce Brandy
- Juice of ¼ Lemon

Combine ingredients in a large bar glass. Fill with shaved ice, then shake well. Garnish with seasonal fruits and serve with a straw.

TEA PUNCH

- Green Tea, best available (1 ounce Tea Leaf infused with 4 cups of boiling water)
- 8 ounces good Brandy
- 8 ounces Rum
- .25 lb. Lump Sugar
- Juice of a large Lemon

Rub a few lumps of Sugar over the Lemon Peel. Place a silver or other metal bowl over a fire and heat until very hot (this punch may also be made in a china bowl, but in that case the flame goes off more rapidly). Put in the Brandy, rum, Sugar, and Lemon Juice. Set this mixture alight and pour in the Tea gradually, mixing it from time to time with a ladle. It will remain burning for some time and should be poured into the glasses while still burning.

UNCLE TOBY PUNCH (ENGLISH)

- 2 large Lemons with rough skins, extra ripe
- 8 oz double-refined Sugar Lumps
- 10 cups Boiling water (soft water is best)
- 1 pint Rum + 1 pint Brandy OR 2 pints Rum
- 8 ounces Porter (on page 143) (optional)

Rub Sugar over Lemons until it has absorbed all the yellow part of the skins. Put these Sugar lumps into a large bowl, along with as much Lemon Juice as needed (the acidity of a Lemon cannot be known until tried, and therefore must be determined by taste). Using a bruiser, press the Sugar and the juice very well together. A great deal of the richness and fine flavor of this punch depends on the rubbing and mixing process being thoroughly performed. Add to the boiling water and mix well until rather cool. This mixture is called Sherbet and may be strained at this point to remove the pulp. Some people strain the Lemon Juice before they put it into the Sugar. This is not proper, as when the pulp and Sugar are well mixed together, it adds much to the richness of the punch. When the sherbet is to your taste, add equal parts of Brandy and rum (or just rum) to taste. When only rum is used, about 8 ounces of Porter will soften the punch' and even when both rum and Brandy are used, the Porter gives a richness and to some a very pleasant flavor.

Although these ingredients are specified to taste, two good Lemons are generally enough to make 4 quarts of punch, including a quart of liquor, with half a pound of Sugar. But this greatly depends on taste, and the strength of the spirit.

Yorkshire Punch

- 10 Lemons
- 4 Oranges
- 3 Lemons
- Sugar Lumps for rubbing
- 12 ounces dissolved Calf's Foot Jelly
- 8 cups water
- 2 cups Plain White Syrup (on page 136)
- 1 cup Rum
- 1 cup Brandy
- 1 bottle good Orange Shrub or Lemon Shrub (on page 292)

Peel the rind from 1 Lemon and 1 Orange and set aside. Rub the rind of 3 Lemons with Sugar lumps. Put those Sugar lumps into a jug along with the Lemon and Orange rinds. Juice the Lemons and oranges and add them, along with the Calf's Foot Jelly, to the jug. Add the water and mix well. Cover the jug and keep it on a warm fire for 20 minutes. Strain the mixture, then add the syrup, rum, Brandy and shrub.

32ND Regiment or Victoria Punch
Credit: recipe from Wm. H. Herbert, Esq.

Serves a party of 20

- 6 Lemons, sliced
- 8 cups Brandy
- 8 cups Jamaican Rum
- 1 lb. Sugar
- 7 cups water
- 2 cups Milk

Steep the sliced Lemons for 24 hours in the Brandy and rum. Bring the Milk to boiling. Add the Sugar, water and boiling Milk to the Lemon-infused liquors and mix well. Strain through a jelly-bag.

This punch may be bottled and used afterwards hot or cold. For parties of less than twenty, this recipe may be halved or less.

MILK PUNCHES AND NOGGS

Milk Punch, Single Serving • Hot Milk Punch • English Milk Punch
English Milk Punch (another method) • Nectar Punch • Egg Nogg • Hot Egg Nogg
Egg Nogg (for a party) • Baltimore Egg Nogg • General Harrison's Egg Nogg
Sherry Egg Nogg

Egg Nogg is a beverage of American origin, but it has a popularity that is cosmopolitan. At the South it is almost indispensable at Christmas time, and at the North it is a favorite at all seasons. In Scotland they call Egg Nogg "auld man's milk"

MILK PUNCH, SINGLE SERVING

- 1 Tablespoon superfine or powdered White Sugar
- 1 ounce water
- 2 ounces Cognac Brandy
- 1 ounce Santa Cruz Rum
- Milk
- Nutmeg for grating

Fill a large bar glass 1/3 with ice. Add Sugar, water, Brandy and rum to the glass. Fill with Milk and shake well. Grate Nutmeg on top, then serve.

HOT MILK PUNCH

This punch is made the same as MILK PUNCH, except that hot Milk is used, and no ice.

ENGLISH MILK PUNCH

- Juice of 6 Lemons
- Rind of 2 Lemons
- 1 lb. Sugar
- 1 Pineapple, peeled, sliced and pounded
- 6 Cloves
- 20 Coriander Seeds
- 1 small stick of Cinnamon
- 16 ounces Brandy
- 16 ounces Rum
- 4 ounces Arrack (*See notes in Arrack Punches* on page 39)
- 1 cup strong Green Tea
- 32 ounces boiling water

Put the ingredients into a very clean pitcher, adding the boiling water last. Cork this down to prevent evaporation and allow these ingredients to steep for at least six hours. Then add:

- 1 quart hot Milk
- Juice of 2 Lemons

Mix and filter through a jelly bag. When the punch has passed bright, put it away in tight-corked bottles. This punch is intended to be iced for drinking.

ENGLISH MILK PUNCH (ANOTHER METHOD)
Makes about 6 bottles

This seductive and nectarous drink can also be made by the following directions:

- 2 quarts water
- 1 quart Milk
- 1 quart Jamaican Rum
- 2 quarts French Brandy

Combine the water and Milk. In a separate container, combine the rum and Brandy. Pour the alcohol into the Milk mixture, stirring it for a short time. Let stand for one hour. (Do not let anyone with a delicate appetite see this mixture during this stage, or you may ruin their desire to try the punch when finished). Filter through blotting paper into bottles. The liquid should not be cloudy, but if it is you may clarify it by adding a small portion of Isinglass to each bottle.

NECTAR PUNCH

- 15 Lemons
- 9 cups Rum
- 8 cups cold water
- 8 cups boiling Milk
- 1 grated Nutmeg nut
- 2.5 lbs. Sugar

Take the peels of the Lemons and infuse them with 3 cups of the rum for 48 hours. Then add the cold water, the juice from the Lemons, and the remaining 6 cups of rum. Add in the Milk and Nutmeg, then cover close. Let this mixture stand for 24 hours. After 24 hours add the Sugar and mix well. Strain through a flannel bag until quite fine, and then bottle it for use. It is fit to serve as soon as bottled.

EGG NOGG

- 1 Tablespoon fine Sugar
- 1 Tablespoon cold water
- 1 Egg
- 2 ounces Cognac Brandy
- 1 ounce Santa Cruz Rum
- 1/3 a tumblerful of Milk
- Fresh Nutmeg for grating

Dissolve the Sugar into the water and Egg. Fill a large bar glass ¼ with shaved ice and add the mixture along with the Brandy, rum and Milk. Shake until the ingredients are thoroughly mixed. Grate fresh Nutmeg on top.

Jerry Thomas: "Every well-ordered bar has a tin Egg-Nogg "shaker", which is a great aid in mixing this beverage."

HOT EGG NOGG

Jerry Thomas: "This drink is very popular in California and is made in precisely the same manner as the cold Egg Nogg above, except that you must use boiling water instead of ice."

EGG NOGG (FOR A PARTY)
Serves a party of 40

- 12 Eggs, separated
- 2 quarts Brandy
- 1 pint Santa Cruz Rum
- 2 gallons Milk
- 1.5 lbs. White Sugar
- Colored Sugar to garnish

Beat the Egg whites and yolks separately with an eggbeater until the yolks are well cut up and the whites assume a light fleecy appearance. Mix all the ingredients, except the Egg whites and Colored Sugar, in a large punch bowl, then float the whites on top. Ornament with Colored sugars. Cool in a tub of ice and then serve.

BALTIMORE EGG NOGG
Serves a party of 15

- 16 Eggs, separated
- .75 cup Powdered Sugar
- Fresh Nutmeg for grating
- 8 ounces good Brandy or Jamaican Rum
- 4 ounces Madeira Wine
- 12 cups good rich Milk

Combine the Egg yolks and Sugar and beat them until they have the consistency of cream. Grate into this mixture ⅔ of a Nutmeg nut and beat well together. Mix in the Brandy (or rum) and the wine. Have the Egg whites ready, beaten into a stiff froth. Fold the Egg whites into the mixture. Stir in the Milk and serve. There is no heat used.

Jerry Thomas: "Egg Nogg made in this manner is digestible and will not cause headache. It makes an excellent drink for debilitated persons, and a nourishing diet for consumptives."

GENERAL HARRISON'S EGG NOGG

- 1 Egg
- 1 ½ teaspoon Sugar
- 2 or 3 small lumps of ice
- Hard Cider

Add the Egg, Sugar, ice and Cider to a mixing glass and shake very well.

Jerry Thomas: "This is a splendid drink and is very popular on the Mississippi River. It was General Harrison's favorite beverage."

SHERRY EGG NOGG

- 1 Tablespoon White Sugar
- 1 Egg yolk
- 4 ounces Sherry
- Milk
- Fresh Nutmeg for grating

Dissolve the Sugar with a little water into a large bar glass. Add the Egg yolk into the glass and add ¼ glass of broken ice. Fill with Milk and shake up until the Egg is thoroughly mixed with the other ingredients. Grate Nutmeg over the top and quaff the nectar cup.

ARRACK PUNCHES

Arrack Punch • Arrack Punch (another method) • Cold Punch
Nuremberg Punch • United Service Punch • Ruby Punch • Royal Punch

*Most of the Arrack imported into this country is distilled from rice and comes from Batavia. It is but little used in America, except to flavor punch. The taste of it is very agreeable in this mixture. Arrack improves very much with age. It is much used in some parts of India, where it is distilled from toddy or tuba, the juice of the Coconut tree. An imitation of Arrack Punch is made by adding to a bowl of punch a few grains of **Benzoin**, commonly called **Flowers of Benjamin**. See Arrack (Faux) (on page 164) in "A Manual for the Manufacture of Cordials, etc.," in the end of this volume.*

ARRACK PUNCH
Serves 3

- 4 ounces Rum
- 6 ounces Arrack
- Sugar to taste
- 2 ounces Lemon Juice or Lime Juice
- 12 ounces water

Jerry Thomas: "In making 'rack punch, you ought to put 4 ounces of rum for every 6 ounces of Arrack. A good deal of Sugar is required, but sweetening, after all, must be left to taste. Lemons and Limes are also a matter of palate, but two Lemons are enough for the above quantity. Put an equal quantity of water (i.e., Not 10, but 12 ounces to allow for the Lemon Juice) and you have a very pretty three tumblers of punch."

ARRACK PUNCH (ANOTHER METHOD)

- 1 quart old Batavia Arrack
- 6 Lemons, cut into thin slices
- 1 lb. Sugar
- 1 quart boiling water

Let the Lemons steep in the Arrack for 6 hours. Remove the Lemons without squeezing. Dissolve the Sugar into the boiling water and add the hot solution to the Arrack. Let it stand to cool.

Jerry Thomas: "This is a delightful liqueur and should be used as such. See Arrack Punch Syrup (on page 270) in 'The Manual for the Manufacture of Cordials, etc.' in the end of this volume."

"Bimbo is made nearly in the same way as the previous recipe, except that Cognac Brandy is substituted for Arrack." See Bimbo Punch (on page 8)

COLD PUNCH

- 4 cups Arrack
- 4 cups Port Wine
- 4 cups water
- 1 lb. Sugar
- Juice of 8 Lemons

NOTE: NO DIRECTIONS WERE PROVIDED IN THE ORIGINAL TEXT.

NUREMBERG PUNCH

Credit: From a recipe in the possession of Hon. Giuliano C. Verplanck

Serves a party of 15

- ¾ lb. Sugar
- 2 or more good-sized Oranges
- 1 quart boiling water
- Batavia Arrack
- 1 bottle French Wine, red or white (red is best)

Reserve a few pieces of the Orange peels, cut thin, then juice the oranges and strain through muslin. Combine Sugar and Orange Juice. Add the boiling water. Measure the total liquid and add 1/3 the volume of Arrack. Heat the wine until hot, but not boiling. Add the hot wine and stir. Let cool and bottle. This is excellent when served cold and will improve with age.

UNITED SERVICE PUNCH

- 2 pints hot Tea
- ¾ lbs. Sugar
- 8 Lemons
- 1 pint Arrack

With 4 of the Lemons, rub the yellow peel off with the Sugar. Juice all the Lemons and set aside. Dissolve the Sugar into the hot Tea. Add the Lemon Juice and the Arrack.

RUBY PUNCH

- 6 cups hot Tea
- 1 lb. Sugar
- Juice of 6 Lemons
- 1 pint Arrack
- 1 pint Port Wine

Dissolve the Sugar into the hot Tea. Add the remaining ingredients and mix.

ROYAL PUNCH

- 1 pint hot Green Tea
- 1 cup Brandy
- 1 cup Jamaican Rum
- 2 ounces Curaçao (on page 226)
- 2 ounces Arrack
- Juice of 2 Limes
- 1 thin slice Lemon
- White Sugar to taste
- 4 ounces of warm Calf's Foot Jelly or 2 Egg whites beaten to a froth

Combine ingredients and drink as hot as possible. If too strong, add more Green Tea to taste.

Jerry Thomas: "This is a composition worthy of a king, and the materials are admirable when blended. The inebriation effects of the spirits being deadened by the Tea, whilst the jelly softens the mixture, and destroys the acrimony of the acid and Sugar."

JULEPS

Mint Julep • *Brandy Julep* • *Gin Julep* • *Whiskey Julep* • *Pineapple Julep*

The julep is peculiarly an American beverage, and in the Southern states is more popular than any other. It was introduced into England by Captain Marryatt, where it is now quite a favorite. The gallant captain seems to have had a penchant for the nectarous drink and published the recipe in his work on America. We give it in his own words: "I must descant a little upon the Mint julep, as it is, with the thermometer at 100 degrees, one of the most delightful and insinuating potations that ever was invented, and may be drunk with equal satisfaction when the thermometer is as low as 70 degrees. There are many varieties, such as those composed of Claret, Madeira, etc, but the ingredients of the real Mint julep are as follows. I learned how to make them and succeeded pretty well. Put into a tumbler about a dozen sprigs of the tender shoots of Mint. Upon them put a spoonful of White Sugar and equal proportions of Peach and common Brandy, so as to fill it up one-third, or perhaps a little less. Then take rasped or pounded ice and fill up the tumbler. Epicures rub the lips of the tumbler with a piece of fresh Pineapple, and the tumbler itself is very often encrusted outside with stalactites of ice. As the ice melts, you drink. I once overheard two ladies talking in the next room to me, and one of them said 'Well if I have a weakness for any one thing, it is for a Mint julep!'- a very amiable weakness and proving her good sense and good taste. They are, in fact, like the American ladies, irresistible."

MINT JULEP

- 1 Tablespoon Powdered Sugar plus a little more for garnish
- 2 ½ Tablespoons water
- 3 or 4 sprigs of fresh Mint
- 3 ounces Cognac Brandy
- Seasonal Berries
- Orange slice
- Dash Jamaican Rum

In a large bar glass, dissolve the Sugar into water. Add the Mint sprigs and press until the flavor of the Mint is extracted. Add the Cognac and fill the glass with fine shaved ice. Extract the Mint sprigs and insert them in the ice with the stems downward, so that the leaves will be above, in the shape of a bouquet. Arrange berries and small pieces of sliced Orange on top in a tasty manner. Dash with rum and sprinkle Sugar on top. Place a straw as shown in the illustration, and you have a julep that is fit for an emperor.

BRANDY JULEP
The Brandy julep is made the same as the Mint Julep, omitting the fancy fixings.

GIN JULEP
The Gin Julep is made the same as the Mint Julep, omitting the fancy fixings.

WHISKEY JULEP
The whiskey julep is made the same as the Mint Julep, but with Whiskey, omitting all fruits and berries.

PINEAPPLE JULEP
Serves a party of 5

- 1 ripe Pineapple, peeled, sliced and cut up
- Juice of 2 Oranges
- 4 ounces Raspberry Syrup (on page 309)
- 4 ounces of Maraschino Liqueur (on page 235)
- 4 ounces Old Gin
- 1 bottle Sparkling Moselle Wine
- About 1 pound of pure ice in shaves
- Seasonal Berries for garnish

Place the Pineapple into a glass bowl. Add the Orange Juice, Raspberry syrup, maraschino, Gin, Moselle and shaved ice. Mix and ornament with berries in season. Serve in flat glasses.

THE SMASH

Brandy Smash • Gin Smash • Whiskey Smash

This beverage is simply a julep on a small plan.

Brandy Smash

- ½ Tablespoon of White Sugar
- 1 Tablespoon water
- 2 ounces Brandy
- 2 sprigs Mint
- 2 small slices of Orange
- Seasonal Berries

In a small bar glass, dissolve Sugar in water and press Mint to extract flavor. Add Brandy. Extract the Mint sprigs. Fill the glass ⅔ with shaved ice. Place the Mint sprigs stem down into the ice to make a bouquet as with the julep. Ornament with Orange slices and berries.

Gin Smash

- ½ Tablespoon White Sugar
- 1 Tablespoon water
- 2 ounces Gin
- 2 sprigs Mint
- 2 small slices of Orange
- Seasonal Berries

Dissolve Sugar in water and press Mint to extract flavor. Add the Gin. Extract the Mint sprigs. Fill the glass ⅔ with shaved ice. Place the Mint sprigs stem down into the ice to make a bouquet as with the julep. Ornament with Orange slices and berries.

Whiskey Smash

- ½ Tablespoon White Sugar
- 1 Tablespoon water
- 2 ounces Whiskey
- 2 sprigs Mint

Dissolve Sugar in water and press Mint to extract flavor. Add whiskey. Extract the Mint sprigs. Fill the glass ⅔ with shaved ice. Place the Mint sprigs stem down into the ice to make a bouquet as with the julep.

THE COBBLER

Catawba Cobbler • Claret Cobbler • Hock Cobbler • Sauternes Cobbler
Champagne Cobbler • Sherry Cobbler • Whiskey Cobbler

Like the julep, this delicious potation is an American invention, although it is not a favorite in all warm climates. The "cobbler" does not require much skill in compounding, but to make it acceptable to the eye, as well as to the palate, it is necessary to display some taste in ornamenting the glass after the beverage is made. We give an illustration showing how a cobbler should look when made to suit an epicure.

CATAWBA COBBLER

- 1 teaspoon Sugar
- 1 Tablespoon of water
- 4 ounces Catawba Wine (or Madeira Wine)
- 2 or 3 Orange slices
- Berries in season

In a large bar glass, dissolve the Sugar into the water, then add the wine. Fill the glass with shaved ice and ornament with Orange slices and berries. Place a straw as shown in the illustration.

CLARET COBBLER

This drink is made the same way as the Catawba cobbler, using Claret Wine instead of Catawba.

HOCK COBBLER

This drink is made the same way as the Catawba cobbler, using Hock Wine (German white wine) instead of Catawba.

SAUTERNES COBBLER

The same as Catawba cobbler, using Sauternes Wine instead of Catawba.

CHAMPAGNE COBBLER

- 1 Tablespoon Sugar
- 1 piece of Orange
- 1 slice Lemon Peel
- Champagne

Place the Sugar, Orange piece and Lemon Peel in a large tumbler, then fill ⅓ full with shaved ice. Fill the balance with wine, and ornament in a tasty manner with berries in season. This beverage should be sipped through a straw.

SHERRY COBBLER

- 4 ounces Sherry
- 1 Tablespoon Sugar
- 2 or 3 slices of Orange
- Berries in season

Add Sugar, Orange and sherry to a tumbler and fill with shaved ice. Shake well and ornament with the berries. Place a straw as represented in the illustration.

WHISKEY COBBLER

- 4 ounces Whiskey
- 1 Tablespoon Sugar
- 2 or 3 slices of Orange.

Add the Sugar, Orange and whiskey to a large bar glass, then fill with ice and shake well. Imbibe through a straw.

THE COCKTAIL AND CRUSTA

Bottle Cocktail • Brandy Cocktail • Fancy Brandy Cocktail
Whiskey Cocktail • Champagne Cocktail • Gin Cocktail • Fancy Gin Cocktail
Japanese Cocktail • Jersey Cocktail • Soda Cocktail • Brandy Crusta
Whiskey Crusta • Gin Crusta

The "Cocktail" is a modern invention, and is generally used on fishing and other sporting parties, although some patients insist that it is good in the morning as a tonic. The "Crusta" is an improvement on the "Cocktail" and is said to have been invented by Santina, a celebrated Spanish caterer.

BOTTLE COCKTAIL

- ⅔ bottle Brandy, Gin, or Whiskey
- ⅓ bottle water
- 1 ounce Bogart's Bitters (on page 353)
- 2 ounces Gum Syrup (on page 305)
- ½ ounce Curaçao (on page 226)

Jerry Thomas: This makes a splendid bottle of Brandy cocktail. "The author has always used this recipe in compounding the above beverage for connoisseurs. Whiskey and Gin cocktails, in bottles, may be made by using the above recipe, and substituting those liquors instead of Brandy."

BRANDY COCKTAIL

- 3 or 4 dashes of Gum Syrup (on page 305)
- 2 dashes Bogart's Bitters (on page 353)
- 2 ounces Brandy
- 1 or 2 dashes Curaçao (on page 226)
- Lemon Peel for garnish

In a small bar glass, add liquid ingredients. Squeeze Lemon Peel. Fill ⅓ with ice and stir with a spoon.

FANCY BRANDY COCKTAIL
This drink is made the same as the Brandy cocktail, except that it is strained into a fancy wineglass, and a piece of Lemon Peel thrown on top, and the edge of the glass moistened with Lemon.

WHISKEY COCKTAIL

- 3 or 4 dashes Gum Syrup (on page 305)
- 2 dashes Bogart's Bitters (on page 353)
- 2 ounces Whiskey
- 1 piece Lemon Peel

Add ingredients to a mixing glass filled ⅓ with fine ice. Shake and strain into a fancy red wineglass.

CHAMPAGNE COCKTAIL
Serves 6 large glasses for every 1 bottle of champagne. This recipe is per-glass.

- ½ teaspoonful Sugar
- 1 or 2 dashes Bitters
- 1 piece Lemon Peel
- 4 oz. Champagne

Add Sugar, Bitters and Lemon Peel to a large bar glass, then fill ⅓ full of broken ice. Fill the balance with wine. Shake well and serve.

GIN COCKTAIL

- 3 or 4 dashes Gum Syrup (on page 305)
- 2 dashes Bogart's Bitters (on page 353)
- 2 ounces Gin
- 1 or 2 dashes Curaçao (on page 226)
- 1 small piece Lemon Peel

Add ingredients to a mixing glass and fill ⅓ with fine ice. Shake well and strain into a small bar glass.

FANCY GIN COCKTAIL
This drink is made the same as the Gin Cocktail, except that it is strained in a fancy wineglass and a piece of Lemon Peel thrown on top, and the edge of the glass moistened with Lemon.

JAPANESE COCKTAIL

- 1 Tablespoon Orgeat Syrup (on page 307)
- ½ teaspoon Bogart's Bitters (on page 353)
- 2 ounces Brandy
- 1 or 2 pieces of Lemon Peel

Add ingredients to a small bar glass and fill ⅓ with ice. Stir well with a spoon.

JERSEY COCKTAIL

- 1 teaspoon Sugar
- 2 dashes Bitters
- Cider
- Lemon Peel

Fill a small bar glass with Sugar, Bitters, and Cider. Mix well and serve with a Lemon Peel on top.

SODA COCKTAIL

The same as Jersey cocktail, using Soda Water instead of Cider and using a large bar glass.

Brandy Crusta

- 3 or 4 dashes of Gum Syrup (on page 305)
- 2 dashes Bogart's Bitters (on page 353)
- 2 ounces Brandy
- 1 or 2 dashes Curaçao (on page 226)
- 1 Lemon Peel (to squeeze)
- 1 large Lemon Peel ring (to garnish)
- Splash Lemon Juice

A Crusta is made the same as a fancy cocktail, with a little Lemon Juice and a small lump of ice added. First, mix the syrup, Bitters, Brandy, Curaçao and Lemon Juice in a small tumbler with the lump of ice. Squeeze the Lemon Peel over it. Prepare a fancy red wineglass by rubbing a sliced Lemon around the rim. Dip the rim in pulverized White Sugar, so that the Sugar adheres to the edge of the glass. Peel half a Lemon the same as you would an Apple (all in one piece) so that the paring will fit in the wineglass, as shown in the illustration. Strain the Crusta from the tumbler into it. Then smile.

Whiskey Crusta

The Whiskey Crusta is made the same as the Brandy Crusta, using Whiskey instead of Brandy.

Gin Crusta

Gin Crusta is made like the Brandy Crusta, using Gin instead of Brandy

MULLS AND SANGAREES

Mulled Wine without Eggs • Mulled Wine with Eggs
Mulled Wine with Egg Whites • Mulled Wine (in verse) • Mulled Claret
Port Wine Sangaree • Sherry Sangaree • Brandy Sangaree • Gin Sangaree
Ale Sangaree • Porter Sangaree

MULLED WINE WITHOUT EGGS

- 1 pint Wine
- 1 small tumblerful of water
- Sugar to taste
- Spice to taste (Cloves, Nutmeg, Cinnamon, Mace, etc.)
- Dry Toasted Bread or Biscuits to garnish

Combine the water and spices and bring to a boil until the flavor is extracted. Add the wine and bring the whole to the boiling point. Serve with strips of crisp dry toast or biscuits.

Jerry Thomas: "In making preparations like the above, it is very difficult to give the exact proportions of ingredients like Sugar and spice as what quantity might suit one person would be to another, quite distasteful. Any kind of wine may be mulled but Port or Claret are those usually selected for the purpose, and the latter requires a large proportion of Sugar. The vessel that the wine is boiled in must be delicately clean."

MULLED WINE WITH EGGS

- 1 quart Wine
- 1 pint water
- 1 Tablespoon Allspice
- Nutmeg to taste
- 6 Eggs
- Sugar to taste

Boil the wine, water and spices together for a few minutes. Beat the Eggs with Sugar to taste. Slowly pour the boiling wine ON THE EGGS, stirring all the time. Be careful not to pour the Eggs into the wine, or they will curdle.

MULLED WINE WITH EGG WHITES

- 1 pound Sugar
- 4 cups hot water
- 5 cups good Sherry
- 12 Egg whites
- Nutmeg for grating

Dissolve Sugar into water. Add sherry and let sit on the fire until it is almost ready to boil. Meantime, beat up the Egg whites to a froth. Pour whites into the hot mixture, stirring rapidly. Add a little Nutmeg.

MULLED WINE (IN VERSE)

- 9 Eggs, separated
- 2-4 Tablespoons Sugar
- 1 Bottle good Wine
- 2 cups water, divided
- Nutmeg for grating

First, my dear madam, you must take
Nine Eggs, which carefully you'll break-
Into a bowl you'll drop the white,
The yolks into another by it.
Let Betsy beat the whites with switch,
'Till they appear quite frothed and rich-
Another hand the yolks must beat
With Sugar, which will make them sweet'
Three or four spoonfuls may be'll do,
Though some, perhaps would take but two.
Into a skillet next you'll pour
A bottle of good wine, or more-
Put half a pint of water too,
Or it may prove too strong for you';
And while the Eggs (by two) a beating,
The wine and water may be heating;
But, when it comes to boiling heat,
The yolks and whites together beat
With half a pint of water more-
Mixing them well, then gently pour
Into the skillet with the wine,
And stir it briskly all the time.
Then pour it off into a pitcher'
Grate Nutmeg in to make it richer.
Then drink it hot, for he's a fool,
Who lets such precious liquor cool.

MULLED CLARET
Credit: Lord Saltoun

- 1 Peel of one Lemon
- Sugar
- 2 ounces Sherry
- 1 bottle good everyday Claret Wine
- 1 sprig Verbena
- 1 bottle Soda Water (on page 300)
- Ground Nutmeg (optional)

Muddle the Lemon Peel with some Sugar. Add the Sherry and Claret, then add more Sugar to taste. Add the Verbena, soda, and Nutmeg (if using). Heat it and serve hot.

Also see Claret Cup (on page 82)

PORT WINE SANGAREE

- 3 ounces Port Wine
- 1 teaspoon Superfine Sugar
- Nutmeg

Add wine and Sugar to a small bar glass and fill ⅔ with ice. Shake well and serve with grated Nutmeg on top.

SHERRY SANGAREE

- 2 ounces Sherry
- 1 teaspoon Superfine Sugar
- Nutmeg

Add wine and Sugar to a small bar glass and fill 1/3 with ice. Shake well and serve with grated Nutmeg on top.

BRANDY SANGAREE

- 1 teaspoon Sugar
- 1 ounce water
- 2 ounces Brandy
- 1 teaspoon Port Wine

In a small bar glass, dissolve the Sugar into water. Add the Brandy, fill ⅔ with ice and float the port on top.

GIN SANGAREE

- 1 teaspoon Sugar
- 1 ounce water
- 2 ounces Gin
- 1 teaspoon Port Wine

In a small bar glass, dissolve the Sugar into water. Add the Gin, fill ⅔ with ice, and float the port on top.

ALE SANGAREE

- 1 teaspoon Sugar
- 1 Tablespoon water
- Ale
- Nutmeg

In a large bar glass, dissolve the Sugar into the water. Fill the tumbler with ale, and grate Nutmeg on top.

PORTER SANGAREE

The beverage is made the same as an Ale Sangaree but with Porter, and is sometimes called Porteree.

TODDIES AND SLINGS

Apple Toddy • Brandy Toddy • Hot Brandy Toddy • Brandy Sling
Whiskey Toddy • Hot Whiskey Sling • Gin Toddy • Gin Sling

APPLE TODDY

- 1 Tablespoon superfine White Sugar
- 2 ounces Cider Brandy (Applejack or Calvados)
- ½ of a baked Apple
- Nutmeg for grating

Add the Sugar, Apple and Brandy to a small tempered bar glass. Fill the glass ⅔ with boiling water. Grate Nutmeg on top.

BRANDY TODDY

- 1 teaspoon Sugar
- 1 ounce water
- 2 ounces Brandy
- 1 small lump of ice

Add ingredients to a small bar glass and stir.

HOT BRANDY TODDY
For a hot Brandy toddy, omit the ice and fill 2/3 with boiling water.

BRANDY SLING
Grate fresh Nutmeg on top.

WHISKEY TODDY

- 1 teaspoon Sugar
- 1 ounce water
- 2 ounces Whiskey
- 1 small lump of ice

Add ingredients to a small bar glass and stir.

HOT WHISKEY SLING
Omit the Sugar and ice. Fill 1/3 with boiling water. Grate fresh Nutmeg on top.

GIN TODDY

- 1 teaspoon Sugar
- 1 ounce water
- 2 ounces Gin
- 1 small lump of ice

Add ingredients to a small bar glass and stir.

GIN SLING
Grate fresh Nutmeg on top.

FIXES AND SOURS

The Fix • The Sour

In making fixes and sours, be careful and put the Lemon skin in the glass.

THE FIX

- 1 Tablespoon Sugar
- ¼ Lemon
- 1 ounce water
- 2 ounces Base Spirit (Brandy, Gin, Santa Cruz Rum, etc.)

Add ingredients to a small bar glass. Fill ⅔ with shaved ice and stir. Dress the top with seasonal fruit.

THE SOUR

Same ingredients as the fix, omitting the fruits except a small piece of Lemon. Press the Lemon Juice into the glass.

FLIP, NEGUS AND SHRUB

Rum Flip • Rum Flip (another method) • Ale Flip • Egg Flip
Egg Flip (another method) • Brandy Flip • Port Wine Negus (Large Batch)
Port Wine Negus (Single Serving) • Soda Negus • Cherry Shrub
White Currant Shrub • Currant Shrub • Raspberry Shrub • Brandy Shrub
Rum Shrub • English Rum Shrub

"Charles Dibdin has immortalized [the flip] as the favorite beverage of sailors (although we believe they seldom indulge in it) – The essential in "flips" of all sorts is, to produce the smoothness by repeatedly pouring back and forward between two vessels, and beating up the Eggs well in the first instance."

Rum Flip

- 4 ounces Rum
- 2 pints Beer (or water when Malt liquor is not available)
- 3-4 Eggs
- Sugar and spices to taste.

Beat the Eggs well. Combine all the ingredients, then pour back and forth between two pitchers until smooth.

Rum Flip (Another method)
Serves: 1 quart of flip

- 2 pints Ale
- 4 oz Sugar (moistened)
- 3-4 Eggs
- 4 ounces old Rum or Brandy
- 1 teaspoon ground Ginger or Nutmeg
- Dried and Powdered Lemon Peel

Rub the Ginger or Nutmeg with a little bit of the Lemon Peel together in a mortar. Put the ale on the fire to warm. Combine the Eggs, Sugar, rum or Brandy, along with the Ginger or Nutmeg mixture, and beat well. When the ale is near to boiling, put it into one pitcher, and the rum and Eggs etc., into another pitcher. Turn it from one pitcher to another till it is as smooth as cream.

Ale Flip

- 2 pints Ale
- 2 Egg whites, well beaten separately
- 4 Egg yolks, well beaten separately
- 4 Tablespoons moist Sugar
- .5 Tablespoon grated Nutmeg

In a saucepan, bring the ale to a boil. Place the Sugar and Nutmeg in a bowl and slowly add the Egg whites and yolks. Mix well. While stirring constantly, slowly pour the ale into the Egg mixture. When combined, pour the entire mixture rapidly back and forth between two jugs until the flip is smooth and finely frothed.

Jerry Thomas: "This is a good remedy to take at the commencement of a cold."

EGG FLIP

- 2 pints Ale
- 2 Egg white
- 4 Egg yolks
- 4 Tablespoons Brown Sugar
- Nutmeg to taste

In a tinned saucepan bring the Ale to a boil. In another saucepan, combine the Egg whites, yolks, Sugar, and Nutmeg, and beat well. Pour the ale into the Egg mixture slowly, beating constantly to prevent the mixture from curdling. Then pour back and forth repeatedly from pan to pan, raising the hand as high as possible to produce the smoothness and frothing essential to a good quality flip.

Jerry Thomas: "This is excellent for a cold, and, from its fleecy appearance, is sometimes designated a 'Yard of Flannel'."

EGG FLIP (ANOTHER METHOD)

- 4 Egg yolks
- 2 Egg whites
- 6 large Sugar Lumps
- 12 ounces Cognac
- 6 ounces aged Jamaican Rum
- 4-5 cups boiling water

In a large jug, beat the Eggs well. Add the Sugar and mix until well combined. Pour in the boiling water, about 1 cup at a time, stirring constantly. When the jug is nearly full, add the Cognac and rum.

BRANDY FLIP

- 1 teaspoon Sugar
- 2 ounces Brandy
- Toasted Cracker
- Nutmeg for grating

Add Sugar and Brandy to a small bar glass and fill ⅓ full of hot water. Mix, then place the cracker on top, and grate Nutmeg over it.

PORT WINE NEGUS (LARGE BATCH)

- 1 pint Port Wine (or Sherry, or any other sweet wine)
- 2 pints boiling water
- 4 oz Sugar Cubes
- 1 Lemon
- Grated Nutmeg to taste.

These portions can be multiplied to the batch size desired.

Put the wine into a jug. Rub the Sugar on the Lemon rind until all the yellow part of the skin is absorbed, then squeeze the juice and strain it. Add the Sugar and Lemon Juice to the port wine with the grated Nutmeg. Add the boiling water and cover the jug. Serve when slightly cooled.

Jerry Thomas: "This beverage is named after Colonel Negus, who is said to have invented it."

PORT WINE NEGUS (SINGLE SERVING)

- 2 oz Port Wine.
- 1 teaspoonful Sugar

Place the Sugar and wine into a small bar glass, then fill 1/3 with hot water.

SODA NEGUS

- 8 oz Port Wine
- 4 teaspoons Sugar
- 3 Cloves
- Nutmeg for grating
- 1 bottle Soda Water (on page 300)

In a saucepan, combine the wine, Sugar, Cloves and about 1" diameter (24mm) grated Nutmeg. Heat to just below boiling temperature. Transfer to a large bowl or jug and mix in the Soda Water.

Jerry Thomas: "A most refreshing and elegant beverage, particularly for those who do not take punch or grog after supper."

CHERRY SHRUB

- 6 -7 lbs. ripe Cherries (no stems)
- Sugar to taste
- 4 ounces Brandy (optional)

Place the washed Cherries into a double-boiler. Boil until the juice is extracted. Strain through a cloth thick enough to filter out the pulp. Sweeten it to your taste as you filter it until perfectly clear. In a 1-liter bottle, add the Brandy, then fill with the Cherry Juice.

By adding the Brandy, it will keep through the summer. It is delicious mixed with water. Irish or Monongahela whiskey can be substituted instead of the Brandy, though not as good.

WHITE CURRANT SHRUB

- 3.5 lbs. White Currants (yields 8-9 cups juice)
- 1 gallon Rum
- 2 lbs. Sugar

Strip and clean the fruit, then add to a double boiler. Boil until the juice is extracted, then strain. Add the Sugar and rum, then strain through a jelly bag.

CURRANT SHRUB

- 1 lb. Sugar
- 1 pint strained Currant Juice (1 lbs. Currants)
- 2-3 ounces Brandy

Combine juice and Sugar and boil gently for eight or ten minutes, skimming well. Remove from heat, and when lukewarm, add 2 oz Brandy to every pint of the mixture. Bottle tight.

RASPBERRY SHRUB

- 2 pints Vinegar
- 6 pints ripe Raspberries
- 6 lbs. Sugar
- 18 oz Brandy

Combine the Raspberries and Vinegar. After standing for a day, strain it. It should yield about 12 cups of liquid. For each pint of liquid, add a pound of Sugar. Bring to a boil for about 30 minutes, skimming it clear. Let the mixture cool, then add 2 ounces of Brandy for every pint of the resulting mixture.

Jerry Thomas: "Two spoonsful of this shrub mixed with a tumbler of water, is an excellent drink in warm weather and in fevers."

BRANDY SHRUB

- 5 Lemons
- 4 pints Brandy
- 2 pints Sherry
- 2 lbs. Sugar

Peel the rinds thinly from two of the Lemons, then juice all five. Combine the Lemon Peels and juice with the Brandy. Cover and let sit for 3 days. Then mix in the sherry and Sugar. Strain through a jelly bag and bottle.

RUM SHRUB

- 3 pints Orange Juice
- 1 lb. Sugar
- 1 gallon Rum

Put all ingredients into a cask and leave for six weeks.

ENGLISH RUM SHRUB

- 3 gallons best Jamaican Rum
- 2 pints Orange Juice
- 16 Lemons (2 cups juice)
- 6 lbs. Powdered Sugar
- 3 pints Milk

Thinly peel the Lemons, then juice them. Combine the rum, Orange Juice, Lemon Peels, Lemon Juice and Powdered Sugar. Cover tight and let sit overnight. The next day, boil the Milk and let it cool. Add the cooled Milk to the rum and juice mixture and mix well. Let stand for 1 hour, then filter through a flannel bag lined with blotting paper. Bottle and cork immediately.

FANCY DRINKS

---

*Badminton • Balaklava Nectar • Bishop • Archbishop • Cardinal • Pope
Prusse Bishop • A Bishop (Protestant) • Bottled Velvet
Champagne, Hock or Chablis Cup • Cider Nectar • Claret Cup
Brunow Claret Cup • Brunow Champagne Cup • Saltoun Claret Cup
Crimean Cup, a la Marmora • Crimean Cup • English Curaçao
Italian Lemonade • Knickerbocker • Locomotive • Porter Cup • Pousse Café's
Parisian Pousse Café • Faivre's Pousse Café • Pousse l'Amour
Santina's Pousse Café • Scaffa • Brandy Champerelle
Brandy Scaffa • Rumfustian • Sleeper • Tom and Jerry • Tom and Jerry Batter
White Lion • White Tiger's Milk*

---

*The following miscellaneous collection of fancy beverages embraces a number of
French, Spanish, English, Russian, Italian, German and American recipes.*

BADMINTON

- ½ medium-size Cucumber, peeled
- 4 oz Powdered Sugar
- 1 pinch ground Nutmeg
- 1 bottle Claret Wine
- 1 bottle Soda Water (on page 300)

Put the Cucumber into a silver punch bowl along with the Powdered Sugar and Nutmeg. Add the Claret and mix until Sugar dissolves. Add the Soda Water.

BALAKLAVA NECTAR

Credit: by Soyer

Serves a party of fifteen.

- 2 Lemons
- 2 Tablespoons crushed Sugar
- .5 small Cucumber, unpeeled and sliced thin
- 2 bottles Soda Water (on page 300)
- 2 bottles Claret Wine
- 1 bottle Champagne

Thinly peel the rind from half of one Lemon and shred it fine. Juice the Lemons and add along with the peel into a punch bowl. Add the Sugar and Cucumber and toss the mixture several times. Add the soda, Claret and Champagne. Stir well and serve.

BISHOP

- 1 Orange
- Cloves
- 1 quart Port Wine
- Sugar to taste

Heat the wine in a large saucepan. Stick the Orange full of Cloves, and roast it over a fire. When brown enough, cut it into quarters, then add it to the hot wine. Add Sugar to taste and let the mixture simmer for half an hour. Serve warm in a glass.

ARCHBISHOP

The same as Bishop, substituting Claret Wine as the wine.

CARDINAL

Same as Bishop, substituting Champagne as the wine.

POPE
Same as Bishop, substituting Burgundy Wine as the wine.

PRUSSE BISHOP
Credit: a la Prusse

- 4 good-sized Bitter Oranges (or Lemons)
- .5 lb. Sugar
- 1 bottle Claret Wine (or Port Wine)

Roast the oranges until they are pale brown. Place them in a container. Add the Sugar and about 6 ounces of the wine. Let this stand for 24 hours. Transfer to a double boiler and heat. Muddle the fruit and strain through a sieve. Boil the remaining wine, being careful not to burn it, and then add it to the strained mixture. Serve warm in a glass.

Lemons can be substituted for the oranges, but is not done often when using Port instead of Claret. See recipe Bishop (on page 293) in "The Manual for the Manufacture of Cordials, etc." at the latter part of this work.

A BISHOP (PROTESTANT)
- 4 Tablespoons of White Sugar
- 2 Tumblers of water
- 1 Lemon, sliced
- 1 bottle Claret Wine
- 4 Tablespoons Santa Cruz Rum or Jamaican Rum
- Ice

BOTTLED VELVET
Credit: Sir John Bayley

- 1 bottle Moselle Wine
- 8 oz Sherry
- Lemon Peel to taste
- 2 Tablespoons Sugar
- 1 sprig Verbena

Combine the Moselle, sherry, and Lemon Peel (not too much to where it dominates the flavor). Add the Sugar and Verbena. Mix well and strain. Chill with ice and serve.

CHAMPAGNE, HOCK OR CHABLIS CUP
Credit: Goodriche

- 4-5 Sugar Lumps
- 4 ounces boiling water
- 1 thin Lemon Peel
- 1 bottle Champagne, Hock Wine, or Chablis Wine
- 1 sprig Verbena
- 2 ounces Sherry
- 1 cup water

Dissolve the Sugar into the boiling water with the Lemon Peel. Let it stand for 15 minutes. Add the wine, Verbena, sherry, and water. Mix well and let stand for 30 minutes. Strain and ice well before serving.

CIDER NECTAR
Credit: Harold Littledale

- 1 quart Cider
- 1 bottle Soda Water
- 2 oz Sherry
- 1 oz Brandy
- Juice of ½ Lemon
- Peel of ¼ Lemon
- Sugar and Nutmeg to taste
- 1 sprig of Verbena
- Pineapple Extract to taste

Combine all the ingredients. Strain and ice it all well.

Jerry Thomas: "This is a delicious beverage, and only requires to be tasted to be appreciated."

CLARET CUP

- 1 bottle Claret Wine, thin
- 8 ounces water
- 1 Tablespoon Powdered Sugar
- 1 teaspoon ground Cinnamon
- 1 teaspoon ground Cloves
- 1 teaspoon ground Allspice
- ½ Lemon Rind, peeled thin

Mix the Sugar, spices, wine and water well. Add the Lemon Rind.

Jerry Thomas: "This is a delicious summer beverage for evening parties." See Mulled Claret (on page 64)

BRUNOW CLARET CUP
Credit: Brunow

Jerry Thomas: "The following Claret and Champagne cup ought, from its excellence, to be called the nectar of the Czar, as it is so highly appreciated in Russia, where for many years it has enjoyed a high reputation amongst the aristocracy of the Muscovite empire."

Serves a party of twenty.

- 3 bottles Claret Wine
- ⅔ pint Curaçao (on page 226)
- 1 pint Sherry
- 1 cup Brandy
- 4 ounces Ratafia of Raspberries (on page 251)
- 3 Oranges, sliced
- 1 Lemon, sliced
- Green Balm sprigs
- Borage
- 1 piece Cucumber rind
- 2 bottles German Seltzer Water
- 3 bottles Soda Water (on page 300)
- Capillaire (on page 94) or Superfine Sugar to taste

For the Claret Cup, stir the ingredients together, and sweeten with Capillaire or pounded Sugar, until it ferments (settles). Let it stand for one hour, then strain it and ice it well. It is then fit for use. Serve in small glasses.

BRUNOW CHAMPAGNE CUP
Credit: Brunow

For the Champagne Cup: use Champagne instead of Claret, and Noyau instead of Ratafia.

SALTOUN CLARET CUP

Credit: Lord Saltoun

- 1 Peel of one Lemon
- Superfine Sugar
- 2 ounces Sherry
- 1 bottle good everyday Claret Wine
- 1 sprig Verbena
- 1 bottle Soda Water (on page 300)
- Ground Nutmeg (optional)

Muddle the Lemon Peel with some Sugar. Add the Sherry and Claret, then add more Sugar to taste. Add the Verbena, soda, and Nutmeg (if using). Shake with ice and strain.

For mulled, heat it and serve hot (see Mulled Claret (on page 64)).

CRIMEAN CUP, A LA MARMORA

Credit: From a recipe by the celebrated Soyer

Serves a party of thirty

- 1 quart Orgeat Syrup (on page 307)
- 1 pint Cognac Brandy
- 8 oz Maraschino Liqueur (on page 235)
- 8 oz Jamaican Rum
- 2 bottles Champagne, well chilled
- 2 bottles. Soda Water (on page 300)
- 6 oz of Sugar
- 4 medium-sized Lemons

Thinly peel the Lemons and place the rinds in a bowl with the Sugar. Macerate them well for a minute or two, to extract the flavor from the Lemon. Next, squeeze in the juice of the Lemons. Add 2 bottles of Soda Water and stir well until Sugar is dissolved. Pour in the Orgeat Syrup and whip the mixture well with an Egg-whisk, to whiten the composition. Then add the Brandy, rum, and maraschino. Strain into a punch bowl. Add the chilled champagne just before serving. While adding the champagne, stir well with the ladle. This will render the cup creamy and mellow.

This recipe can be halved or less as needed.

CRIMEAN CUP
Credit: Wyndham

Serves a party of five

- ½ Orange Rind, thinly peeled
- 1 Tablespoon Superfine Sugar
- 2 oz Maraschino Liqueur (on page 235)
- 1 oz Cognac
- 1 oz Curaçao (on page 226)
- 2 bottles Soda Water (on page 300)
- 1 bottle Champagne
- .5 lbs. pure ice (optional)

Put the Orange peel into a bowl along with the Sugar, and muddle for a minute. Then add the Maraschino, Cognac, and Curaçao. Mix in the Soda Water, then add the Champagne, working it up and down with the punch ladle. Adding the ice greatly improves it.

ENGLISH CURAÇAO

- 1.5 cups (6 ounces) thinly peeled Orange Rinds
- 1 pint genuine Whiskey
- 1 pint Plain White Syrup (on page 136)
- 1 drachm powdered Alum
- 1 drachm Potassium Carbonate

Put the Orange peels and whiskey in a quart-sized sealed container. Let this infuse for 10-12 days, shaking well occasionally. Remove the Orange peel and fill the container with syrup. Shake well and let sit for 3 days. Pour a few ounces into another container and muddle well with the Alum and Potassium Carbonate. Return this to the mixture, shake well and let sit for a week.

Jerry Thomas: "You will find the Curaçao perfectly transparent, and equal in flavor to that imported from Malines or any other place in the universe"

ITALIAN LEMONADE

- 24 Lemons
- 2 lbs. Sugar
- 1 quart good Sherry
- 3 quarts boiling water
- 1 quart boiling Milk

Peel the Lemons, then juice them. Place the peels in a large container and pour the juice over them. Leave them to sit overnight. In the morning, add the Sugar, sherry and boiling water. Mix well, then add the boiling Milk. Strain through a jelly bag until clear.

KNICKERBOCKER

- ½ Lime or Lemon
- 2 teaspoons Raspberry Syrup (on page 309)
- 2 ounces Santa Cruz Rum
- 1 barspoon Curaçao (on page 226)
- Seasonal Berries for garnish

In a small bar glass, muddle the fruit. Add the syrup, rum and Curaçao. Cool with shaved ice. Shake up well, and ornament with berries in season. If this is not sweet enough, put in a little more Raspberry syrup

LOCOMOTIVE

- 2 Egg yolks
- 1 ounce Honey
- 1 dash Essence of Cloves
- 1 oz Curaçao (on page 226)
- 1 pint high Burgundy Wine, heated

Put the Egg yolks in a goblet along with the Honey. Add the Essence of Cloves and Curaçao. Add the hot Burgundy and whisk until well mixed. Serve hot in glasses.

PORTER CUP

- 1 bottle Porter (on page 143)
- 1 bottle Table Ale (on page 141)
- 2 ounces Brandy
- 1 barspoon Ginger Syrup (on page 305)
- 3-4 Sugar Lumps
- ½ Nutmeg, grated
- 1 teaspoon Sodium Carbonate
- Cucumber rind for garnish.

Combine the Ales, Brandy, syrup, Sugar and Nutmeg into a tankard or covered jug. Cover and chill for 30 minutes. Just before serving, add the Sodium Carbonate and garnish with the Cucumber rind.

POUSSE CAFÉ'S

NOTE: A POUSSE CAFÉ IS A LAYERED DRINK, IN WHICH INGREDIENTS ARE CAREFULLY ADDED IN ORDER OF WEIGHT (HEAVIEST TO LIGHTEST). IF MADE PROPERLY, A CLEAN SEPARATION ON INGREDIENTS AND COLORS MAY BE SEEN.

PARISIAN POUSSE CAFÉ

- .5 oz Curaçao (on page 226)
- .5 oz Kirschwasser (on page 212)
- .5 oz Chartreuse

In a small wine glass, carefully layer the ingredients, maintaining separation, in the order given.

Jerry Thomas: "This is a celebrated Parisian drink."

FAIVRE'S POUSSE CAFÉ

- ⅓ Parisian Pousse Cafe (as above)
- ⅓ (1.5 oz) Kirschwasser (on page 212)
- ⅓ (1.5oz) Curaçao (on page 226)

In a small wine glass, carefully layer the ingredients, maintaining separation, in the order given.

Jerry Thomas: "This celebrated drink is from the recipe of M. Faivre, a popular proprietor of a "French Saloon" in New York."

POUSSE L'AMOUR

- .75 oz Maraschino Liqueur (on page 235)
- 1 Egg yolk
- .5 oz Vanilla Cordial (on page 204)
- Splash Cognac Brandy

This delightful French drink is described in the below illustration. To mix it, fill a small wine glass half full of maraschino, then put in the Egg yolk. Surround the yolk with Vanilla Cordial and dash the top with Cognac.

SANTINA'S POUSSE CAFÉ

- .5 oz Maraschino Liqueur (on page 235)
- .5 oz Curaçao (on page 226)
- .5 oz Brandy (Cognac)

In a small wine glass, carefully layer the ingredients, maintaining separation, in the order given.

Jerry Thomas: "This delicious drink is from a recipe by Santina, proprietor of "Santina's Saloon", a celebrated Spanish Cafe in New Orleans."

SCAFFA

NOTE: A SCAFFA IS A MIXED DRINK SERVED NEAT, USUALLY COMPRISED OF A HARD SPIRIT, A SWEETENER OR TWO (LIQUEUR, CORDIAL, SYRUP, ETC.), AND OFTEN BITTERS.

BRANDY CHAMPERELLE

- ⅓ Brandy
- ⅓ Bogart's Bitters (on page 353)
- ⅓ Curaçao (on page 226)

Serve in a small wine glass.

Jerry Thomas: "This is a delicious French cafe drink."

BRANDY SCAFFA

- ½ Brandy
- ½ Maraschino Liqueur (on page 235)
- 2 dashes of Bitters

Serve in a small wine glass.

RUMFUSTIAN

- 12 Egg yolks
- 1 quart strong Beer
- 1 pint Gin
- 1 bottle Sherry
- 1 stick Cinnamon
- 1 Nutmeg, ground
- 12 cubes Sugar
- 1 Lemon Rind, peeled thinly

Whisk the Egg yolks well and combine with the Beer and Gin. Put the sherry, Cinnamon, Nutmeg, Sugar and Lemon Peel in a saucepan. Heat to a boil, then add to the Beer mixture. Serve hot.

Jerry Thomas: "This is the singular name bestowed upon a drink very much in vogue with English sportsmen after their return from a day's shooting"

SLEEPER

- 1 cup water
- 6 Cloves
- 6 Coriander Seeds
- A bit of Cinnamon
- 4 oz old Rum
- 2 Tablespoons (1 oz) Sugar
- 2 Egg yolks
- ½ Lemon, juiced (1 oz)

Boil the Cloves, Coriander, and Cinnamon in the water. Separately combine the rum, Sugar, Egg yolks and Lemon Juice. When the spices have been infused, whisk everything together, and strain into a tumbler.

TOM AND JERRY

- 1 Tablespoon Tom and Jerry Batter (see next recipe)
- 2 ounces Brandy
- Boiling water
- Nutmeg for grating

Place the batter in a small bar glass. Add the Brandy, then fill with boiling water. Grate a little Nutmeg on top.

Bartenders, when serving Tom and Jerry, sometimes use a mixture of ½ Brandy, ¼ Jamaican Rum and ¼ Santa Cruz Rum, instead of Brandy plain. This compound is usually mixed and kept in a bottle and 2 ounces is used in each tumbler of Tom and Jerry.

Jerry Thomas: "This drink is sometimes called Copenhagen and sometimes Jerry Thomas."

TOM AND JERRY BATTER

- 5 lbs. Sugar
- 12 Eggs, separated
- 1 ounce Jamaican Rum
- 1.5 teaspoons ground Cinnamon
- ½ teaspoon ground Cloves
- ½ teaspoon ground Allspice
- 1 teaspoon Cream of Tartar or Sodium Carbonate

Beat the whites of the Eggs to a stiff froth, and the yolks until they are as thin as water. Then mix together and add the spices and rum. Thicken with Sugar until the mixture attains the consistency of a light batter.

Note: A teaspoon of Cream of Tartar, or about as much Sodium Carbonate as you can get on a dime, will prevent the Sugar from settling to the bottom of the mixture.

WHITE LION

- 1.5 teaspoon Superfine Sugar
- ½ Lime (squeeze out juice and put the rind in glass)
- 2 ounces Santa Cruz Rum
- 1 barspoon Curaçao (on page 226)
- 1 barspoon Raspberry Syrup (on page 309)

Combine the Sugar, Lime Juice and rind, rum, Curaçao and Raspberry syrup into a small bar glass. Mix well. Ornament with berries in season, and cool with shaved ice.

WHITE TIGER'S MILK

Credit: From a recipe in the possession of Thomas Dunn English, Esq.

- 2 ounces Applejack
- 2 ounces Peach Brandy (on page 181)
- ½ teaspoon Aromatic Tincture (on page 93)
- Sugar to taste.
- 1 Egg white, beaten to a stiff foam.
- 1 quart of pure Milk
- Ground Nutmeg

Pour the ingredients into the Milk, stirring all the while until all is well mixed. Then sprinkle with Nutmeg.

Jerry Thomas: "The above recipe is sufficient to make a full quart of "white tiger's Milk". If more is wanted, you can increase the above proportions. If you want to prepare this beverage for a party of twenty, use one gallon of Milk to 1 pint of Applejack, etc."

NOTE: JERRY THOMAS'S NOTE ON MAKING THIS RECIPE FOR A PARTY OF 20 CONTRADICTS HIS APPLEJACK PROPORTIONS FOR THE SMALLER BATCH. CONSIDER USING 4 OUNCES OF APPLEJACK INSTEAD OF THE 2 OUNCES LISTED IN THE RECIPE.

RATAFIAS AND TINCTURES

Aromatic Tincture • Capillaire • Capillaire (another recipe)
"Jerry Thomas'" own Decanter Bitters • Quince Liqueur

Every liqueur made by infusions is called ratafia. That is, when the spirit is made to imbibe thoroughly the aromatic flavor and color of the fruit steeped in it. When this has taken place, the liqueur is drawn off and Sugar added to it. It is then filtered and bottled. See recipe Ratafia de Grenades (on page 252) in "The manual for the Manufacture of Cordials, etc." in the latter part of this work.

AROMATIC TINCTURE

- 1 oz Ginger
- 1 oz Cinnamon
- 1 oz Orange Peel
- ½ ounce Valerian Root
- 2 quarts Alcohol

Macerate in a closed vessel for fourteen days, then filter through unsized paper.

CAPILLAIRE

- 2 ounces Curaçao (on page 226)
- 16 ounces Plain White Syrup (on page 136)

Shake syrup and Curaçao together well. A teaspoon of this mixture added to a glass of fair water makes a pleasant "eau sucre" (sweet water). See Capillaire (Maidenhair) Syrup on page 302 in "Manual for the Manufacture of Cordials, etc."

CAPILLAIRE (ANOTHER RECIPE)

- 1 gallon water
- 28 pounds Sugar
- 4 - 5 Egg whites, well beaten
- Orange Flower Water or Bitter Almonds to taste

Combine the water and Sugar and bring to a simmer. While heating, when the mixture reaches Milk-warm, add the Egg whites. As these simmer with the syrup, skim it well. Pour off the mixture, and flavor it with the Orange Flower Water or Bitter Almonds as desired.

JERRY THOMAS' OWN DECANTER BITTERS

- 4 oz Raisins
- 2 oz Cinnamon
- 1 oz Snakeroot (on page 347)
- 1 Lemon, sliced
- 1 Orange, sliced
- 1 oz Cloves
- 1 oz Allspice
- Santa Cruz Rum

Add all ingredients to a decanter and let sit. Serve in pony glasses. As the bitters is used, refill it with more rum.

QUINCE LIQUEUR

- 4 pints Quince Juice (about 4 lbs. Quinces)
- 4 quarts Cognac Brandy
- 2.5 lbs. White Sugar
- 12 oz. Bitter Almonds, bruised
- 1 lb. Coriander Seed
- 36 Cloves

Grate enough quinces to make 4 pints of juice and squeeze them through a jelly bag. Mix all of the ingredients and put them in a sealable container. Let sit for 10 days, shaking well once per day. Strain the liquid through a jelly bag until it is perfectly clear, and bottle for use.

Jerry Thomas: "This is a delightful liqueur, and can be relied upon, as it is from a recipe in the possession of a lady who is famous for concocting delicious potations."

MISCELLANEOUS DRINKS

*Blue Blazer • Burnt Brandy and Peach • Black Stripe • Peach and Honey
Gin and Wood • Gin and Pine • Gin and Tansy • Gin and Wormwood
Scotch Whiskey Skin • Columbia Skin • Hot Rum • Hot Spiced Rum
Stone Fence • Absinthe • Rhine Wine and Seltzer-Water • "Arf and Arf"
Brandy Straight • Brandy and Gum • Gin Straight • Pony Brandy
Brandy and Soda (Stone Wall) • Sherry and Egg • Sherry and Bitters • Sherry and Ice*

BLUE BLAZER

- 2 oz Scotch Whisky
- 2 oz boiling water
- 1 teaspoon Powdered Sugar
- Lemon Peel for garnish

Use two large, silver-plated mugs with handles. Put the whiskey and the boiling water in one mug. Ignite the liquid with fire, and while blazing, mix both ingredients by pouring them four or five times from one mug to the other, as shown in the illustration. If done well, this will have the appearance of a continuous string of liquid fire.

Sweeten with the Powdered Sugar. Serve in a small bar tumbler, with a piece of Lemon Peel.

Jerry Thomas: "The Blue Blazer does not have a very euphonious or classic name, but it tastes better to the palate than it sounds to the ear. A beholder gazing for the first time upon an experienced artist, compounding this beverage, would naturally come to the conclusion that it was a nectar for Pluto, rather than Bacchus. The novice in mixing this beverage should be careful not to scald himself. To become proficient in throwing the liquid from one mug to the other, it will be necessary to practice for some time with cold water."

BURNT BRANDY AND PEACH

- 2 oz Cognac
- ½ Tablespoon Sugar
- 2 or 3 slices dried Peaches

Burn the above ingredients in a saucer or plate. Place the dried fruit in a small bar glass and pour the liquid over them.

Jerry Thomas: "This drink is very popular in the Southern States, where it is sometimes used as a cure for diarrhea."

BLACK STRIPE

- 2 oz Santa Cruz Rum
- 1 Tablespoon Molasses
- 1 Tablespoon water (for cold)
- Boiling water (for hot)
- Nutmeg for grating

This drink can either be made in summer or winter. In the summer, dissolve molasses in the water, add the rum and fill with shaved ice. In the winter, put molasses and rum in a tempered glass and fill with boiling water. Grate a little Nutmeg on top.

PEACH AND HONEY

- 1 Tablespoon of Honey
- 2 oz Peach Brandy (on page 181)

Add to a small bar glass and stir with a spoon

GIN AND WOOD

Jerry Thomas: "The [following] three drinks are not much used except in small country villages."

GIN AND PINE

- 2 oz pencil-sized splints of Green Pine Log Heart
- 1 quart Gin

Add the pine splints to the Gin and let soak for 2 hours. Serve in a wine glass.

GIN AND TANSY

NOTE: TANSY IS KNOWN TO BE TOXIC AND CAN BE FATAL. WHILE IT IS SAID TO BE SAFE IN DISTILLED SPIRITS, I MAKE NO RECOMMENDATION FOR TRYING THIS DRINK.

Fill a quart decanter ½ full of Tansy and pour in Gin to fill up the balance ⅓ Tansy to ⅔ Gin. Serve to customers in a wine glass.

GIN AND WORMWOOD

NOTE: WORMWOOD CONTAINS THUJONE, WHICH IS KNOWN TO BE TOXIC. I DO NOT RECOMMEND PREPARING THIS DRINK.

Put three or four sprigs of Wormwood into a quart decanter and fill up with Gin. Serve in a small bar glass.

SCOTCH WHISKEY SKIN

- 2 oz Scotch Whisky
- 1 piece of Lemon Peel

Add to a small tumbler and then fill up to halfway with boiling water.

COLUMBIA SKIN
This is a Boston drink and is made the same as a Whiskey Skin.

HOT RUM

- 1 teaspoon Sugar
- 2 oz Jamaican Rum
- 1 piece of Butter as large as half of a chestnut
- Nutmeg for grating

Add ingredients to a small glass and fill with hot water. Grate Nutmeg over the top

HOT SPICED RUM

- 1 teaspoon Sugar
- 2 oz Jamaican Rum
- 1 teaspoonful of mixed spices (Allspice and Cloves)
- 1 piece of Butter as large as half of a chestnut

Add ingredients to a small glass and fill with hot water.

STONE FENCE

- 2 oz Bourbon Whiskey
- 2 or 3 small lumps of ice
- Sweet Cider (on page 148)

Add the Bourbon and ice to a large bar glass, then fill with Cider.

ABSINTHE

- 2 oz Absinthe

Pour Absinthe into a small bar glass. Add water, drop by drop, until the glass is full. Never use a spoon.

RHINE WINE AND SELTZER-WATER

- Rhine Wine
- Seltzer Water

Fill a large bar glass half-full with Rhine wine, and fill balance with Seltzer Water.

Jerry Thomas: "This is a German drink and is not very likely to be called for at an American bar."

"ARF AND ARF"

- Porter (on page 143)
- Ale

In London, this drink is made by mixing half Porter and half Ale (pale/mild) in a large bar glass. In America it is made by mixing half new and half old Ale.

BRANDY STRAIGHT

In serving this drink, you simply put a piece of ice in a small tumbler, and hand it to your customer, with the bottle of Brandy.

Jerry Thomas: "This is very safe for a steady drink, but though a straight beverage, it is often used on a bender."

BRANDY AND GUM
Same as Brandy straight, with one dash of Gum Syrup

GIN STRAIGHT
Same as Brandy straight, substituting Gin for Brandy.

PONY BRANDY

- 1 oz best (Sazerac) Brandy

Fill a pony glass, and hand it to your customer.

BRANDY AND SODA (SOMETIMES CALLED STONE WALL)

- 2 ounces Cognac Brandy
- Soda Water (on page 300)

Pour the Cognac into a large bar glass and fill one-third full of fine ice. Fill the rest with the soda.

SHERRY AND EGG

- 2 oz Sherry
- 1 Egg

Serve in a small bar glass.

SHERRY AND BITTERS

- 2 oz Sherry
- 1 dash of Bitters

SHERRY AND ICE

Put two lumps of ice into a small bar glass and fill with Sherry.

TEMPERANCE DRINKS

Lemonade • Plain Lemonade • Lemonade (Fine for Parties)
Draught Lemonade, or Lemon Sherbet • Orangeade • Orgeat Lemonade
Ginger Lemonade • Lemonade Powders • Soda Nectar
Drink for the Dog Days • Sherbet • Imperial Drink for Families • Nectar
Raspberry, Strawberry, Currant, or Orange Effervescing Draughts • Ginger Wine

LEMONADE

- ½ Lemon, juiced
- 1.5 Tablespoons Sugar
- 2 -3 pieces Orange
- 1 Tablespoon Raspberry Syrup (on page 309) or Strawberry Syrup(on page 310)
- 1 dash Port Wine

Add the Lemon Juice, Sugar, Orange and syrup to a large bar glass. Fill the tumbler one-half full with shaved ice and fill the rest with water. Dash with port wine, and ornament with seasonal fruit.

* See Lemonade (on page 299) recipes in "The Manual for the Manufacture of Cordials, etc." at the latter part of this work.

PLAIN LEMONADE
Credit: From a recipe by the celebrated Soyer

- 3 Lemons, sliced very thin
- .5 lb. White Sugar or Brown Sugar
- 1 gallon water

Combine the Lemons and Sugar in a large container and muddle. Add the water and stir well.

LEMONADE (FINE FOR PARTIES)

- 3 large Lemons
- .5 lbs. Lump Sugar
- 1 quart of boiling water
- 1 Egg white, beaten (optional)
- Sherry (optional)

Rub some of the Sugar lumps on two of the Lemons until they have taken in all of the oil from the Lemons. Put these lumps along with the remainder of the Sugar into a jug. Juice the Lemons and add to the jug (no pips). Pour in the boiling water and stir until the Sugar is dissolved. Strain the lemonade through a piece of muslin and, when cool, it will be ready for use.

> *Jerry Thomas: "The lemonade will be much improved by having the white of an Egg beaten up with it. A little sherry mixed with it also makes this beverage much nicer."*

DRAUGHT LEMONADE, OR LEMON SHERBET

- 4 Lemons, sliced
- 4 ounces Sugar
- 2 pints boiling water.

Adjust sweetness to taste. For a cheaper drink:

- 1 oz Cream of Tartar
- 1 oz Tartaric Acid or Citric Acid
- 2 Lemons (the juice and peel)
- ½ pound, or more, of Sugar

ORANGEADE

This agreeable beverage is made the same way as lemonade, substituting oranges for Lemons.

ORGEAT LEMONADE

- 1 oz Orgeat Syrup (on page 307)
- .5 Lemon, juiced

Combine the syrup and juice in a mixing glass. Fill it ⅓ full of ice and the rest with water. Shake well, pour into a large bar glass and ornament with berries in season.

GINGER LEMONADE

- 12.5 lbs. Sugar
- 10 gallons water
- 6 Egg whites
- .5 lbs. Ginger
- 10 Lemons, pared
- 2 Tablespoons Yeast
- .5 oz Isinglass

Place the Lemons in a large container. Heat the water to boiling and then add the Sugar, boiling for 20 minutes. Clear it with the Egg whites. Bruise the Ginger and add it to the boiling mixture. Pour the boiling mixture over the Lemons and let sit until completely cool. Slice the Lemons and then put everything into a cask along with the Yeast and Isinglass. Bung up the cask the next day and let sit for 2 weeks.

LEMONADE POWDERS

- 1 lb. Powdered Sugar
- 1 oz Tartaric Acid or Citric Acid
- 20 drops Essence of Lemon
- 1 ounce Sodium Carbonate (optional for sparkling)

Mix and keep very dry. To serve, place 2-3 teaspoons in a tumbler. Add cold water and stir briskly.

SODA NECTAR

- 1 Lemon
- 12 oz water
- Powdered White Sugar to taste
- 1 barspoon of Sodium Carbonate

Fill a large tumbler ¾ with water. Strain the juice of the Lemon, and add it to the water, with sufficient White Sugar to sweeten the whole nicely. When well mixed, put in the Sodium Carbonate, stir well, and drink while the mixture is in an effervescing state.

DRINK FOR THE DOG DAYS

- 1 bottle Soda Water (on page 300)
- 1 Lemon Ice Cube

Combine in a large goblet.

Jerry Thomas: "Forms a deliciously cool and refreshing drink, but should be taken with some care, and positively avoided whilst you are very hot."

SHERBET

- 8 oz Sodium Carbonate
- 6 oz Tartaric Acid
- 2 lbs. Powdered Sugar
- 3 drachms of Essence of Lemon

Combine all ingredients and make sure the powders are *very dry*. Mix them very well and store them for use in a wide-mouthed bottle, closely corked. To serve, put two good-sized teaspoonfuls into a tumbler. Pour in a cup of cold water and stir briskly.

IMPERIAL DRINK FOR FAMILIES

- 2 oz Cream of Tartar
- 2-3 Lemons (peel and juice of)
- .5 lb. Coarse Sugar
- 1 gallon boiling water

Put the Cream of Tartar, Lemon Juice, Lemon Peels and Sugar into a gallon pitcher. Add in the boiling water. Let cool completely before serving.

NECTAR

- 1 drachm Citric Acid
- 1 scruple Potassium Bicarbonate
- 1 oz Powdered Sugar (2.75 Tablespoons)

Fill a soda water bottle nearly full of water. Drop in the Potassium Bicarbonate and Sugar, and lastly the Citric Acid. Cork the bottle up *immediately* and shake. As soon as the crystals are dissolved, the nectar is fit for use. It may be colored with a small portion of Cochineal.

RASPBERRY, STRAWBERRY, CURRANT, OR ORANGE EFFERVESCING DRAUGHTS

- 1 quart base Fruit Juice of choice
- 1 lb. Powdered Sugar
- 1.5 oz Tartaric Acid
- 1 teaspoon Sodium Carbonate for each serving

Boil the juice and Sugar into a syrup, and strain. Add Tartaric Acid. When cold, put it into a bottle, and keep it well corked. For serving, pour 6 ounces of water into a tumbler, and add 2 Tablespoonfuls of the syrup. Then briskly stir in the Sodium Carbonate, and a very delicious drink will be formed. The color may be improved by adding a very small portion of Cochineal to the syrup at the time of boiling.

GINGER WINE

- 12 lbs. Sugar
- 6 oz Powdered Ginger
- 6 gallons water
- 6 Egg whites
- 6 Lemons, sliced
- 2 oz Yeast

Put the Sugar, Ginger, and water into a pot and bring to a boil. Let it boil for an hour. Beat up the Egg whites with a whisk. Mix them well with the liquor and then let cool. When quite cold, put it into a barrel along with the Lemons, and Yeast. Let it work for three days, then put in the bung and let it sit for 1 week. It can be bottled and used immediately.

A MANUAL FOR THE MANUFACTURE OF CORDIALS, LIQUORS, FANCY SYRUPS, etc., etc.

After The Most Common And Approved Methods Now Used In The Distillation Of Liquors And Beverages, Designed For The Special Use Of Manufacturers, Dealers In Wines And Spirits, Grocers, Tavern Keepers And Private Families.

The Same Being Adapted To The Trade Of The United States And The Canadas

PROF. CHRISTIAN SCHULTZ
PRACTICAL CHEMIST AND DISTILLER

CHRISTIAN SCHULTZ, *author of the Manual for the Manufacture of Cordials, Syrups, Etc., begs to inform dealers and others, who do not desire to trouble themselves with manufacturing their Cordials, etc., that he will furnish them with the concentrated extract of any recipe in this book at a low price, for cash.*

Address: Christian Schultz, Care of Dick & Fitzgerald, 18 Ann Street, New York

Modern Adaptation by Ben Hammer.
Original 1862 edition by Christian Schultz

INTRODUCTION

TO THE READER:

The Author of the following work, in presenting it as a useful and valuable practical Manual to Manufacturers, Distillers, and Dealers in Cordials, Liquors, etc., in this country, thinks, that long experience as a practical distiller and vender of the above articles, gives him strong claims to the favorable considerations of the public at large.

A close and uniform practice of fifteen years in Switzerland, as well as in the city of New York; a thorough acquaintance with the method used in the best distilleries in Paris and Bordeaux; and manufacturing, as he has been, for many years for wholesale houses in this city, he flatters himself that in this Manual he has furnished all the facilities necessary, the recipes used, and the directions required, for the best preparations of the most celebrated Cordials, Liquors, Syrups, etc., ever yet introduced. The book contains the easiest, shortest, and the most economical manner of preparing the various articles; the style is concise and clear, so that it can be readily comprehended, and its matter, with great method and order, is alphabetically arranged under proper heads and references. Measures and weights referred to are those of the United States.

The Author, in this compendium, did not deem it necessary to describe the raw materials generally used in macerating and distilling. Such a description would only unnecessarily enlarge the work, thereby increasing the price, with but little or no advantage to the reader. A well informed and practical druggist will at once be able to understand, and property furnish, the articles contained in each recipe.

Manufacturing Instruments

The first to be described are the "Manufacturing Instruments", for without these nothing can be affected. The arrangements and preparations of the articles described in this work do not contemplate an expensive and costly apparatus, nevertheless the author recommends that the best materials and most substantial instruments should be provided, by reason of their durability, and the certainty of obtaining in its perfection a good product.

The instruments deemed indispensable in the process of distilling are as follow:

- a furnace
- two boilers of tinned copper
- a copper skimmer
- a few filter-bags, filtering holders, and a percolator
- tubs and pails for various uses
- measure from one gallon to that of the smallest
- weights and scales
- areometer
- funnels
- alcohol lamps with tinned dishes for different colors of bottle wax
- a cork-press and siphon
- casks, demi-johns, bottles.

Those who wish to engage in this business on a large scale, would do well to purchase

- a brass mortar; one of iron would often change the color of the material
- a stone mortar is required for the preparation of Orgeat Syrup
- Sieves for separating the coarse powdered materials from the fine
- a large knife for cutting and preparing roots, etc., etc., for the powdered state.

Necessary Preparations

There should always be on hand:

- Well clarified White and Brown Sugar syrups, put up in well-corked demijohns and labeled.
- Clean Spirit, or Rectified Whiskey Alcohol of 95 percent
- Sugar Coloring for brandies, rum, etc.
- Tincture of Turmeric, for Essence of Peppermint
- Tincture of Cochineal for red cordials.

All other colors prepared when wanted. Flavoring essences can be prepared in some larger quantity when wanted, and put up in bottles, labeled for further use.

Fruit syrups, such as Raspberry, Strawberry, etc., are prepared in summer; others, such as orgeat, gum, sarsaparilla, etc., at any season.

In preparing the following work, the author has had in view brevity and utility. He believes that such a Manual is much wanted in the business of distillation, and has spared no pains, which thorough experience and a practical knowledge of the subject could bring to his aid. It contains four hundred improved recipes of the various preparations now known, and each one can be readily referred to from the excellent alphabetical arrangements adopted.

To the liberal patronage and favorable consideration of his friends and the public at large, he most respectfully submits the result of his labors.

New York, January 2, 1862

WEIGHTS AND MEASURES

VOLUME MEASURES OF THE UNITED STATES (DISTILLED WATER)

1 gallon = 8 lbs. = 2 halves
½ gallon = 4 lbs. = 2 quarts
1 quart = 2 lbs. = 2 pints
1 pint = 1 lb. = 4 gills = 16 fl oz
½ pint = ½ lb. = 2 gills = 8 fl oz
1 ounce = 8 fl drams

A large and a small pair of scales must be provided. The large scale for weighing Sugar, etc. The smaller scale for drugs, etc.

WEIGHT MEASURES

1 pound = 16 ounces = 453.6g
½ pound = 8 ounces = 226.8g
¼ pound = 4 ounces = 113.4g
1 ounce = 8 drachms = 28.35g
1 drachm = 60 grains = 3.54 grams
1 scruple = 20 grains = 1.18 grams
1 grain = .06g

All other articles and utensils, such as mortars, mills, funnels, demijohns, casks, bottles, labels, pumps, areometers, bung-hammers, bung-bores, boxes, cases, hammer and nails, and siphon, must be supplied, as necessary to the operations of distilling and preparing liquors, syrups, cordials, etc.

NOTE: SEVERAL RECIPES IN THIS SECTION CALL FOR A 12.5% ALCOHOL SOLUTION. IF YOU ARE NOT DISTILLING YOUR OWN SPIRITS, YOU CAN CREATE THIS SOLUTION BY USING 80-PROOF BASE SPIRIT WITH DISTILLED WATER IN THE FOLLOWING RATIO 5:11. FOR INSTANCE, TO MAKE 1 GALLON OF 12.5% ALCOHOL, USE 5 CUPS OF 80-PROOF SPIRIT AND 11 CUPS OF DISTILLED WATER. A SIMPLE SEARCH ONLINE FOR "ALCOHOL DILUTION CALCULATOR" IS SURE TO PROVIDE YOU WITH MORE TOOLS TO CREATE ANY DILUTION REQUIRED.

THE DISTILLING APPARATUS

The first and most important is the furnace: temporary accommodations, under the name of furnaces, only prolong the operations of the distiller, and render his products very often imperfect. With a good fire, and proper apparatus, work can be accomplished with readiness and comparative ease, whereas the ordinary measures of every day's experiments often fail to succeed.

The portable furnace (1) is most excellent for boilers of from 5 to 10 gallons and may be used as a heating or cooking stove for families, as well as for the purposes of distillation. Coal can be filled in without moving the boiler, it having a good draught of air, and being laid out with firebricks, with a fall-grate for extinguishing the coal after using. The above can be obtained, ready-made, of J. Murphy, at No. 256 Water street, complete for $5

The *cucurbit*, or boiler (2), belonging to the furnace, contains 10 gallons of liquid, and is formed of tinned copper – the smaller part of the bottom standing on the fire-bricks, while the upper bottom covers the top of the furnace. This construction enables the first heat of the coal to give its whole strength on the under bottom, and rising up by the door, continues around the boiler, between the top and the brickwork, and in the stove-pipe. By this process, time and coal are both saved.

Distilling consists essentially in converting a liquid into vapor in a closed vessel, by means of heat, and then conveying the vapor into another cool vessel, where it is condensed again into a liquid.

To accomplish this, the liquids are placed in the boiler (2), and when heat is applied to the boiler, spirit begins to rise in vapor at 176 degrees, and water is converted into vapor at 212 degrees. These vapors pass from the boiler through the tube into the *worm* (3), and in passing through the worm, become condensed by the cold. The refrigerator, or worm-tub (4), must be kept full, by a constant stream of cold water, or else the water at the bottom will be cold, while that of the surface will be very hot. The cold water is supplied at 5, and escapes at 6.

With respect to the practical part of distilling, we shall observe that **the heat should, in all cases, be as gentle and uniform as possible**. Accidents may be effectively prevented by distilling spirits in a water bath, which, if sufficiently large, will perform the operation with all the dispatch requisite for the most extensive business. The vessel in which the distillation is effected ought to be immersed in another filled with water up to the neck. The process will thus be managed as expeditiously as if the vessel were placed over an open fire, and without the apprehension of being disappointed by having your spirits burned; nor will it be necessary at any time to raise the water in the bath to a boiling heat. By looking at the engraving of the still, you will see what we mean. The inner boiler or *cucurbit*, marked (2), is the vessel in which the liquids to be distilled are put, and the outer boiler or bath (A) is the vessel that should be filled with water. This is sometimes called a **Bain Marie**.

The cover of the inner boiler must be well luted, that is, closed completely, to prevent evaporation. Take a lute made of equal proportions of flour, whitening and salt, mixed together with the blade of a knife, and diluted with water; spread this on a piece of rag, and close all the crevices.

The object of distillation is to separate one substance from others with which it may be mixed. For example, in the recipe for making Aqua de Paradiso (on page 171), or Paradise Water, 7 pints of Neutral Spirits, and 20 pints of water are distilled with a quantity of Cacao and spice. Now as the alcohol distills at 176 degrees, and water at 212 degrees, it is perfectly apparent that the 7 pints of alcohol will all distill from off the water and become impregnated with the flavor and taste of the Cacao and spices before the water begins to distill.

The greater the surface exposed, and the less the height the vapors have to ascend, the more rapidly does the distillation proceed; and so well are these principles understood by the Scotch distiller, that they do not take more than three minutes to discharge a still containing fifty gallons of fluid. The body of the still or boiler should never be filled above one-half, sometimes not above one-fourth, to prevent the possibility of boiling or spiriting over.

As a necessary appendage to the boiler, furnace, etc., a copper skimmer, with small holes, such as is used in kitchens, should be provided.

FILTRATION

The filtering Apparatus consists of a long, high, narrow, but strong table, in the middle of which are cut out round holes of 4 inches diameter, 2 feet distant from each other.

On the under part of the table around the holes are placed 4 hooks equidistant from each other, for hanging up the filtering-bags:

For filtering-bags, cut a yard of Canton flannel in three square pieces as exact at you can. Double one of the square pieces, sew it on one side and let the other remain open, so that you form a triangle. The soft or cotton substance of the bag must form the inner side, with brass rings to hang the bag to the table sewed on. For every hole in the table there should be a correspondent filtering-bag hung up. In connection with this process there must be provided as many pails as there are filterers in use. For each pail there must be apportioned half of a sheet of blotting paper, prepared as follows: rub each piece of paper in your hands until it becomes smooth and pliant, as near to cloth as possible. Then place it in the pail with a little water, constantly beating it and rubbing it together with the hands until it comes to the consistency of a soft or pulpy matter. Afterward more water should be added, continuing the process of beating up the pulpy substance similar to the usual mode of beating up Eggs. The pail must then be filled, and the contents thrown into the filterer.

When the water has run through, fill up again so as to keep the filterer full, and when the water runs _clear_ let the whole of the water pass through, and the bag is prepared to filter. Place a five-gallon demijohn under the filterer, with funnel, fill another demijohn with the liquor to be filtered. Let the mouth of it, turned down, be placed (in the hole on the top of the table) in the bag, so that the neck of the demijohn will descend one inch in the filtering-bag. The liquor from the upper demijohn will just fill the bag to the neck, the product of which will run clear, pure and bright into the demijohn below. In this way the distiller can employ as many filterers as he may desire or produce as many different liquors as are wanted.

Spirits which are largely loaded with essential oils, such as those of Anise Seed, etc., usually require the addition of a spoonful or two of **magnesia** before they will flow quite clear.

TINCTURE

A tincture is an alcohol based solution of extracted flavors through the process of displacement or maceration.

DISPLACEMENT

The kind of filtration commonly called the *process of displacement*, for extracting the essence from roots, herbs, seeds, barks, etc., is to be effected in the following manner: It is first necessary that the articles to be acted upon should be ground in a drug-mill to the condition of a coarse powder. Then weigh each powder by itself, and mix them together in the proportions demanded by the recipe, and moisten the mass thoroughly with alcohol, allowing it to **macerate*** for twelve hours in a vessel well covered. Next you require a hollow instrument of cylindrical form, having one end shaped like a funnel, so that it can be inserted in the neck of a demijohn and having inside near the lower end, a partition pierced with numerous small holes, like the strainer of a French Coffee pot. In the absence of such a partition, soft cotton, or any insoluble substance, may be substituted, and being placed in the inside at the lower end of the instrument, will answer as well as the strainer. This instrument is called a percolator. Having let the ingredients be acted upon, macerate for the time we have named – introduce them into the percolator, and slightly press them upon the partition. Any portion of the liquid used in the maceration, not absorbed by the powder, should be poured upon the mass in the instrument, and allowed to percolate. You must now gradually pour into the percolator sufficient of the alcohol, or other liquid to be filtered, to drive before it, or **displace**, the liquid contained in the mass. The portion introduced must in like manner be **displaced** by another portion; and so on, until you obtain the required quantity of filtered liquor. This extract is called **tincture**. In case the liquor which first passes through, should be thick and turbid, you must again introduce it into the instrument, and be very careful not to have the powder too coarse or loosely pressed, or it will permit the liquid to pass too quickly, and on the other hand it should not be too fine and compact, or it may offer an unnecessary resistance. Should the liquor flow too rapidly, you must return it to the instrument, and close it beneath for a time, and thus permit the finer parts of the powder to subside and cause a slower percolation. If you have sufficient time, you can avoid the trouble of going through the process of displacement, by simply macerating the articles for two weeks, being careful to stir them up thoroughly once in every 24 hours.

MACERATION

Maceration is simply the immersing of certain substances in spirits or any other liquid, for a given length of time. By this process, the strength and flavor are taken from the roots, seeds, etc., and imparted to the liquid. To macerate, the liquid should be at blood-heat.

FINING (CLARIFYING)

Fining with Milk • Fining with Eggs • Fining with Potash • Fining with Alum

FINING (CLARIFYING) WITH MILK

- .75 pints good Milk
- 10 gallons Liquor

Boil the Milk, then cool. Mix with the liquor. It will soon settle.

FINING (CLARIFYING) WITH EGGS

- 2 Egg whites
- Splash Alcohol
- 10 gallons Liquor

Beat the Egg whites to a froth. Add a little alcohol, then mix it with the liquor. It will soon settle.

FINING (CLARIFYING) WITH POTASH

- 1.5 oz Potassium Carbonate
- 1 pint water
- 10 gallons Liquor

Dissolve the Potassium Carbonate into the water, then mix with the liquor. It will soon settle.

FINING (CLARIFYING) WITH ALUM

- 3 drachms Alum powder
- Splash Alcohol
- 10 gallons Liquor

Dissolve the Alum powder into a little bit of alcohol, then mix with the liquor. It will soon settle.

COLORING

Base Coloring • Blue • Green • Yellow (Saffron) • Purple • Red • Violet

---

BASE COLORING

- 100 lbs. White Sugar
- 3 gallons regular water
- 6.25 gallons boiling water

In a 50-gallon copper or iron boiler, dissolve the Sugar into the regular water. It is necessary to have the boiler this size, as in manufacturing, coloring the liquid is apt to run over when made in a small vessel. Put the boiler on a hot fire, and stir the Sugar constantly, so as to prevent it from burning on the bottom. Keep it boiling until it gets as black as tar when dropped on a cold stone. Then slowly add the boiling water – *at first, only a little at a time*, and increase the quantity gradually – constantly stirring as the whole is dissolved. Pass it through a flannel.

COLOR, BLUE (INDIGO)

- 3 oz Sulphuric Acid (smoking)
- 1 oz finest powdered Indigo
- 3 quarts water
- .5 lbs. Chalk Powder
- 1.5 pints Neutral Spirits

Put the acid into a 1-gallon glass jar. Add, in very small portions, the Indigo, being very careful to stir the ingredients constantly during the process of mixing them. Let the jar stand in a warm place for several days. Very slowly add the water, then add, in small quantities, the Chalk Powder, and continue stirring it until it no longer froths. Let it stand for 24 hours, then decant and filter. Mix in the alcohol and bottle for use.

COLOR, GREEN (SAFFRON/INDIGO)

By mixing the tincture of Saffron and the tincture of Indigo together in different proportions, you can obtain any shade of green you desire. For a light green, increase the Saffron; for a dark green, increase the Indigo.

COLOR, YELLOW (SAFFRON)

- .25 lbs. American Saffron, cut very fine
- 1 quart Neutral Spirits

Mix the Saffron and alcohol. Put this in a covered jar and let it stand in a warm place for 8 days. Then press, filter, and bottle for use.

A yellow coloring may also be made of **Turmeric** instead of Saffron. Observe the same proportions, and make it in the same way.

COLOR, PURPLE (ELDERBERRIES)

- .5 lbs. Elderberries, mashed to a pulp
- 1 quart Neutral Spirits

Combine the Elderberries and alcohol. Macerate in a warm place for 9 days. Press, filter, and bottle for use.

COLOR, RED (COCHINEAL)

- 1 oz finely powdered Cochineal
- .5 drachm Alum
- 1 quart Neutral Spirits

Boil the Cochineal and Alum with a quart of water, in an earthen dish. Add the alcohol, then press, filter, and bottle for use.

COLOR, VIOLET (INDIGO/COCHINEAL)

- 1 pint Blue color
- 2 pints Red color

Mix together

DEGREES FOR BOILING SUGAR

NOTE: I HAVE TRIED TO FIND TEMPERATURE REFERENCES FOR THE DEGREES MENTIONED IN THIS CHAPTER. I HAVE NOTATED THEM NEXT TO THE CORRESPONDING ENTRY HEADINGS. FINER DETAIL (AND CONFLICTING ANSWERS) MAY BE FOUND BY SEARCHING THE WEB. FYI, MY OWN CANDY THERMOMETER LISTS THE FOLLOWING DEGREES:

1. SYRUP - 230° F / 110° C
2. SOFT BALL - 240° F / 116° C
3. FIRM BALL - 248° F / 120° C
4. HARD BALL - 260° F / 127° C
5. SOFT CRACK - 285° F / 141° C
6. HARD CRACK - 302° F / 150° C

You should have a perfect knowledge of the degrees of boiling Sugar after it has been clarified. There are nine essential points, or degrees, in boiling Sugar. They are called:

1. Small Thread
2. Large Thread
3. Little Pearl
4. Large Pearl
5. The Blow
6. The Feather
7. The Ball
8. The Crack
9. The Caramel

THE THREAD (215° F–220° F / 102° C–105° C)

SMALL THREAD
The Sugar being clarified, put it on the fire, and after boiling a few moments, gently dip the top of your forefinger into the syrup, and apply it to your thumb, when, on separating them immediately, the Sugar forms a fine thread, which will break at a *short distance*, and remain as a drop on the finger and thumb. This is termed the "Small Thread"

LARGE THREAD

Boil a little longer, and again dip the forefinger into the syrup, and apply it to the ball of the thumb. This time a *somewhat longer* string will be drawn. This is termed the "Large Thread"

THE PEARL (220° F–222° F / 104° C–106° C)

LITTLE PEARL

This is when you separate the thumb and finger, and the fine thread reaches, without breaking, from one to the other.

LARGE PEARL

When the finger and thumb are spread as far as possible, without the thread being broken, it is termed the "Large Pearl". Another sign, also, is sometimes shown by the boiling syrup exhibiting bubbles on the surface. But this should be considered more as a hint than as a rule for guidance.

THE BLOW (230° F–235° F / 110° C–113° C

Continue boiling the syrup. Take your skimmer and dip it into the Sugar, then shake it over the pan, hold it before you, and blow through the holes. If you perceive small bubbles, or little sparkling bladders, on the other side of the skimmer, these are signs that you have produced what is called "The Blow".

THE FEATHER (230° F–235° F / 110° C–113° C)

When you have boiled the mixture a little more, and again dipped the skimmer into it, and after shaking it, find, upon blowing through the holes, that bubbles are produced in much greater quantities, then you may be sure the "Feather" has been made. Another sign, after dipping the skimmer, is to shake it extra hard, in order to get off the Sugar; if it has acquired this degree, you will see the melted Sugar hanging from the skimmer like silk or flying flax; whence it is termed by the French *d la grande plume.*

THE BALL (234° F–268° F / 112° C–131° C)

SMALL BALL

To know when the "Ball" has been acquired, you must first dip the forefinger into a basin of cold water. Now apply your finger to the syrup, taking up a little on the tip. Then quickly dip it into the water again. If upon rolling the Sugar with the thumb, you can make it into a small ball, you may be sure that what is termed the "Small Ball" has been produced.

LARGE BALL

When you can make a *larger and harder* ball, which you could not bite without adhering unpleasantly to the teeth, you may be satisfied that it is the "Large Ball".

THE CRACK

CRACK (270° F–290° F / 132° C–143° C)

Boil the syrup a very little more, dip the finger into the Sugar, and if upon taking it out, the Sugar adhering to the finger breaks with a slight noise, and will not stick to the teeth when bitten, the "Crack" has been produced.

GREAT CRACK (300° F–310° F / 148° C–154° C)

Now boil the syrup up again, dip the finger into the cold water, then into the syrup, and as quickly into the water again. If the Sugar breaks short and brittle upon doing this, it is the "Great Crack".

You cannot be too careful when the boiling syrup is at this degree because it rapidly passes to what is termed the "Caramel". Be quick and cautious, as an additional stir of the fire, or one minute's delay, may cause the syrup to be scorched beyond cure.

THE CARAMEL (320 ° F + / 160 ° C +)

When the Sugar has been boiled to the "Crack", as just stated, it quickly changes to the next degree. The syrup rapidly loses its whiteness and begins to be slightly colored. You must now add to the syrup a few drops of Lemon acid or juice, to *prevent its graining*. A little Vinegar or a few drops of pyroligneous acid (wood Vinegar), will produce the desired effect.

Dropping the acid in is termed *greasing it*. Having given the syrup another slight boil, so as to assume a yellow color, take the pan from the fire and place it in a dish of cold water, two or three inches deep. This will prevent burning… a circumstance most to be feared in this process.

Unless care is used, it will soon turn from yellow to brown, and then to black. Especially be careful not to use too much acid or Lemon Juice, for this will spoil the syrup, and probably produce the very graining you are trying to avoid. A small piece of Butter put into the pan will prevent the syrup from rising over the sides, and will grease or smooth it, and thus act like the acid in keeping it from graining. A little Cream of Tartar also on the point of a knife, will prevent it from candying. All this time a good red fire (not a blaze) should be kept up underneath. A small piece of wet rag or flannel will keep the top edges of the pan from crusting with Sugar, which might soon cake up and burn.

When boiling Sugar, it is a good plan to keep the top somewhat covered after it has begun to boil, and before the syrup has been boiled to the "Crack". The steam by this plan is kept within; the sides are moistened, and no crust is formed. If at any time you boil the syrup a little too much, or produce a degree beyond what you wish for, pour in a little water and boil it up again. Sugar that has been boiling too often loses many of its good qualities. Some sugars are not well adapted for boiling to the degrees, and no rules laid down would enable the practitioner to know when the "Crack" is near. Great care must, therefore, be used, and nothing but practice will enable you to be uniformly successful. It is an old axiom with confectioners and dealers in syrup, that "*there are twenty ways to* **grease** *syrup, but none to make it grain when it is* **greasy**".

With regard to the ninth degree of boiling Sugar, the "Caramel", the name is derived from a Count Albufage Caramel, of Nismes, France, who discovered this stage of boiling

PLAIN SYRUPS AND CLARIFICATION

Plain White Syrup • *Plain Extra-White Syrup* • *Brown/Moist Sugar Syrup*

On the whole, clarification is preferable for syrups to filtration. They need only be beaten up while cold with a little white of Egg, and then heated. A scum rises which must be removed as soon as it becomes consistent, and the skimming continued until the liquid becomes clear. Any floating portions of scum that may have escaped notice, are easily removed by running the syrup through a coarse flannel strainer whilst hot.

NOTE: THE BASE RATIO FOR SYRUP IN THIS BOOK IS APPROXIMATELY 2:1 SUGAR TO WATER. THIS WOULD BE CALLED "HEAVY SYRUP" TODAY, AS THE STANDARD FOR "SIMPLE SYRUP" IS NOW 1:1 SUGAR TO WATER. ONE OF THE REASONS FOR THIS CHANGE IS THE LARGER OVERALL SIZE OF TODAY'S COCKTAILS.

FROM THE Flavored Syrups (on page 300) CHAPTER IN THIS BOOK: "IN BOILING TO THE DEGREES, IT IS FROM THE 'small thread' (on page on page 131)TO THE 'large pearl' (on page 132) THAT SYRUP IS PRODUCED."

PLAIN WHITE SYRUP

- 10 lbs. Sugar
- 5 pints water
- 2 Egg whites

Place the Sugar into a copper pan large enough to allow the boiling Sugar to rise without spilling over. Beat the Egg whites until frothy, mix with the water, then pour over the Sugar. You should have extra cold water ready to be used during the boiling process.

Place the pan on the heat source and heat until the Sugar begins to rise. Throw in a little bit of the cold water to prevent the Sugar from boiling over. Let the Sugar rise two more times, using the cold water to control spillover. When the Sugar rises for the fourth time, begin to skim it, using cold water as necessary. Continue to take the scum off (which is rather white) until no more comes to the surface. Strain the mixture through a fine sieve made of cloth, or a flannel bag. The scum can be saved instead of throwing away and clarified when enough has been collected.

PLAIN EXTRA-WHITE SYRUP

- 10 lbs. Sugar (very best quality)
- 5 pints water
- 2 Egg whites
- 1 lb. Ivory-Black

Use the very best Loaf Sugar and place it in a copper pan. Beat the Egg whites until frothy and mix with the water. Pour into the pan with the Sugar. Add the Ivory-Black and mix thoroughly. When heating, the mixture should be as close to boiling as possible without actually boiling. Strain three or four times until it's extra fine and clear.

BROWN/MOIST SUGAR SYRUP

- 10-12 lbs. Brown Sugar
- 4 pints water
- 1 Egg white
- 1 pound Charcoal (hedge wood or small branches)

Place the Sugar into a copper pan that is large enough to allow the boiling Sugar to rise without spilling over. Beat the Egg whites to a froth and mix into the water. Combine with the Sugar in the pan. Crush the charcoal very fine and add it to the mixture. Have extra cold water ready to use during the boiling process.

Place the pan on the heat source and heat until the Sugar begins to rise. Throw in a little bit of the cold water to prevent the Sugar from boiling over. Let the Sugar rise two more times, using the cold water to control spillover. When the Sugar rises for the fourth time, begin to skim it, using cold water as necessary. Continue to take the scum off until no more comes to the surface. Strain the mixture through a fine sieve made of cloth, or a flannel bag. At first, the mixture will be very black, and you must repeatedly strain it until perfectly clear.

RECIPE NOTES

NOTE: I HAVE CHANGED THE ORGANIZATION OF THESE RECIPES FROM NUMBERED TO GROUPING BY CATEGORY FOR EASIER REFERENCE. MANY OF THE RECIPES, HOWEVER, DID NOT FIT CLEANLY INTO THEIR CATEGORY, EITHER BY THE RATIO OF INGREDIENTS OR THE CATEGORY NAMED IN THE RECIPE TITLE.

RATHER THAN REPEAT THE SAME INSTRUCTIONS OVER AND OVER, MANY OF THE RECIPES REFER TO A COMMON PROCESS (SUCH AS CREATING A TINCTURE). THE INSTRUCTIONS FOR THESE PROCESSES ARE FOUND IN THE BEGINNING SECTIONS OF THIS MANUAL.

MOST OF THESE RECIPES YIELD 10 GALLONS.

BEERS

Table Ale • White Devonshire Ale • Grout's Extract • Hop Beer • Porter
Porter en Cercles • Spring Beer • Spruce Beer
Hydromel Vineux (Metheglin) (Wine Mead)

TABLE ALE

- 2 gallons ground Malt
- 12 gallons water, at 142-deg heat.
- 2 oz Hops
- 1 Egg white
- 1/3 lb. Yeast

Combine Malt and 6 gallons of the water. Stir well. Let it stand for 1.5 hours. Draw off the liquid as much as possible and reserve. Repeat the same operation with 3 gallons more water. Draw off the liquid again. Repeat a third time with 3 gallons more water. Draw off the liquid a final time.

Mix the 3 liquors together and boil them with the Hops. Clarify the whole with the Egg white. Filter while hot, then cool it as quickly as possible. Stir in the Yeast, and let it ferment.

WHITE DEVONSHIRE ALE

- 2 gallons of ground Malt (Barley)
- 12 gallons of water, at 142-deg heat
- ⅓ lb. Hops
- 2 lbs. Grout's Extract
- .75 lb. Yeast

Combine Malt and 6 gallons of the water. Stir well. Let it stand for 1.5 hours. Draw off the liquid as much as possible and reserve. Repeat the same operation with 3 gallons more water. Draw off the liquid again. Repeat a third time with 3 gallons more water. Draw off the liquid a final time.

Mix the 3 liquors together and boil them with the Hops. Clarify the whole with the Egg white. Filter while hot, then cool it as quickly as possible. Stir in the Grout's Extract and Yeast, and let it ferment. After the fermentation is complete, and the ale settled, it is to be put in bottles and tied up.

GROUT'S EXTRACT

- 2 lbs. ground Malt
- 2 pints water

Mix the Malt and water, filling in a bottle and covering. Let it stand in a warm place until the fermentation has evaporated. The mixture to be of the consistency of an extract.

HOP BEER

- 2 oz Hops
- 10 gallons water
- 16 lbs. Sugar
- 1.5 pints Brewers' Yeast

Combine the Hops, Sugar and water, then boil for 10 minutes. Skim and strain. Let it cool to 80 degrees Fahrenheit. Add the Brewers' Yeast and let it stand for 24 hours. Filter, then fill it in an iron-bound and well-pitched cask and bung it up tight.

PORTER

- 2.5 gallons Brown Malt
- 3.75 oz Hops
- 2.5 oz Molasses
- 3.75 oz Licorice
- 6 grains Pimento
- 24 grains Extract of Spanish Licorice
- 7.5 grains Cocculus Indicus
- 22.5 grains Ginger
- 3 grains Heading, or Extract of Dark Burned Malt
- 8 oz Base Coloring (on page 128)
- 8 oz half-burnt Base Coloring (on page 128)
- 12 gallons water, 144 degrees Fahrenheit
- 1-2 Egg whites
- 8 oz Yeast

All substantial items should be ground. Combine with 6 gallons the water and stir well. Let stand for 1.5 hours. Draw off the liquor as much as possible. Repeat the same operation two more times, using just 3 gallons of water. Mix these liquors. Boil and clarify with the white of 1 or 2 Eggs. Cool as quickly as possible to 50-degrees Fahrenheit (see No. 6). Add the Yeast, and when the fermentation is over, transfer to cask.

PORTER EN CERCLES

- 11 pints Pale Malt
- 8.5 pints Yellow Malt
- 4.5 pints Brown Malt
- 12 gallons water, 144 degrees Fahrenheit
- 1-2 Egg whites
- 3 oz Hops
- .5 drachm Salt
- 8 oz Yeast

All substantial items should be ground. Combine with 6 gallons of the water. Stir and mix well, then macerate for 1.5 hours. Draw off the liquor as clear and as much as possible. Repeat the same operation two more times, using just 3 gallons of water. Mix these liquors. Boil and clarify with the white of 1 or 2 Eggs. Add the Hops and salt. Strain and cool as quickly as possible to 50 degrees Fahrenheit. Add the Yeast. Transfer to cask and let it ferment.

SPRING BEER

- 3 small bunches Sweet Fern
- 3 small bunches Sarsaparilla
- 3 small bunches Wintergreen
- 3 small bunches Sassafras
- 3 small bunches Prince Pine
- 3 small bunches Spice Wood
- 12 gallons water
- 8 oz Hops
- 1 gallon Molasses
- 1.5 lbs. Roasted Bread, soaked in Brewers' Yeast
- 1 Egg white

Combine the bunches with 8 gallons of the water. Boil down to 6 gallons of decoction or extract. Strain. Combine the remaining 4 gallons of water with the Hops, then boil down to 3 gallons of decoction. Strain. Mix the two extracts/decoctions together. Dissolve the molasses into the mixture. When cooled to 80-degrees, Fahrenheit, mix in the roasted Bread. Fill up a 10 gallon keg. When fermentation is over, mix with the white of one Egg beaten to froth. Bung it and bottle when clear.

SPRUCE BEER

- 9.5 gallons water
- 9 lbs. Sugar
- 1 oz Essence of Spruce
- 1 pint good Brewers' Yeast
- 1 handful Brick Powder
- 2 Egg whites, beaten to a froth

Boil the water, then let it cool to 80-degrees Fahrenheit. Mix the Sugar with the essence of spruce, then dissolve Sugar into the water. Add the Yeast. Fill a 10 gallon keg. After fermentation is over, add the brick powder then the Egg whites. Mix and let it stand until clear. Bottle.

HYDROMEL VINEUX (METHEGLIN) (WINE MEAD)

- 16 lbs. Honey
- 9 gallons water
- 8 oz good Brewers' Yeast

Heat the water to 84 degrees, Fahrenheit. Mix in the Honey until dissolved, then add the Brewers' Yeast, making sure all is well mixed. Fill a clean 10-gallon keg to the bung with the mixture and reserve the rest of the liquid. Leave the keg in a warm place. During fermentation, keep the keg full using the reserved liquid. When fermentation is over, keep the keg well sealed in a cool place.

CIDERS

Champagne Cider • Strong Cider • Sweet Cider

CHAMPAGNE CIDER

- 10 gallons of Cider, old and clear
- 2.5 pints Plain White Syrup (on page 136)
- 5 oz Tartaric Acid
- 7.5 oz Potassium Bicarbonate

Put the Cider in a strong iron-bound cask, pitched inside (like beer casks). Dissolve the Tartaric Acid into the syrup, then add to the cask. With the bung ready in hand, add the Potassium Bicarbonate and bung it as quickly and well as possible

STRONG CIDER

- Apples for juicing
- 1 drachm Brimstone (sulfur)

Take as many Apples as will make juice sufficient to fill a strong cask. Make them into a pulp by passing them through a Cider-mill. Spread this pulp out on a large surface in the open air and leave it for 24 hours. Press out the juice as thoroughly as possible. Fill the cask up to the bung-hole with the juice and keep it full as long as the fermentation is going on, by adding some juice kept aside for that purpose. Prepare another clean cask by burning the Brimstone in it by hanging an iron vessel through the bunghole. When the fermentation has ended, transfer the liquid to the prepared cask. Bung it up carefully and keep it in a cool place.

SWEET CIDER

- Apples for juicing
- 1.5 oz Brimstone (sulfur)

Procure a cask, pitched inside (like a beer-cask); then take as many sweet Apples as will make juice sufficient to fill it. Press the Apples as quickly as possible, being careful to let the juice settle a little while; then decant the juice and put it in the cask in the following manner:

Burn .5 oz of Brimstone in the cask by hanging an iron vessel through the bunghole.

1. Bung up the cask and let it stand awhile.
2. Fill the cask ⅓ full with the juice, being very careful to shake it well.

Go through this process three times, and be very particular to observe the above directions each time. After you have put the last ⅓ of the juice in the cask, bung it carefully, and put it in a cool place for use.

WINES

Calabre a Chaud (Hot) • Calabre a Froid (Cold) • Blackberry Wine
Black Currant Wine • Birch Wine • Champagne • English Champagne
Cherry Wine • Red Currant Wine • Damson Wine • Frontignan Wine of.
Ginger Wine • Greek Wine • Juniper Wine • Lemon Wine
Liqueur (Cordial) Wine • Mixed Fruit Wine • Orange Wine • Parsnip Wine
Peach Wine • Plain Wine • Quince Wine • Raisin Wine • Raspberry Wine
Rose Wine • St. George Wine • Imitation Wines

CALABRE A CHAUD (HOT)

- 36 gallons of white or red Wine Must
- 1.25 gallons Neutral Spirits.

Boil and skim the wine down to 8.75 gallons. Combine with the alcohol.

Use: For the manufacture of Malaga wine.

CALABRE A FROID (COLD)

- 9 gallons of fresh, pure red or white Wine Must
- 1 gallon Neutral Spirits

Combine the Wine Must with the alcohol. Let it clarify itself by standing. Decant.

Use: for manufacture of different wines.

BLACKBERRY WINE

- 10 lbs. Sugar
- 5 gallons water
- .5 oz ground Cinnamon
- .25 oz ground Cloves
- .5 drachm Cardamom
- 1 drachm Nutmeg
- 5 gallons Blackberries, pulped
- 1 gallon Neutral Spirits

Dissolve the Sugar into the water, then heat to 100 degrees Fahrenheit. Mix in the spices and fruit. Reserve ½ a gallon of the liquid and put the rest in a 10 gallon keg, leaving it in a warm place. Keep the keg constantly full as it ferments, using the reserved liquid. After fermentation has ended, strain and press. Add the alcohol to this mixture, then filter or fine the mix. (See Fining on page 124)

BLACK CURRANT WINE

- 5 gallons Black Currants, pulped
- 10 lbs. Sugar
- 5 gallons water
- 1 gallon Neutral Spirits

Dissolve the Sugar into the water then heat to 100 degrees Fahrenheit. Mix in the fruit. Reserve ½ gallon of the liquid and transfer the rest to a 10 gallon keg, leaving it in a warm place. Keep the keg constantly full as it ferments, using the reserved liquid. After fermentation has ended, strain and press. Add the alcohol to this mixture, then filter or fine the mix. (See Fining on page 124)

BIRCH WINE

- 9 gallons Birch Juice, drawn in the month of February or March from the Birch tree by boring holes in it
- 9 lbs. Sugar
- 2 oz Lemon Peel, finely cut
- 1 pint Gluten

Boil the Birch Juice, skim and cool down to 100 degrees Fahrenheit. Dissolve the Sugar into the juice and add the Lemon Peel. Add the Gluten to produce fermentation. Put the ingredients in a keg and keep it constantly full until fermentation is over. Filter or fine it (see Fining on page 124). Put in another keg, in which you have previously burnt a strip of Brimstone paper (see Brimstone Paper on page 325).

CHAMPAGNE

- 10 gallons Light White Wine, such as Sauterne or Rhine, well clarified.
- 3 lbs. whitest Rock Candy
- 1.5 gallons water
- .5 gallons Wine Alcohol (bon gout) or any other perfectly free of flavor

Combine the wine, Rock Candy, water and wine alcohol. When all this is perfectly clear, fill it in a soda water apparatus, and impregnate it with Carbonic Acid (for family use, 1.5 drachm Citric Acid and 1.5 drachm Sodium Bicarbonate). Bottle, cork, wire, cap and label.

ENGLISH CHAMPAGNE

- 5 gallons Currant Juice
- 15 lbs. Sugar
- 5 gallons water
- 1.25 gallons pure Neutral Spirits, free of flavor

Dissolve the Sugar into the water. Add the juice and let the liquid settle for 3 days. Decant and then add the alcohol. Put it in a keg and let it stand unbunged for 6 weeks. Bung up tight. Let it stand for a year and then bottle.

CHERRY WINE

- 10 gallons fresh-pressed Cherry Juice
- 5 lbs. Sugar

Dissolve Sugar into juice and put in a keg. Keep it constantly full of the liquid during the process of fermentation. Filter (on page 119) or fine (on page 124) it, then fill in a pitched keg or bottle.

RED CURRANT WINE

- 8 lbs. Honey
- 10 lbs. Sugar
- 7.5 gallons water
- 1 Egg white
- 11 pints Red Currant Juice
- 1 pint Yeast

Boil the water and dissolve the Honey and Sugar into it. Clarify with the Egg white. Skim and strain. Add the Currant Juice and Yeast. Put in a keg and keep it full of the liquid during fermentation. Filter (on page 119) or fine (on page 124) it. Put in a clean pitched keg and bung tight or bottle.

DAMSON WINE

- 80 lbs. Damsons (Plums)
- 10 gallons water
- 25 lbs. Sugar
- 2.5 pints French Brandy

Boil the water, then add the Damsons. Macerate for 2 days , then strain and press. Dissolve the Sugar into the liquid. Add the French Brandy and let it stand for a few days. Filter, bottle, and be careful to add another .5 oz ground Sugar to each bottle. Cork and string it.

FRONTIGNAN WINE.

- 4.5 gallons Red Wine
- 4.5 gallons White Wine
- 1 gallon Quarter-Proof Spirit (12.5% ABV alcohol).

Mix all ingredients.

GINGER WINE

- 12.5 gallons boiling water
- 19 lbs. Sugar
- 9 oz washed and cut Ginger
- 6 lbs. Malaga Raisins
- 3 lbs. Muscat Raisins
- 1 oz Isinglass
- 8 oz water
- 4 Lemons, sliced
- 1 pint good Brewers' Yeast

Combine the Ginger and ½ gallon of the boiling water and let macerate until cold. Strain and press. Make a syrup by boiling the Sugar and the remaining 12 gallons of water. Combine the two mixtures. Mash the Raisins to a pulp. Soak the Isinglass in the 8 oz of water. Now combine all of the ingredients and put in a keg to ferment for 3 weeks. During fermentation, keep the keg full by adding leftover liquid. After fermentation is finished, transfer to a keg in which a strip of Brimstone has been burned. (see Brimstone Paper on page 325). Bung tight.

GRAPE WINE

- 11 gallons Grape Juice (lightly-pressed from sweet grapes)

Fill a 10 gallon keg to the bung. Let it stand in a warm place and keep it full during fermentation. After it has settled, draw it off in a clean keg. Filter the dregs of the first keg and add the clear to the liquid that has been drawn off. In the month of March, the second fermentation begins, then lift the bung. When the second fermentation is over, if the wine is red, Fine (on page 124) it with Egg. If the wine is white, fine it with a mixture composed of 1 oz Isinglass steeped in a pint of the wine, and beaten and mixed as with Egg fining.

Put red wine in a pitched keg or white wine in a Brimstone keg (See Brimstone Paper on page 325), and bung tight.

GREEK WINE

- 165 lbs. perfectly ripe Grapes
- 5 oz Sea-Salt

Take a sufficient quantity of perfectly ripe Grapes to make 10 gallons of juice and expose them to the sun for 10 days. Press out the juice in a boiler and keep it over a fire until it attains the boiling point. Add the sea-salt. Remove it from the fire and let it stand for 8 days. Bottle.

JUNIPER WINE

- 12.5 gallons hot water
- .5 oz ground Coriander Seed
- 55 lbs. ground Juniper Berries
- 5 lbs. Brown Sugar
- 1 pint good Brewers' Yeast

Combine the hot water, Coriander, Juniper and Sugar, and when the liquid is cooled to 100-degrees Fahrenheit, add the Yeast. Put it all in a keg with the top out. Fix the top again as tight as possible, and when fermentation is over and the wine clear, draw off. Press and filter the balance and put it in a new, clean pitched keg.

LEMON WINE

- 11 gallons water
- 15 lbs. Sugar
- 50 Lemons, very thinly sliced
- 1 quart fresh Brewers' Yeast
- 1/3 gallon good Sherry or Madeira Wine

Boil the Sugar and water together until the Sugar is perfectly dissolved. Skim and strain. When cooled to 100-degrees Fahrenheit, add the Lemons and Yeast. Put a 10 gallon keg in a warm place and fill it full to the bung and keep it full with the liquid until fermentation is over. Strain, press and filter. Add ⅓ gallon good sherry or Madeira wine.

LIQUEUR (CORDIAL) WINE

- 105 lbs. sweet Grapes
- 3 gallons Neutral Spirits
- 1 oz Cinnamon, ground

Take a sufficient quantity of Grapes to make 7 gallons of juice. Expose them to the sun for 10 days before pressing them. As soon as they are pressed, put the juice in a 10 gallon keg. Add the Cinnamon and alcohol. Mix well, bung it. After settling (about 1 month), bottle it.

MIXED FRUIT WINE

- 1.75 gallons fresh-pressed Currant Juice
- 1.75 gallons fresh-pressed Grape Juice
- 1.75 gallons fresh-pressed Raspberry Juice
- 1.75 gallons fresh-pressed English Cherry Juice
- 24 lbs. Sugar
- 1 quart good Brewers' Yeast
- 1.5 gallons good French Brandy

Dissolve the Sugar into the mixed juices. Add the Brewers' Yeast. Fill up a keg holding 8 gallons. Keep the cask full with the remaining juice during fermentation. When fermentation is over, add 1.5 gallon good French Brandy. Let it stand together for a few days longer. Filter and bottle.

ORANGE WINE

- 15 lbs. Sugar
- 11 gallons water
- 50 Oranges, cut into thin slices
- 2 pints fresh Brewers' Yeast
- 4 pints Brandy

Boil the Sugar and water, then skim and strain. When cooled to 100-degrees Fahrenheit, add the oranges and Yeast. Fill a keg to the bung and keep it in a warm place. Keep it full with the remaining liquid during fermentation. When fermentation is over, strain and press, then add the Brandy. Filter.

PARSNIP WINE

- 40 lbs. Parsnips
- 11 gallons water
- 3 Eggs
- 1 oz bruised Bitter Almonds
- 25 lbs. Sugar
- 2 pints Yeast
- 3 pints Quarter-Proof Cognac (12.5% ABV)

Boil the parsnips and water down to 9 gallons. Press out the liquid, beat the Eggs to a froth and mix with the decoction. When it is cool, reserve 4 pints of liquid. Add the Almonds to the main mixture. Dissolve the Sugar into the mix and bring to a boil. Let the scum rise 3 times, stopping the rising each time by adding from the .5 gallon of cool liquid. Skim, strain and cool down to 100 degrees Fahrenheit. Add the Yeast. After fermentation is over, add the Cognac. Filter.

PEACH WINE

- 10 gallons Peach Juice, pressed from the ripest fruits + the stones (unbroken)
- 5 lbs. Sugar
- 1 oz Cloves, ground
- 4 pints pure Neutral Spirits

Dissolve the Sugar into the Peach Juice and stones. Put in a keg and ferment. Keep the keg constantly full with the extra liquid until fermentation ends. Add the Cloves, then strain. Mix in the alcohol, then filter.

PLAIN WINE

- 9.5 gallons water at 86-degrees Fahrenheit
- 10 lbs. Sugar
- 4 lbs. Raisins, mashed
- 3 oz Tartaric Acid
- 1 pint strong Vinegar
- 2 pints Brewers' Yeast
- 1 gallon Neutral Spirits

Combine the water, Sugar, Raisins, Tartaric Acid, Vinegar and Yeast, and mix well. Fill up a keg and put it in a warm place. While fermenting, keep it constantly full with the liquid. After fermentation is over, add the alcohol. Strain, press and filter.

QUINCE WINE

- 8 gallons Quince Juice
- 10 lbs. Sugar
- 2 pints Brewers' Yeast
- 2.5 gallons good Sherry or Madeira Wine

To produce the juice, wipe off quinces, cut them in slices and mash into a pulp. Press out the juice.

Heat the Quince Juice to near boiling. Dissolve the Sugar into the juice. Skim, strain and let it cool to 86-degrees Fahrenheit. Fill a keg and put it in a warm place. Add the Yeast and mix well. During the fermentation, keep the keg filled with the leftover liquid. When fermentation is over, add the Sherry or Madeira wine.

RAISIN WINE

- 80 lbs. Malaga Raisins
- 10 gallons boiling water
- 6 oz powdered Rock Candy
- 4 Orange Rinds
- 2 Lemons
- 1 oz Bitter Almonds, bruised
- 2 pints Brewers' Yeast
- 2 pints best French Brandy

Macerate the Raisins with the boiling water until cool. Rub the Raisins between the hands, taking care not to hurt the stones. Pass the pulp through a sieve. Press slowly, to get 11 gallons of the liquid with the water used to wash out the pulp. Dissolve the Rock Candy into the liquid. Add the Orange rinds, Lemons, Almonds and Yeast. Fill a 10 gallon keg and keep it full with the extra liquid during fermentation. Strain and press, then add the Brandy.

RASPBERRY WINE

- 10 gallons fresh Raspberry Juice
- 7.5 lbs. Sugar
- 2 Egg whites
- 1 pint good Brewers' Yeast
- 1 oz ground Mace
- 1.25 gallons good Port Wine

Combine the juice and Sugar. Boil, then clarify with the Egg whites. Skim and strain. When nearly cool, add the Yeast. Fill a 10 gallon keg and hang a little bag with the Mace inside it. Keep the keg full with the extra juice until fermentation is over. When fermentation is over, add the wine. Filter.

ROSE WINE

- 10 gallons water
- 30 lbs. Sugar
- 1.25 gallons Red Rose Petals
- 1 pint Yeast
- .5 drachm Rose Oil
- 2 oz Neutral Spirits

Combine the water, Sugar and rose petals, then boil for 2 minutes. When lukewarm, fill up a keg. Put it in a warm place. Add the Yeast and let ferment. Fill up constantly with the spare liquid until fermentation ceases. Dissolve the Rose Oil into the alcohol and mix it with the above wine. Strain. Color the mixture rose with Red Coloring (on page 129), then filter.

St. George Wine

- 5 gallons dark red Claret Wine
- 5 gallons Piquepoul Wine
- 4 oz Raspberry Tincture (on page 251)
- 4 oz Lemon Balm Tincture
- 4 oz Orris Root Tincture

Combine all ingredients.

IMITATION WINES

Red Bordeaux Wine (Imitation) • White Bordeaux Wine (Imitation)
Cyprus Wine (Imitation) • Madiera Wine (Imitation)
Malaga Wine (Imitation) • Muscat Wine (Imitation) • Port Wine (Imitation)
Sherry Wine (Imitation) • Tokay (Tokaji) Wine (Imitation)

RED BORDEAUX WINE (IMITATION)

- 4 gallons high-flavored Red Bordeaux Wine
- 6 gallons Plain Wine, colored to the same shade with Purple Coloring (on page 129).

WHITE BORDEAUX WINE (IMITATION)

- 4 gallons high-flavored White Wine
- 6 gallons Plain Wine, colored to the same shade with Base Coloring (on page 127) or Yellow Coloring (on page 128).

CYPRUS WINE (IMITATION)

- 8 ⅔ gallons water
- 8 ⅔ pints Elderberries
- 7 ⅜ lbs. Sugar
- 7 drachms ground Ginger
- 3.5 drachms Cloves
- 10.5 oz mashed Raisins
- 1 pint Yeast

Combine the water, Elderberries, Sugar, Ginger and Cloves and boil together for 1 hour. Skim. Strain when cooled to 100-degrees Fahrenheit. Put in a 10 gallon keg along with the Raisins. Add the Yeast. During fermentation be careful and keep the keg full with the balance of the liquid. Filter or fine (on page 124) it.

MADEIRA WINE (IMITATION)

- 4 gallons good Madeira Wine, high flavored
- 6 gallons Plain Wine

Mix and color to the same shade with Base Coloring (on page 127) or Yellow Coloring (on page 128).

MALAGA WINE (IMITATION)

- 4 gallons Malaga Wine, best quality
- 6 gallons Plain Wine
- 2.5 pints Plain White Syrup (on page 136)

Mix and color with Purple Coloring (on page 129) and Base Coloring (on page 127).

MUSCAT WINE (IMITATION)

- 10 gallons Plain Wine
- 20 lbs. Muscat Raisins, bruised
- 12 oz Alder Flowers, hanging in a bag

Combine and macerate for 2 or 3 months. Press and filter or fine (on page 124).

PORT WINE (IMITATION)

- 4 gallons high-flavored Port Wine
- 5 $\frac{5}{8}$ gallons Plain Wine
- $\frac{3}{8}$ gallons Plain White Syrup (on page 136)

Combine and color the mixture with Purple Coloring (on page 129).

SHERRY WINE (IMITATION)

- 4 gallons high-flavored Sherry
- 6 gallons Plain Wine

Combine the wines and color the mixture with Base Coloring (on page 127).

TOKAY (TOKAJI) WINE (IMITATION)

- 4 gallons Tokay Wine, best quality
- 6 gallons Plain Wine
- Sugar to taste

Combine the wines and sweeten and color (on page 126) to taste.

BASE SPIRITS

Angelica Brandy • Anisette Fausse (Imitation) [D] • Arrack (Faux)
British Brandy • Spice Brandy • Domestic Gin • English Gin • Holland Gin
London Gin Cordial • Rum, Jamaica [D] • Rum, Jamaica, Imitation [D]
Rum, St. Croix (Santa Cruz Rum) [D] • Whiskey (Imitation) Irish, Monongahela, Scotch

ANGELICA BRANDY
Flavoring:

- 4 oz Pimpinella Root, ground
- 12 oz Angelica Root, ground
- 2 oz Lavender Flowers, ground
- 1 quart Neutral Spirits

Mixing:

- 4 gallons Neutral Spirits
- 6 gallons water

Create a tincture using the flavoring ingredients. Combine the mixing ingredients, then add the tincture. Filter. Color the mixture pale brown with Sugar-color (on page 127).

ANISETTE FAUSSE (IMITATION) [D]

Distilling	Mixing
26.5 oz ground Anise Seed	32.5 pints Plain Extra-White Syrup (on page 136)
17.5 oz ground Star Anise Seed	
4.5 oz ground Coriander Seed	
4.5 oz ground Fennel Seed	
47.5 pints of Neutral Spirits	
27 pints water	

Combine distilling ingredients. Distill 47.5 pints of alcohol from off the water. Slowly add the syrup. Filter if necessary. Color the mixture white.

ARRACK (FAUX)

- 21 ⅓ pints of fine Batavia Arrack
- 58 ⅔ pints pure Quarter-Proof Rice Spirit
- ½ oz Coconut Oil

Combine the ingredients, then filter. Color the mixture white.

BRITISH BRANDY

- 1 oz Catechu (Acacia Extract)
- ½ drachm Vanilla, finely powdered
- 1 gallon good Cognac
- 9 gallons 50% Alcohol

Combine all ingredients. Color the mixture pale or dark.

SPICE BRANDY

- 2.5 oz Cinnamon
- .75 oz Cloves
- .75 oz Cardamom
- 1 oz Galangal Root
- 1 oz Ginger
- 10 gallons good French Brandy

Grind dry ingredients to a coarse powder. Combine with the Brandy and let macerate for 7 days. Filter.

DOMESTIC GIN

- 3 drachms Juniper Oil
- 5.25 gallons Neutral Spirits
- 37 pints water
- 1 pint Plain White Syrup (on page 136)

Dissolve the oil into the alcohol. Add the water and syrup.

ENGLISH GIN

- 3 drachms Juniper Oil
- 1 drachms Turpentine Oil
- 5.25 gallons Neutral Spirits
- 4.75 gallons water

Dissolve the oils into the alcohol, then add the water.

HOLLAND GIN

- 2.5 gallons Holland Gin
- 3.75 gallons Neutral Spirits
- 3.75 gallons water

Mix all of the ingredients

LONDON GIN CORDIAL

- 3 drachms Juniper Oil
- 1 drachm Angelica Oil
- 10 drops Coriander Oil
- 5.25 gallons Neutral Spirits
- 4 pints Plain White Syrup (on page 136)
- 4.25 gallons water

Dissolve the oils into the alcohol. Add the syrup and water, then filter.

RUM, JAMAICA [D]

- 35 gallons Sugar Scum, from refineries
- 7 gallons West India Molasses
- 35 gallons water
- 1 gallon good Brewers' Yeast
- 4 pints Plain White Syrup (on page 136)

Dissolve the Sugar scum and molasses into the water, hot enough to get the mixture at 80-degrees Fahrenheit. Add the Brewers' Yeast. When fermentation is over, distill and add the syrup. Color the mixture dark yellow with Oak Bark.

RUM, JAMAICA, IMITATION [D]

Distilling	Mixing
7 lbs. fragments of Sugar Cane	3.75 gallons water
6 gallons Neutral Spirits	2 pints Plain White Syrup (on page 136)
4 gallons water	
18 oz Salt	

Combine the Sugar Cane, alcohol and water, then macerate for 24 hours. Add the salt, then distill over 6 gallons of flavored spirit. Add the mixing ingredients to the flavored alcohol. Color the mixture dark yellow with Oak Bark.

RUM, ST. CROIX (SANTA CRUZ RUM) [D]

- 62 lbs. Brown Sugar
- 40 gallons boiling water
- 1 gallon Brewers' Yeast

Dissolve the Brown Sugar into the water, then let cool to 80 degrees, Fahrenheit. Add the Brewers' Yeast and let ferment. Distill when the fermentation is over.

WHISKEY (IMITATION)

Christian Shultz: "Without large distilleries, these whiskeys, Irish and Scotch cannot be manufactured with profit. It is a humbug to make them with essences, and a nuisance as regards health. The best imitation is mixing in proportion to the price."

IRISH WHISKEY

- 3 gallons genuine Irish Whiskey
- 7 gallons best Pure Spirit

MONONGAHELA WHISKEY

- 3 gallons Monongahela Whiskey
- 7 gallons Pure Spirit

Mix and color yellow.

SCOTCH WHISKEY

- 3 gallons best genuine Scotch Whisky
- 7 gallons best Pure Spirit

AQUA (WATER)

Anisette de Bordeaux [D] • Anisette de Hollande [D] • Anisette de Martinique [D]
Aqua del Paradiso (Water of Paradise) [D] • Aqua Divina (Divine Water) [D]
Aqua Persicana (Persicot Water) [D] • Aqua Romana (Water of Rome) [D]
Alkermes de Florence • Amour Sans Fin (Love Without End)
Beaume Humain (Balsam of Man) • Canelin de Corfou • Canelle
Cedrat (Citron) • Citron • Escubac d'Irelande [D] • Espirit de Manuel

IN MID-19TH-CENTURY AMERICA, **AQUA** (LATIN FOR "WATER") DESIGNATED A FAMILY OF SPIRIT-BASED CORDIALS THAT BALANCED DISTILLED OR INFUSED BOTANICALS WITH A HEAVY SUGAR SYRUP. FAR FROM SIMPLE FLAVORED SPIRITS, THESE "WATERS" EXEMPLIFIED THE ERA'S FUSION OF PHARMACY AND HOSPITALITY: POTENT ENOUGH TO CARRY BOTANICAL ESSENCES, YET SWEET AND VISCOUS ENOUGH FOR LEISURELY SIPPING. THE RECIPES IN THIS BOOK MEASURE AT ROUGHLY 30-35% ABV. THESE AQUA CORDIALS WOULD CUSTOMARILY BE SERVED NEAT IN SMALL CORDIAL GLASSES AS AFTER-DINNER DIGESTIFS. THEY COULD ALSO BE ADDED IN DASHES OR SPOONFULS TO PUNCH BOWLS AND MIXED DRINKS, LEVERAGING THEIR CONCENTRATED FLAVORS TO PERFUME LARGER BATCHES WITHOUT EXCESS DILUTION.

ANISETTE DE BORDEAUX [D]

Distilling	Mixing
2.5 lbs. ground Anise Seed	20 pints Neutral Spirits
2.25 oz ground Coriander Seed	53 pints Plain Extra-White Syrup (on page 136)
7 oz ground Ceylon Cinnamon	
7 pints of Neutral Spirits	
20 pints water	

Combine distilling ingredients. Distill 7 pints of alcohol from off the water. Mix this flavored alcohol with the 20 pints of mixing alcohol, then slowly add the syrup. Filter if necessary. Color the mixture white.

ANISETTE DE HOLLANDE [D]

Distilling	Mixing
54 oz ground Anise Seed	26 pints Neutral Spirits
27 oz ground Star Anise Seed	47 pints Plain Extra-White Syrup (on page 136)
7 pints Neutral Spirits	
20 pints water	

Combine distilling ingredients. Distill 7 pints of alcohol from off the water. Mix this flavored alcohol with the 26 pints of mixing alcohol, then slowly add the syrup. Filter if necessary. Color the mixture white.

ANISETTE DE MARTINIQUE [D]

Distilling	Mixing
54 oz ground Anise Seed	20 pints Neutral Spirits
13.5 oz ground Star Anise Seed	53 pints Plain Extra-White Syrup (on page 136)
7 pints Neutral Spirits	
20 pints water	

Combine distilling ingredients. Distill 7 pints of alcohol from off the water. Mix this flavored alcohol with the 20 pints of mixing alcohol, then slowly add the syrup. Filter if necessary. Color the mixture white.

AQUA DEL PARADISO (WATER OF PARADISE) [D]

Distilling	Mixing
40 ½ ounces roasted and ground Cacao	20 pints Neutral Spirits
6 ⅔ oz ground Cardamom seeds	53 pints Plain Extra-White Syrup (on page 136)
6 ⅔ oz ground Ceylon Cinnamon	
7 pints Neutral Spirits	
20 pints water	

Combine distilling ingredients. Distill 7 pints of alcohol from off the water. Mix this flavored alcohol with the 20 pints of mixing alcohol, then slowly add the syrup. Filter if necessary. Color the mixture white.

AQUA DIVINA (DIVINE WATER) [D]

Distilling	Mixing
6 ⅔ oz ground Ceylon Cinnamon	20 pints Neutral Spirits
6 ⅔ oz Gum Myrrh	53 pints Plain Extra-White Syrup (on page 136)
26 ⅔ oz Roasted Cacao Caracas	
7 pints Neutral Spirits	
20 pints water	

Combine distilling ingredients. Distill 7 pints of alcohol from off the water. Mix this flavored alcohol with the 20 pints of mixing alcohol, then slowly add the syrup. Filter if necessary. Color the mixture white.

AQUA PERSICANA (PERSICOT WATER) [D]

Distilling	Mixing
6 ⅔ oz ground common Cinnamon	20 pints Neutral Spirits
6 ¾ lbs. ground Peach Kernels	53 pints Plain Extra-White Syrup (on page 136)
7 pints of Alcohol	
20 pints of water	

Combine distilling ingredients. Distill 7 pints of alcohol from off the water. Mix this flavored alcohol with the 20 pints of mixing alcohol, then slowly add the syrup. Filter if necessary. Color the mixture white.

AQUA ROMANA (WATER OF ROME) [D]

Distilling	Mixing
6 ⅔ oz ground Ceylon Cinnamon	20 pints Neutral Spirits
6 ⅔ oz ground aromatic Calamus Root	53 pints Plain Extra-White Syrup (on page 136)
3 ¾ oz ground Nutmeg	
7 pints Alcohol	
20 pints water	

Combine distilling ingredients. Distill 7 pints of alcohol from off the water. Mix this flavored alcohol with the 20 pints of mixing alcohol, then slowly add the syrup. Filter if necessary. Color the mixture white.

ALKERMES DE FLORENCE

- 3 ¾ drachms Vanilla Essence
- 23 drops of Rose Oil
- 27 pints Neutral Spirits
- 13.5 lbs. Figs, cut fine
- 53 pints Plain Extra-White Syrup (on page 136)

Dissolve the Vanilla Essence and Rose Oil in the alcohol. Boil the Figs in the syrup for 5 minutes, then add the syrup to the alcohol. Filter. Color the mixture rose with Red Coloring (on page 129).

AMOUR SANS FIN (LOVE WITHOUT END)

- 36 drops Rose Oil
- 81 drops Neroli Oil
- 108 drops Clove Oil
- 27 pints Neutral Spirits
- 53 pints Plain Extra-White Syrup (on page 136)

Dissolve oils into the alcohol. Slowly add in the syrup. Color the mixture rose with Red Coloring (on page 129).

BEAUME HUMAIN (BALSAM OF MAN)

- 23 drops Rose Oil
- 54 drops Cinnamon Oil
- 162 drops Cedrat Oil
- 54 drops Mace Oil
- 27 pints Neutral Spirits
- 53 pints Plain Extra-White Syrup (on page 136)

Dissolve the oils into the alcohol. Slowly add the syrup. Filter. Color the mixture white.

CANELIN DE CORFOU

- 2 drachms Ceylon Cinnamon Oil
- 3 1/3 gallons Neutral Spirits
- 6 2/3 gallons Plain White Syrup (on page 136)

Dissolve the oils into the alcohol, then add the syrup. Color the mixture yellow with Yellow Coloring (on page 128).

CANELLE

- 6.75 drachms Cinnamon Oil
- 3 1/3 gallons Neutral Spirits
- 6 2/3 gallons Plain White Syrup (on page 136)

Dissolve the oil into the alcohol, then add the syrup.

CEDRAT (CITRON)

- 13.5 drachms Cedrat Oil (Citron Oil)
- 3 1/3 gallons Neutral Spirits
- 6 2/3 gallons Plain White Syrup (on page 136)

Dissolve the oil into the alcohol, then add the syrup. Color the mixture yellow with Yellow Coloring (on page 128).

CITRON

- 1 oz Lemon Oil
- 3 1/3 gallons Neutral Spirits
- 6 2/3 gallons Plain White Syrup (on page 136)

Dissolve the oil into the alcohol, then slowly add the syrup. Color the mixture yellow with Yellow Coloring (on page 128).

ESCUBAC D'IRELANDE [D]

- 12 oz Italian Fennel Seed
- 8 oz Ceylon Cinnamon
- 3 1/3 gallons Neutral Spirits
- 4 gallons water
- 6 2/3 gallons Plain White Syrup (on page 136)

Grind the Fennel and Cinnamon. Combine with the alcohol and water, then macerate for 24 hours. Distill from off the water 3 1/3 gallons of flavored alcohol. Add the syrup, then filter. Color the mixture yellow with Yellow Coloring (on page 128).

ESPRIT DE MANUEL

- 100 drops Peppermint Oil
- 89 drops Clove Oil
- 3 1/3 gallons Neutral Spirits
- 6 2/3 gallons Plain White Syrup (on page 136)

Dissolve the oils into the alcohol, then add the syrup. Color the mixture green with Green Coloring (on page 128).

BRANDY LIQUEURS

Angelica Brandy [D] • *Anise Seed Brandy Liqueur* • *Anise Seed Brandy [D]*
Blackberry Brandy Liqueur • *Calamus Brandy Liqueur* • *Carminative Brandy Liqueur*
Caraway Brandy Liqueur • *Cherry Brandy Liqueur* • *Cinnamon Brandy Liqueur* • *Cloves Brandy Liqueur*
Domestic Brandy Liqueur • *French Brandy Liqueur* • *Ginger Brandy Liqueur*
Grunewald Brandy Liqueur • *Imperial Peach Brandy Liqueur* • *Juniper Brandy Liqueur*
Mint Brandy Liqueur • *Orange Brandy Liqueur* • *Peach Brandy Liqueur*
Peppermint Brandy Liqueur • *Raspberry Brandy Liqueur* • *Stomach Brandy Liqueur (Green)*
Stomach Brandy Liqueur (White) • *Strawberry Brandy Liqueur* • *Wormwood Brandy Liqueur*

THE TERM **BRANDY LIQUEUR** CAN BE DECEPTIVELY SIMPLE, ESPECIALLY IN THE CONTEXT OF HISTORICAL RECIPES. TODAY, WE ASSOCIATE BRANDY WITH GRAPE-BASED DISTILLATES, BUT HISTORICALLY, BRANDY WAS A CATCH-ALL TERM APPLIED TO A VARIETY OF FLAVORED OR FRUIT-BASED SPIRITS. FOR EXAMPLE, PEAR BRANDY TRADITIONALLY REFERS TO THE UNSWEETENED DISTILLATE OF FERMENTED PEARS — NOT A GRAPE SPIRIT AT ALL.

WHEN WE TURN TO LIQUEURS AND CORDIALS, THE TERMINOLOGY GROWS EVEN MORE CONFUSING. A BRANDY LIQUEUR OR BRANDY CORDIAL OFTEN IMPLIES A SWEETENED DRINK BUILT ON A GRAPE BRANDY BASE. YET A LABEL LIKE PEAR BRANDY LIQUEUR COULD MEAN: (1) GRAPE BRANDY INFUSED WITH PEAR, (2) PEAR BRANDY THAT'S BEEN SWEETENED, OR (3) A SWEETENED PEAR INFUSION BUILT ON NEUTRAL SPIRITS.

IN THIS CHAPTER, "BRANDY LIQUEUR" REFERS NOT TO GRAPE-BASED CORDIALS, BUT TO SWEETENED, FLAVORED DRINKS BUILT ON FULLY RECTIFIED SPIRITS. TWO RECIPES (ANGELICA BRANDY AND ANISE SEED BRANDY) BEGIN WITH A FLAVORING DISTILLATE, WHILE THE OTHERS USE NEUTRAL SPIRITS AS A BLANK CANVAS — REIMAGINING BRANDY'S WARMTH AND DEPTH THROUGH LAYERED ADDITIONS OF BOTANICALS, SPICES, AND SUGAR.

THESE LIQUEURS TYPICALLY RANGE FROM 25–40% ABV. HISTORICALLY, THEY MAY HAVE BEEN SERVED NEAT IN THIMBLE-SIZED CORDIAL GLASSES AS AFTER-DINNER DIGESTIFS, ADDED BY THE OUNCE TO PUNCH BOWLS AND MIXED DRINKS, OR EVEN SPOONED INTO SAUCES AND DESSERTS BY AMBITIOUS COOKS.

ANGELICA BRANDY [D]

Distilling	Mixing
1.5 lbs. Angelica Root, ground course	3 pints Plain White Syrup (on page 136)
2.25 oz Cinnamon, ground course	water
1.5 oz Lavender Flowers, ground course	
1.5 oz Licorice Root, ground course	
10 gallons 50% ABV Alcohol	
6 lbs. Rectifier's Charcoal	

Combine distilling ingredients, then distill over to 50 percent. Mix in the syrup and enough water to make 10 gallons of liquid.

ANISE SEED BRANDY LIQUEUR

- 2.5 drachms Anise Seed Oil
- ½ drachm Star Anise Seed Oil
- 4.25 gallons Neutral Spirits
- 6 pints Plain Extra White Syrup (on page 136)
- 5 gallons water

Dissolve the oils into alcohol. Mix the syrup and water together, then combine with the flavored alcohol. Filter. Color the mixture white.

ANISE SEED BRANDY [D]

Distilling	Mixing
3 lbs. Anise Seed, ground course	3 pints Plain White Syrup (on page 136)
2 oz Caraway Seed, ground course	
3 oz Orris Root, ground course	water
10 gallons Proof Alcohol (50% ABV)	
6 lbs. Rectifier's Charcoal	

Combine distilling ingredients, then distill over to 50 percent. Mix in the syrup and enough water to make 10 gallons of liquid.

BLACKBERRY BRANDY LIQUEUR

- .5 oz Cinnamon
- .25 oz Cloves
- .25 oz Mace
- .25 oz Cardamom
- 16 lbs. Blackberries, mashed
- 5 gallons Neutral Spirits
- 10 lbs. Sugar
- 27 pints water

Grind all dry ingredients into a course powder. Combine with the Blackberries and alcohol. Create a tincture by letting macerate for 2 weeks. Create a syrup from the Sugar and water. Combine with the tincture, then filter.

CALAMUS BRANDY LIQUEUR

- .5 drachm Lemon Oil
- .5 oz Calamus Oil
- 5 drops Coriander Oil
- 4.75 gallons Neutral Spirits
- 5 gallons water
- 32 oz Plain White Syrup (on page 136)

Dissolve the oils into the alcohol. Combine the water and syrup and add to the alcohol. Color the mixture flesh-color with Saffron (on page 128) and Cochineal (on page 129) coloring.

CARMINATIVE BRANDY LIQUEUR

- 1.5 drachms Calamus Oil
- 16 drops Anise Seed Oil
- 32 drops Orange Oil
- 16 drops Coriander Oil
- 16 drops Lemon Balm Oil
- 4.75 gallons Neutral Spirits
- 5 gallons water
- 32 ounces Plain White Syrup (on page 136)

Dissolve the oils into the alcohol. Combine the water and syrup and add to the alcohol. Color the mixture yellow with Yellow Coloring (on page 128).

Caraway Brandy Liqueur

- .5 oz Caraway Seed Oil
- 30 drops Anise Seed Oil
- 5 drops Coriander Oil
- 4.75 gallons Neutral Spirits
- 5 gallons water
- 2 pints Plain White Syrup (on page 136)

Dissolve the oils into the alcohol. Combine the water and syrup and add to the alcohol.

Cherry Brandy Liqueur

- 16 lbs. Black Cherries, mashed with the stones
- 5 gallons Neutral Spirits
- 10 lbs. Sugar
- 3.75 gallons water

Create a tincture by macerating the Cherries in the alcohol for 2 weeks. Press the fruit to extract all the juices. Dissolve the Sugar in the water, then add to the tincture. Filter.

Cinnamon Brandy Liqueur

- .5 oz Cinnamon Oil
- 32 drops Cassia Bud Oil
- 32 drops Clove Oil
- 4.75 gallons Neutral Spirits
- 4.75 gallons water
- 4 pints Plain White Syrup (on page 136)

Dissolve the oils into the alcohol. Combine the water and syrup and add to the alcohol. Color the mixture brown with Base Coloring (on page 127).

Cloves Brandy Liqueur

- 4.5 drachms Clove Oil
- .5 drachm Cinnamon Oil
- 4.75 gallons Neutral Spirits
- 4.75 gallons water
- 4 pints Plain White Syrup (on page 136)

Dissolve the oils into the alcohol. Combine the water and syrup and add to the alcohol. Color the mixture brown with Base Coloring (on page 127).

DOMESTIC BRANDY LIQUEUR

- 50 drops Oil of Cognac
- 3 drachms Orris Root Powder
- 1 drachm finely cut Vanilla
- 4 oz Neutral Spirits
- 9.75 gallons 25% ABV Alcohol
- 1.5 pints Plain White Syrup (on page 136)

Combine the Oil of Cognac, Orris root powder Vanilla and Neutral Spirits. Let macerate in a warm place for 24 hours. Filter and then add the 25% ABV alcohol and syrup. Color the mixture pale or dark with Base Coloring (on page 127).

FRENCH BRANDY LIQUEUR

- 1 gallon genuine Otard Brandy
- 8 ⅞ gallons 12.5% ABV Alcohol (pure)
- 4 pints pure Plain White Syrup (on page 136)

Combine all ingredients. Color dark or pale with Base Coloring (on page 127).

GINGER BRANDY LIQUEUR

- 8 ounces White Ginger, cut and washed
- 7.5 lbs. Sugar
- 3 gallons water
- 7 gallons 12.5% ABV Alcohol

Combine Ginger, Sugar and water and bring to a boil for 10 minutes. Strain and add the 12.5% ABV alcohol. Color the mixture pale yellow with Yellow Coloring (on page 128).

GRUNEWALD BRANDY LIQUEUR

- 4 oz Orange Peel
- 4 oz Centaurium
- 1 oz Ginger
- 1 ⅓ oz Calamus Root
- 1 ⅓ oz Blessed Thistle
- 1 oz Wormwood
- ⅔ oz Trefoil
- 1 ⅓ drachm Clove Oil
- 1 ⅓ drachm Cinnamon Oil
- ⅔ drachm Peppermint Oil
- 4.75 gallons Neutral Spirits
- 6 pints Plain White Syrup (on page 136)
- 4.5 gallons water

Combine the dry ingredients, oils and alcohol and let macerate for 24 hours. Strain and filter. Combine the syrup with the water and add to the tincture. Color the mixture brown with Base Coloring (on page 127).

IMPERIAL PEACH BRANDY LIQUEUR

- 4.5 oz powdered Bitter Almonds
- 3.75 gallons Neutral Spirits
- 5.25 gallons water
- 3.75 lbs. Sugar
- 1 pint Peach Jelly
- 2.25 oz Preserved Ginger
- 1 Lemon, sliced
- 1 drachm Nutmeg, grated
- 1 drachm Allspice, powdered
- 5 pints water

Combine the Almonds, alcohol, and 5.25 gallons of water, and let macerate for 24 hours. Create a syrup by bringing the remaining ingredients to a boil for 2 minutes. Mix the syrup into the tincture and filter.

JUNIPER BRANDY LIQUEUR

- 9 drachms Juniper Oil, best quality
- 4.75 gallons Neutral Spirits
- 6 lbs. Sugar
- 39 pints water

Dissolve the oil into the alcohol. Dissolve the Sugar into the water. Mix together, then filter.

Mint Brandy Liqueur

- .5 oz Spearmint Oil
- 30 drops Peppermint Oil
- 3 drops Bergamot Oil
- 4.75 gallons Neutral Spirits
- 3 lbs. Sugar
- 5 1/3 gallons water

Dissolve the oils into the alcohol. Dissolve the Sugar into the water. Mix together. Color the mixture green with Green Coloring (on page 128).

Orange Brandy Liqueur

- 4 ⅓ drachms Orange Oil
- 3 drops Neroli Oil
- 4.75 gallons Neutral Spirits
- 2.5 lbs. Sugar
- 41 pints water

Dissolve the oils into the alcohol. Dissolve the Sugar into the water. Mix together, then filter.

Peach Brandy Liqueur

- 18 lbs. Peaches, mashed with the stones
- 4.75 gallons Neutral Spirits
- 4 gallons water
- 5 pints Plain White Syrup (on page 136)

Combine the Peaches, alcohol, and water. Macerate for 24 hours. Strain, press, and filter. Add the syrup. Color the mixture dark yellow with Base Coloring (on page 127).

Peppermint Brandy Liqueur

- .5 oz Peppermint Oil (English)
- 4.75 gallons Neutral Spirits
- 4.75 lbs. Sugar
- 5 gallons water

Dissolve the oil into the alcohol. Dissolve the Sugar into the water. Mix together, then filter.

RASPBERRY BRANDY LIQUEUR

- 4 gallons Raspberry Juice
- 4.75 gallons Neutral Spirits
- 1.25 gallons Plain White Syrup (on page 136)

Combine the juice and alcohol, then let macerate for 2 days. Add the syrup, then filter.

STOMACH BRANDY LIQUEUR (GREEN)

- .25 lb. Cubebs, coarsely ground
- 2.5 oz Centaurium, coarsely ground
- 1.25 oz Trefoil, coarsely ground
- 2 oz Cassia Buds, coarsely ground
- 4.75 gallons Neutral Spirits
- .5 drachm Rosemary Oil
- .5 drachm Sage Oil
- .5 drachm Chamomile Oil
- .5 drachm Peppermint Oil
- .5 drachm Spearmint Oil
- .5 drachm Lavender Oil
- .25 drachm Caraway Oil
- .25 drachm Origanum Oil
- .25 drachm Lemon Oil
- .25 drachm Coriander Seed Oil
- .25 drachm Anise Seed Oil
- .75 drachm Fennel Seed Oil
- 4 lbs. Sugar
- 5 gallons water

Combine the dry ingredients with the alcohol and let macerate for 7 days. Filter, then dissolve the oils into the mixture. Dissolve the Sugar into the water and add to the flavored mixture. Color the mixture green with Green Coloring (on page 128).

STOMACH BRANDY LIQUEUR (WHITE)

- .25 drachm Anise Seed Oil
- .5 drachm Coriander Seed Oil
- .5 drachm Spearmint Oil
- 1 drachm Orange Oil
- .25 drachm Clove Oil
- .25 drachm Cinnamon Oil
- 2 drachm Calamus Oil
- 4.75 gallons Neutral Spirits
- 4 lbs. Sugar
- 5 gallons water

Dissolve the oils into the alcohol. Dissolve the Sugar into the water. Mix together, then filter.

STRAWBERRY BRANDY LIQUEUR

- 4 gallons Strawberry Juice
- 4.75 gallon Neutral Spirits
- 1.25 gallons Plain White Syrup (on page 136)

Macerate juice with the alcohol for 2 days, then add the syrup. Filter.

WORMWOOD BRANDY LIQUEUR

- 2.5 drachms Wormwood Oil
- 1.25 oz Herb of Wormwood
- .75 oz Calamus Root
- 4.75 gallons Neutral Spirits
- 4 lbs. Sugar
- 5 gallons water

Grind the herb and root. Add to the alcohol along with the oil. Macerate for a few days. Make a syrup from the Sugar and water and add to the mixture. Filter. Color the mixture green, with tincture of Indigo and Saffron.

CORDIALS

Anise Seed Cordial • Bright Pearl (Jelly) Cordial • Caraway Cordial Celery Cordial • Champ d'Asile [D] • Cherry Cordial • Christine Christophelet [D] • Cinnamon Cordial • Citronelle [D] • Cloves Cordial [D] Coquette Flatteuse • Cordial • Ginger Cordial • Gerofline Greengage Cordial • Imperial Nectar [D] • Lait de Vieillesse (Milk of Old Age) Lait Virginale (Virgin's Milk) • Lait de Vecchia (Milk of Vecchia) [D] Lemon Cordial [D] • French Macaron Cordial [D] • Mint Cordial Noyau Cordial [D] • Orange Cordial • Peach Cordial • Peppermint Cordial Persicot Cordial [D] • Quince Cordial [D] • Smallage Cordial

CORDIALS ARE SWEETENED AND FLAVORED SPIRITS THAT OCCUPIED A SPACE BETWEEN MEDICINE AND HOSPITALITY IN MID-19TH-CENTURY AMERICA. THE TERM *CORDIAL* DERIVES FROM THE LATIN *CORDIALIS*, MEANING "INVIGORATING" OR "HEART-STRENGTHENING," AND ORIGINALLY REFERRED TO APOTHECARIAL TONICS. BY THE 1860S, AMERICAN HOUSEHOLD MANUALS AND PHARMACY GUIDES ALIKE PUBLISHED RECIPES BLENDING NEUTRAL SPIRITS WITH FRUITS, SPICES, NUTS, OR HERBS, SWEETENED WITH SUGAR SYRUP, CLARIFIED, AND OFTEN TINTED FOR VISUAL APPEAL. IN REFINED PARLORS, CORDIALS LIKELY APPEARED AT THE CLOSE OF FORMAL DINNERS—SERVED IN SMALL GLASSES AS BOTH A DIGESTIF AND A SYMBOL OF HOSPITALITY. BARTENDERS OFTEN USED CORDIALS AS FLAVORING AGENTS IN PUNCHES, JULEPS, COBBLERS, AND OTHER MIXED DRINKS. THEIR CONCENTRATED SWEETNESS AND AROMATIC DEPTH MADE THEM INDISPENSABLE IN BUILDING LAYERED BEVERAGES. THE CORDIALS IN THIS SECTION RANGE WIDELY IN ALCOHOL CONTENT FROM 8-61% ABV.

ANISE SEED CORDIAL

- 3 drachms Anise Seed Oil
- 2.75 gallons Neutral Spirits
- 2.5 gallons Plain Extra-White Syrup (on page 136)
- 4.75 gallons water

Dissolve the oils into the alcohol. Mix the syrup and water together, then combine with the flavored alcohol. Filter. Color the mixture white.

BRIGHT PEARL (JELLY) CORDIAL

Jelly	Citrus-Ginger Flavoring
6 lbs. Malaga Raisins	2 oz Candied Lemons
4 oz Currant Jelly	2 oz Lemon Peel
2 oz Almonds, blanched and broken	3 oz Candied Ginger
1 oz Bitter Almonds, blanched and broken	4 oz raw Ginger
2 oz Carob, broken and mashed	2 gallons water
1 oz Conserve of White Roses	
1 oz Powdered Ginger	
1 oz Cinnamon powdered	
1 oz Mace powdered	
8 oz Lemon Juice	
7 gallons of Quarter-Proof Spirit (12.5% ABV)	
2 oz Isinglass, dissolved in water	

Mix the jelly ingredients except the Raisins into a well-covered earthenware pot. Boil the Raisins in 1 gallon of water then add to the mixture. Press and filter through a flannel while hot. Combine the Citrus-Ginger ingredients and boil for 20 minutes. Strain. Add in the jelly mixture.

CARAWAY CORDIAL

- 6 drachms Caraway Oil
- 3 gallons Neutral Spirits
- 42 lbs. Sugar
- 4.75 gallons water

Dissolve the oil into the alcohol. Make a syrup from the Sugar and water and add it to the flavored alcohol. Filter.

CELERY CORDIAL

- 1 lb. Celery Seed
- 5 lbs. Celery Root
- 7 gallons Plain White Syrup (on page 136)
- 3 gallons Neutral Spirits

Combine the Celery seed and root with the syrup, then boil for 2 minutes. Add in the alcohol. Strain and filter. Color the mixture with Tincture of Turmeric (on page 128).

CHAMP D'ASILE [D]

Distilling	Mixing
8 oz Caraway Seed	42 lbs. Sugar
4 oz Ambrette seeds	4.75 gallons water
1 ⅓ oz Ceylon Cinnamon, coarsely ground	
3 gallons Neutral Spirits	
3.5 gallons water	

Macerate the distilling ingredients, then distill 3 gallons of alcohol off the water. Make a syrup from the mixing ingredients. Slowly add to the flavored alcohol. Filter.

CHERRY CORDIAL

- 30 lbs. Sour Red Cherries without stems
- 4.5 gallons Neutral Spirits
- 42 lbs. Sugar
- 3.5 gallons water

Pulp the Cherries and macerate in the alcohol. Press. Make a syrup from the Sugar and water and add it to the alcohol mixture. Filter.

CHRISTINE

- 2 drachms of Vanilla Essence
- 8 drops Rose Oil
- 24 drops Neroli Oil
- 48 drops Cinnamon Oil
- 3 gallons Neutral Spirits
- 42 lbs. Sugar
- 4.75 gallons water

Dissolve the oils into the alcohol. Make a syrup from the Sugar and water and add it to the flavored alcohol.

CHRISTOPHELET [D]

Distilling	Mixing
6 ⅘ drachms of Spanish Saffron	1.25 gallons St. Julien Medoc Wine
14 ⅕ drachms Cinnamon	1.25 gallons distilled water
6 ⅘ drachms Cardamom	13 drops Ambergris Tincture
10 ⅕ oz Figs	2.5 gallons Plain White Syrup (on page 136)
10 ⅕ drachms Galangal Root	
4.25 oz Orris Root	
2.5 oz Sage	
4.25 oz Star Anise	
2.5 oz Coriander Seed	
6 gallons Neutral Spirits	
1.5 gallons water	

Coarsely grind the dry distilling ingredients. Macerate with the distilling liquids. Distill 5 gallons of flavored alcohol off the water. Combine the mixing ingredients, then add slowly to the flavored alcohol. Color the mixture purple with Purple Coloring (on page 129).

CINNAMON CORDIAL

- .5 oz Cinnamon Oil
- 3 gallons Neutral Spirits
- 42 lbs. Sugar
- 3.5 gallons water

Dissolve the oil into the alcohol. Make a syrup from the Sugar and water and add it to the flavored alcohol. Filter.

CITRONELLE [D]

Distilling	Mixing
1 lb. Lemon Peel, only the yellow part	2 gallons Plain White Syrup (on page 136)
2 oz Orange Peel, only the yellow part	
1 drachm Cloves	
1 drachm Nutmeg	
5 gallons Neutral Spirits	
5 gallons water	

Cut the distilling flavorings into small pieces. Macerate with the alcohol and water. Distill off 8 gallons of flavored spirit, and mix it with the syrup. Color the mixture yellow with Yellow Coloring (on page 128).

CLOVES CORDIAL [D]

Distilling	Mixing
12 oz Cloves	24 lbs. Sugar
3 oz Orris Root	3.5 gallons water
2 oz Cinnamon	
.5 oz Cardamom	
5.5 gallons Neutral Spirits	
5.5 gallons water	

Coarsely grind the dry distilling ingredients. Macerate or displace with the distilling alcohol and water. Distill off 5 gallons of flavored alcohol. Make a syrup from the mixing ingredients, then add to the flavored alcohol. Color the mixture brown with tincture of Cloves.

COQUETTE FLATTEUSE

- 24 drops Rose Oil
- 48 drops Mace Oil
- 32 drops Ambergris Essence
- 3 gallons Neutral Spirits
- 42 lbs. Sugar
- 4.75 gallons water

Dissolve the oils and essence into the alcohol. Make a syrup from the Sugar and water and add it to the flavored alcohol. Color the mixture rose with Red Coloring (on page 129).

CORDIAL

- 32 drops Cinnamon Oil
- 24 drops Clove Oil
- 24 drops Mace Oil
- 48 drops Peppermint Oil
- 3 gallons Neutral Spirits
- 42 lbs. Sugar
- 4.75 gallons water

Dissolve the oils into the alcohol. Make a syrup from the Sugar and water and add it to the flavored alcohol. Filter.

GINGER CORDIAL

- 10 oz of ground Ginger
- 5 drops Bergamot Oil
- 3 gallons Neutral Spirits
- 42 lbs. Sugar
- 4.75 gallons water

Macerate the Ginger and oil with 3 the alcohol. Press and filter. Make a syrup with the Sugar and water and add it to the flavored alcohol. Color the mixture pale yellow (on page 128), or red (on page 129).

GEROFLINE

- .5 oz Clove Oil
- 3 gallons Neutral Spirits
- 2.5 gallons Plain White Syrup (on page 136)
- 4.5 gallons water

Dissolve the oil into the alcohol. Add the syrup and water. Filter. Color the mixture yellow (on page 128).

GREENGAGE CORDIAL

- 8 lbs. ripe Greengages
- 42 lbs. Sugar
- 4.75 gallons of water
- 4 oz Currant Jelly
- 4 oz Dates, cut in small pieces
- 4 oz Figs cut in small pieces
- 8 oz Orange Juice
- 3 pints Sherry
- 1 pint Calf's Foot Jelly
- 1 oz Candied Lemon
- 1 oz Cinnamon, coarsely ground
- 1 oz Cloves, coarsely ground
- 2 oz Ginger, coarsely ground
- 1 oz Nutmeg, coarsely ground
- 1 oz Pimento, coarsely ground
- 2 gallons Neutral Spirits

Boil the Greengages and Sugar in the water until the greengages are tender and make them into a pulp. Skim and take from the fire. Add the remaining ingredients, except for the alcohol, and macerate for 7 days. Add the alcohol. Strain, press and filter

IMPERIAL NECTAR [D]

Distilling	Mixing
8 Lemons, yellow rinds only	20 lbs. Sugar
10 Oranges, yellow rinds only	4.5 gallons water
6 oz Ceylon Cinnamon	4 pints Rose Water
.5 oz Mace	
8 oz Star Anise Seed	
8 oz Coriander Seed	
4 oz Juniper Berries	
2 oz Angelica Seed	
2 drachms Spanish Saffron	
4 gallons Neutral Spirits	
5 gallons water	

Grind and cut the dry distilling ingredients. Combine with the distilling alcohol and water, then macerate for 10 days. Distill from off the water 4 gallons of flavored alcohol. Make a syrup by boiling the mixing Sugar and water. When nearly cold, mix in the rose water. Filter. Color the mixture rose with Red Coloring (on page 129).

LAIT DE VIEILLESSE (MILK OF OLD AGE)

- 1 drachm Peruvian Balsam Tincture
- 3 gallons Neutral Spirits
- 20 lbs. Sugar
- 5.5 gallons water
- 2 pints Orange Flower Water

Combine the Balsam tincture and alcohol. Dissolve the Sugar into the water, then add to the alcohol mixture. Add the Orange Flower Water, then filter.

LAIT VIRGINALE (VIRGIN'S MILK)

- .5 oz Lemon Oil
- 3 gallons Neutral Spirits
- 20 lbs. Sugar
- 47 pints water
- 2 pints Vinegar
- 1 pint Lemon Juice

Dissolve the oil into the alcohol. Dissolve the Sugar into the water and combine with the flavored alcohol. Add the Vinegar and Lemon Juice, then filter

LAIT DE VECCHIA (MILK OF VECCHIA) [D]

Distilling	Mixing
1.5 lb. Roasted Cacao, ground	20 lbs. Sugar
4 oz Cinnamon, ground	5.75 gallons water
4 oz Carrot Seed, ground	
3 gallons Neutral Spirits	
3.5 gallons water	

Combine the distilling ingredients and macerate for 24 hours. Distill from off the water 3 gallons of flavored alcohol. Dissolve the Sugar into the mixing water, then add to the flavored alcohol.

LEMON CORDIAL [D]

Distilling	Mixing
2 lbs. of fresh Lemon Peel	30 drops Lemon Oil
4 oz roasted Wheat Bread Crusts	24 lbs. Sugar
4 oz Cinnamon, crushed	3.5 gallons water
.5 oz Nutmeg, crushed	
5.5 gallons Neutral Spirits	
5.5 gallons water	

Cut the Lemon Peel and crusts small and macerate for one week with 5.5 gallons of Neutral Spirits and 5.5 gallons water. Distill from off the water 5 gallons of flavored alcohol. Make a syrup from the mixing Sugar and water. Mix in the Lemon Oil and slowly add to the flavored alcohol. Color the mixture pale yellow with Yellow Coloring (on page 128).

FRENCH MACARON CORDIAL [D]

Distilling	Mixing
22 oz Bitter Almonds	24 lbs. Sugar
1.5 oz Cinnamon	3.5 gallons water
1.5 oz Cloves	
1.5 oz Cardamom	
5.25 gallons Neutral Spirits	
5.5 gallons water	

Coarsely grind the dry distilling ingredients. Combine with the distilling alcohol and water, then let it macerate for one week. Distill from off the water 5 gallons of flavored alcohol. Make a syrup with the mixing Sugar and water and slowly add to the flavored alcohol. Filter.

MINT CORDIAL

- .5 oz Spearmint Oil
- 3 gallons Neutral Spirits
- 42 lbs. Sugar
- 4.75 gallons water

Dissolve the oil into the alcohol. Make a syrup from the Sugar and water and add it to the flavored alcohol. Color the mixture green (on page 128).

NOYAU CORDIAL [D]

Distilling	Mixing
1.25 lb. Apricot Kernels	42 lbs. Sugar
.5 lb. Peach Kernels	4.75 gallons water
.5 lb. Prune Kernels	
Rinds of 12 Oranges, cut in small pieces.	
3.5 gallons Neutral Spirits	
3.5 gallons water	

Combine the distilling ingredients and macerate for 24 hours. Distill from off the water 3 gallons of flavored spirit. Make a syrup from the mixing ingredients. Add to the flavored alcohol, then filter.

ORANGE CORDIAL

- 1 oz Orange Oil
- 3 gallons Neutral Spirits
- 42 lbs. Sugar
- 4.75 gallons water

Dissolve the oil into the alcohol. Make a syrup from the Sugar and water and add it to the flavored alcohol. Color the mixture yellow with Saffron (on page 128).

PEACH CORDIAL

- 12 lbs. Peaches with kernels, mashed to a pulp
- 7 gallons Plain White Syrup (on page 136)
- 3 gallons Neutral Spirits

Let the Peaches ferment for eight days. Combine with the syrup and boil for 2 minutes. Strain, then add the alcohol. Filter. Color the mixture yellow (on page 128).

PEPPERMINT CORDIAL

- .5 oz Peppermint Oil
- 3 gallons Neutral Spirits
- 7 gallons Plain White Syrup (on page 136)

Dissolve the oil into the alcohol. Mix in the syrup and then filter.

PERSICOT CORDIAL [D]

- 3 lbs. Peach Kernels
- 6 oz Lemon Peel
- 2 oz Cinnamon
- .5 oz Cloves
- .5 oz Nutmeg
- 3.5 gallons Neutral Spirits
- 3.5 gallons water
- 7 gallons Plain White Syrup (on page 136)

Combine all ingredients except the syrup and macerate for 24 hours. Distill from off the water 3 gallons of flavored spirit, then slowly add in the syrup. Color Peach-blossom, with Red Coloring (on page 129).

QUINCE CORDIAL [D]

- 48 oz Quinces, grated
- 3.5 gallons Neutral Spirits
- 3.5 gallons water
- 7 gallons Plain White Syrup (on page 136)

Combine all ingredients except the syrup and macerate for 8 days. Distill from off the water 3 gallons of flavored spirit, then slowly add the syrup.

SMALLAGE CORDIAL

- 3 lbs. of Raisins, seeded
- 5 lbs. young sprouts of Smallage (cut and washed)
- 7 gallons Plain White Syrup (on page 136)
- 3 gallons Neutral Spirits

Combine the Raisins, sprouts and syrup, then boil for 2 minutes. Strain, then add the alcohol. Filter.

CRÈME'S

Crème d'Absinthe [D] • *Crème d'Angelique [D]* • *Crème de Anise [D]*
Crème de Barbadoes [D] • *Crème de Cacao [D]*
Crème de Cedrat with Champagne • *Crème de Chocolat [D]*
Crème de Cinnamon • *Crème de Cinq fruits (Five Fruits) [D]*
Crème de Dattes (Date) • *Crème Imperiale [D]* • *Crème de Martinique*
Crème de Menthe (Mint) [D] • *Crème de Mocha (Coffee) [D]*
Crème de Nymphe • *Crème d'Orange with Champagne* • *Crème de Portugal*
Crème de Roses • *Crème Royale [D]* • *Crème de Truffles*
Crème de Vanille (Vanilla) • *Crème Virginal* • *Cuckold's Comfort*

IN AMERICAN PARLOURS AND TAVERNS OF THE 1860S, *CRÈMES* WERE ULTRA-SWEET CORDIALS (40-48% ABV) — CRAFTED BY DISSOLVING GENEROUS QUANTITIES OF REFINED SUGAR INTO NEUTRAL SPIRITS, THEN AROMATIZED WITH FLORAL WATERS, FRUIT ESSENCES, AND EXOTIC SPICES. TYPICALLY SERVED IN THIMBLE-SIZED GLASSES AT THE CLOSE OF A MEAL, THESE LIQUEURS ALSO FOUND A PLACE IN PUNCHES, POSSETS, AND ICED DESSERTS. WHETHER SIPPED TO SOOTHE THE STOMACH AFTER A HEARTY MEAL OR OFFERED AS A TOKEN OF HOSPITALITY DURING AFTERNOON RECEPTIONS, CRÈMES EVOKE BOTH THE DOCUMENTED CUSTOMS AND THE INFERRED TASTES OF MID-19TH-CENTURY AMERICAN REFINEMENT.

CRÈME D'ABSINTHE [D]

Distilling	Mixing
24 oz Wormwood, ground fine	53 lbs. Sugar
8 oz Anise Seed, ground fine	3.25 gallons water
3 1/3 gallons Neutral Spirits	
3 2/3 gallons water	

Combine the distilling ingredients and macerate for 24 hours. Distill from off the water 3 ⅓ gallons of flavored spirit. Make a syrup from the mixing ingredients at near boiling heat, then mix into the flavored alcohol. Color green (on page 128).

CRÈME D'ANGELIQUE [D]

Distilling	Mixing
12 oz Angelica Root, powdered	53 lbs. Sugar
3 2/3 gallons Neutral Spirits	3.25 gallons water
3 2/3 gallons water	

Combine the Angelica with the alcohol and macerate for 24 hours. Add the distilling water. Distill from off the water 3.5 gallons of flavored spirit. Make a syrup from the mixing ingredients at near boiling heat, then mix into the flavored alcohol.

CRÈME DE ANISE [D]

Distilling	Mixing
24 oz Green Anise Seed	53 lbs. Sugar
8 oz Star Anise Seed	3.25 gallons water
4 oz Cinnamon	
3 1/3 gallons Neutral Spirits	
3 2/3 gallons water	

Grind the dry distilling ingredients then macerate with the alcohol and water for 24 hours. Distill from off the water 3 1/3 gallons of highly flavored spirit. Make a syrup from the mixing ingredients at near boiling heat, then mix into the flavored alcohol.

CRÈME DE BARBADOES [D]

Distilling	Mixing
4 Lemons, rinds only	53 lbs. Sugar
4 Oranges, rinds only	3.25 gallons water
5.5 oz ounces Ceylon Cinnamon	
3 drachms Cloves	
11 drachms Coriander Seed	
11 drachms Bitter Almonds	
1.5 drachms Nutmeg	
3 1/3 gallons Neutral Spirits	
3 2/3 gallons water	

Grind and cut the dry distilling ingredients then macerate for 24 hours with the alcohol and water. Distill from off the water 3 1/3 gallons of flavored spirit. Make a syrup from the mixing ingredients at near boiling heat, then mix into the flavored alcohol.

CRÈME DE CACAO [D]

Distilling	Mixing
5 lbs. Roasted Cacao	53 lbs. Sugar
1 oz Ceylon Cinnamon	3.25 gallons water
3 1/3 gallons Neutral Spirits	1 oz Vanilla Tincture
3 2/3 gallons water	

Grind the dry distilling ingredients, then macerate for 24 hours with the alcohol and water. Distill from off the water 3 1/3 gallons of flavored spirit. Make a syrup from the mixing Sugar and water at near boiling heat. Mix the syrup into the flavored alcohol, then add the Vanilla tincture.

CRÈME DE CEDRAT WITH CHAMPAGNE

- 1 oz Cedrat Oil
- 2 ⅓ gallons of Neutral Spirits
- 4 quarts Champagne
- 53 lbs. Sugar
- 3.25 gallons water

Dissolve the oil into the alcohol, then add the Champagne. Bring the water to near boiling heat and add the Sugar to make a syrup. Combine with the alcohol mixture.

CRÈME DE CHOCOLAT [D]

Distilling	Mixing
8 lbs. Roasted Cacao	53 lbs. Sugar
12 oz Cinnamon	3.25 gallons water
4 oz Vanilla	
.5 oz Cloves	
3 1/3 gallons Neutral Spirits	
3 2/3 gallons water	

Grind the dry distilling ingredients, then macerate for 48 hours with the distilling alcohol and water. Distill from off the water 3 1/3 gallons of high-flavored spirit. Make a syrup from the mixing ingredients at near boiling heat, then mix into the flavored alcohol.

CRÈME DE CINNAMON

- 162 drops Cinnamon Oil
- 3 1/3 gallons Neutral Spirits
- 53 lbs. Sugar
- 3.25 gallons water

Dissolve the oil into the alcohol. Make a syrup from the mixing ingredients at near boiling heat, then mix into the flavored alcohol. Color the mixture yellow (on page 128).

CRÈME DE CINQ FRUITS (FIVE FRUITS) [D]

Distilling	Mixing
6 Bergamots, rinds only	53 lbs. Sugar
6 Bitter Oranges, rinds only.	3.25 gallons water
6 Cedrats, rinds only	
6 Lemons, rinds only	
9 Oranges, rinds only	
3 1/3 gallons Neutral Spirits	
3 2/3 gallons water	

Cut the rinds small, then macerate for 24 hours with the distilling alcohol and water. Distill from off the water 3 ⅓ gallons of flavored spirit. Make a syrup from the mixing ingredients at near boiling heat, then mix into the flavored alcohol.

CRÈME DE DATTES (DATE)

- 8 lbs. Dates, pounded
- 53 lbs. Sugar
- 3.25 gallons water
- 72 drops Neroli Oil
- 3 1/3 gallons Neutral Spirits

Combine the Dates, Sugar and water and boil to make a syrup. Strain and press. Dissolve the Neroli Oil into the alcohol, then combine with the syrup.

CRÈME IMPERIALE [D]

Distilling	Mixing
4 oz Carrot Seed	53 lbs. Sugar
4 oz Ceylon Cinnamon	3.25 gallons water
8 oz Angelica Seed	
8 oz Orris Root	
3 1/3 gallons Neutral Spirits	
3 2/3 gallons water	

Grind the dry distilling ingredients, then macerate for 24 hours with the distilling alcohol and water. Distill from off the water 3 1/3 gallons of flavored spirit. Make a syrup from the mixing ingredients at near boiling heat, then mix into the flavored alcohol.

CRÈME DE MARTINIQUE

- 4 drachms Vanilla Tincture
- 32 drops Neroli Oil
- 14 drops Rose Oil
- 24 drops Cinnamon Oil
- 3 1/3 gallons Neutral Spirits
- 53 lbs. Sugar
- 3.25 gallons water

Dissolve the oils and tincture into the alcohol. Bring the water to a near boil and combine with the Sugar to make a syrup. Mix the syrup into the flavored alcohol. Color the mixture rose with Red Coloring (on page 129).

CRÈME DE MENTHE (MINT) [D]

Distilling	Mixing
5 lbs. Spearmint	5 drachms Peppermint Oil
25 Lemons, rinds only	53 lbs. Sugar
3 1/3 gallons Neutral Spirits	3.25 gallons water
3 2/3 gallons water	

Cut the distilling ingredients, then macerate for 24 hours with the distilling alcohol and water. Distill from off the water 3 ⅓ gallons of flavored spirit. Dissolve the Peppermint Oil into the flavored alcohol. Bring the mixing water to a near boil, then add the Sugar to make a syrup. Mix the syrup into the flavored alcohol.

CRÈME DE MOCHA (COFFEE) [D]

Distilling	Mixing
32 oz Mocha Coffee roasted and ground	1 drachm Vanilla Essence
3 1/3 gallons Neutral Spirits	53 lbs. Sugar
3 2/3 gallons water	3.25 gallons water

Macerate the distilling ingredients for 24 hours. Distill from off the water 3 ⅓ gallons flavored spirit. Dissolve the Vanilla Essence into the flavored alcohol. Bring the mixing water to a near boil, then add the Sugar to make a syrup. Mix the syrup into the flavored alcohol.

CRÈME DE NYMPHE

- 97 drops Cinnamon Oil
- 49 drops Mace Oil
- 24 drops Rose Oil
- 3 1/3 gallons Neutral Spirits
- 53 lbs. Sugar
- 3.25 gallons water

Dissolve the oils into the alcohol. Bring the water to a near boil, then add the Sugar to make a syrup. Mix the syrup into the flavored alcohol. Color the mixture rose with Red Coloring (on page 129).

CRÈME D'ORANGE, WITH CHAMPAGNE

- 1 oz Orange Oil
- 2 1/3 gallons Neutral Spirits
- 4 quarts Champagne
- 53 lbs. Sugar
- 3.25 gallons water

Dissolve the oil into the alcohol. Bring the water to a near boil, then add the Sugar to make a syrup. Mix the syrup into the flavored alcohol.

CRÈME DE PORTUGAL

- 1 oz Oil of Portugal
- 3 1/3 gallons Neutral Spirits
- 53 lbs. Sugar
- 3.25 gallons water

Dissolve the oil into the alcohol. Bring the water to a near boil, then add the Sugar to make a syrup. Mix the syrup into the flavored alcohol.

CRÈME DE ROSES

- 1 drachm Rose Oil
- 3 1/3 gallons Neutral Spirits
- 53 lbs. Sugar
- 3.25 gallons water

Dissolve the oil into the alcohol. Bring the water to a near boil, then add the Sugar to make a syrup. Mix the syrup into the flavored alcohol. Color the mixture rose with Red Coloring (on page 129).

CRÈME ROYALE [D]

Distilling	Mixing
4 oz Cloves	53 lbs. Sugar
4 oz Cinnamon	3.25 gallons water
8 oz Carrot Seed	
10 Oranges, rinds only	
3 1/3 gallons Neutral Spirits	
3 2/3 gallons water	

Combine the distilling ingredients and macerate for 24 hours. Distill from off the water 3 ⅓ gallons of flavored spirit. Bring the mixing water to a near boil, then add the Sugar to make a syrup. Mix the syrup into the flavored alcohol.

CRÈME DE TRUFFLES

- 1 lb. Truffles, ground
- 3 1/3 gallons Neutral Spirits
- 53 lbs. Sugar
- 3.25 gallons water

Combine the Truffles with the alcohol and macerate for 8 days. Strain and press. Bring the water to a near boil, then add the Sugar to make a syrup. Mix the syrup into the flavored alcohol. Color the mixture dark yellow (on page 128).

CRÈME DE VANILLE (VANILLA)

- 2 drachms Vanilla Bean, cut fine
- 3 1/3 gallons Neutral Spirits
- 53 lbs. Sugar
- 3.25 gallons water

Combine the Vanilla with the alcohol and macerate for 2 days. Bring the water to a near boil, then add the Sugar to make a syrup. Mix the syrup into the flavored alcohol.

CRÈME VIRGINAL

- 13 pints Rose Water
- 13 pints Orange Flower Water
- 53 lbs. Sugar
- 3 1/3 gallons Neutral Spirits

Dissolve Sugar into the Rose and Orange waters. Mix in the alcohol, then filter.

CUCKOLD'S COMFORT

- 4.5 lbs. fresh Poppies, mashed
- 4 gallons Proof Spirit (50% ABV)
- 1 gallon Plain White Syrup (on page 136)
- .5 oz Vanilla Essence
- 24 drops Rose Oil
- 2 oz Neutral Spirits

Combine the Poppies with the proof spirit, and macerate for 7 days. Strain and press. Dissolve the Vanilla Essence and Rose Oil into the Neutral Spirits, then add to the syrup. Mix the syrup into the flavored alcohol, then filter.

EAU'S

Eau d'Abricots (Apricot) • *Eau d'Absinthe (Absinthe) [D]* • *Eau d'Anis (Anise Seed)*
Eau d'Anis Compose (Compound Water of Anise Seed) [D] • *Eau Arohi-Episcopale [D]*
Eau d'Argent (Silver Water) • *Eau Aromatique (Aromatic Water) [D]* • *Eau de Belles Dames*
Eau de Bergamotte (Bergamot) [D] • *Eau de Cannelle (Cinnamon)* • *Eau de Carvi (Caraway) [D]*
Eau de Cedrat (Cedrat) [D] • *Eau de Celery (Kirschwasser) [D]* • *Eau de Cerises (Cherry) [D]*
Eau de Chasseurs (Hunter's Dew) • *Eau de Cologne, pure (Cologne)*
Eau de Cologne, a l'Amberegris (Ambergris Cologne) • *Eau de Cologne au Musc (Musk Cologne)*
Eau Cordiale (Cordial) [D] • *Eau de Cumin* • *Eau Divine [D]* • *Eau de Fleurs d'Oranges*
Eau de Fraises (Strawberry) • *Eau de Framboises (Raspberry)* • *Eau de Genievre (Juniper)*
Eau de Girofle (Clove) [D] • *Eau de Groseilles (Currant)* • *Eau de la Cote, St. Andre [D]*
Eau de Lucrece • *Eau de Malte (Water of Malta) [D]* • *Eau de Menthe (Mint)* • *Eau de Mere*
Eau de Millefleur (All Flower) [D] • *Eau de Noix (Walnut)* • *Eau de Noyaux de Pfalzburg [D]*
Eau d'Oilets (Pinks) [D] • *Eau d'Or (Golden Water) [D]* • *Eau des Pacificateurs de Grece [D]*
Eau de Quatre Graines (Four Seeds) [D] • *Eau de The (Tea)* • *Eau Verte Stomachique [D]*
Eau de Vie d'Andaye [D] • *Eau de Vie de Danzig [D]* • *Eau de Vie de Languedoc*

EAUX ("WATERS") REFERS TO SPIRIT-BASED INFUSIONS, DISTILLATES, AND AROMATIC
DILUTIONS, ORGANIZED HERE INTO THREE TYPES:

- EAUX DISTILLÉES: SWEET, SYRUPY DIGESTIFS (~30–35% ABV), E.G., *EAU DE CELERY (KIRSCHWASSER)*.

- EAUX SUCRÉES: MEDIUM-SWEET FLORAL OR FRUIT WATERS (~30% ABV), USED AS APERITIFS OR COCKTAIL ACCENTS, E.G., *EAU DE FRAISES*.

- EAUX D'ARÔMES: HIGH-PROOF (80–90% ABV), UNSWEETENED AROMATIC WATERS WITH ADDED ESSENTIAL OILS; USED BY THE DROP FOR FLAVOR OR SCENT, E.G., *EAU DE COLOGNE À L'AMBREGRIS*.

EAU D'ABRICOTS (APRICOT WATER)

- 80 Apricots, very ripe
- 4 gallons White Wine
- 1.25 gallons Plain White Syrup (on page 136)
- .5 oz Cinnamon Tincture
- 4.75 gallons Neutral Spirits

Cut the Apricots into small pieces, then boil them up with the wine. Strain, then add the remaining ingredients. Let sit for 2 weeks, then filter.

EAU D'ABSINTHE (ABSINTHE WATER) [D]

Distilling	Mixing
22 oz Wormwood	8 lbs. Sugar
3 gallons Neutral Spirits	6.5 gallons water
3.5 gallons water	

Combine the distilling ingredients and macerate for 24 hours. Distill from off the water 3 gallons of flavored alcohol. Dissolve the Sugar into the mixing water, then mix with the flavored alcohol. Filter.

Color the mixture green (on page 128).

EAU D'ANIS (WATER OF ANISE SEED)

- 1 oz Anise Seed Oil
- 3 gallons Neutral Spirits
- 8 lbs. Sugar
- 6.5 gallons water

Dissolve the oil into the alcohol. Dissolve the Sugar into the water, then mix into the flavored alcohol. Filter.

Eau d'Anis Compose (Compound Water of Anise Seed) [D]

Distilling	Mixing
8 oz Green Anise Seed	3 lbs. Sugar
8 oz Star Anise Seed	6.5 gallons water
8 oz Angelica Seed	
3 gallons Neutral Spirits	
3.5 gallons water	

Grind the dry distilling ingredients, then combine with the distilling alcohol and water. Macerate for 24 hours. Distill from off the water 3 gallons flavored spirit. Dissolve the Sugar into the mixing water, then add to the flavored alcohol. Filter.

Eau Arohi-Episcopale [D]

Distilling	Mixing
24 Cedrats	8 lbs. Sugar
18 oz Lemon Balm	6.5 gallons water
3 drachms Mace	
6 oz Angelica Root	
2 drachms Reseda Flowers	
2 drachms Jasmine Flowers	
3 quarts Orange Flower Water	
3 gallons Neutral Spirits	
3.5 gallons water	

Combine the distilling ingredients and macerate for 24 hours. Distill over 3 gallons of flavored alcohol. Dissolve the Sugar into the mixing water, then add to the flavored alcohol. Filter.

EAU D'ARGENT (SILVER WATER)

- 4 drachms Cedrat Oil
- 10 drops Rose Oil
- 3 gallons Neutral Spirits
- 20 lbs. Sugar
- 5.75 gallons water
- 40 sheets edible Silver Foil

Dissolve the oils into the alcohol. Dissolve the Sugar into the water. Combine the two mixtures, then filter. Tear or cut the Silver Foil, then add to the mixture.

EAU AROMATIQUE (AROMATIC WATER) [D]

Distilling	Mixing
13 oz Ceylon Cinnamon	8 lbs. Sugar
5 oz Cardamom	6.5 gallons water
6.5 oz Sassafras	
3 gallons Neutral Spirits	
3.5 gallons water	

Grind the dry distilling ingredients, then combine with the distilling alcohol and water. Macerate for 24 hours. Distill from off the water 3 gallons flavored spirit. Dissolve the Sugar into the mixing water, then add to the flavored alcohol. Filter.

EAU DE BELLES DAMES

- 2.75 drachms Vanilla Essence
- 12 drops Neroli Oil
- 8 drops Rose Oil
- 3 gallons Neutral Spirits
- 20 lbs. Sugar
- 5.75 gallons water

Dissolve the essence and oils into the alcohol. Dissolve the Sugar into the water and add to the flavored alcohol. Filter. Color the mixture rose with Red Coloring (on page 129).

EAU DE BERGAMOTTE (BERGAMOT WATER) [D]

Distilling	Mixing
10 Oranges, rinds only	20 lbs. Sugar
10 Bergamots, rinds only	5.75 gallons water
5 Lemons, rinds only	
3 gallons Neutral Spirits	
3.5 gallons water	

Cut rinds into small pieces, and macerate with the alcohol for 24 hours. Add the distilling water. Distill from off the water 3 gallons of flavored spirit. Dissolve the Sugar into the mixing water and combine with the flavored alcohol. Filter.

EAU DE CANNELLE (CINNAMON WATER)

- 1 oz Cinnamon Oil
- 3 gallons Neutral Spirits
- 8 lbs. Sugar
- 6.5 gallons water

Dissolve the oil into the alcohol. Dissolve the Sugar into the water, then combine with the flavored alcohol. Filter.

EAU DE CARVI (CARAWAY WATER) [D]

Distilling	Mixing
1.5 lbs. Caraway Seed, ground	8 lbs. Sugar
3 gallons Neutral Spirits	6.5 gallons water
3.5 gallons water	

Combine the distilling ingredients and macerate for 24 hours. Distill from off the water 3 gallons of flavored alcohol. Dissolve the Sugar into the mixing water, then mix with the flavored alcohol. Filter.

EAU DE CEDRAT (CEDRAT WATER) [D]

Distilling	Mixing
48 Cedrats, rinds only	24 lbs. Sugar
24 Oranges, rinds only	5.5 gallons water
3 gallons Neutral Spirits	
3.5 gallons water	

Cut the rinds. Combine the distilling ingredients and macerate for 24 hours. Distill from off the water 3 gallons of flavored alcohol. Dissolve the Sugar into the mixing water, then mix with the flavored alcohol. Filter.

EAU DE CELERY (KIRSCHWASSER) [D]

Distilling	Mixing
12 oz Celery Seed, ground	24 lbs. Sugar
3 gallons Neutral Spirits	5.5 gallons water
3.5 gallons water	

Macerate the distilling ingredients for 24 hours. Distill from off the water 3 gallons of flavored alcohol. Dissolve the Sugar into the mixing water, then mix with the flavored alcohol. Filter.

EAU DE CERISES (CHERRY WATER) [D]

- 9 bushels Black Cherries, without stems, pulped
- 2 handfuls Cherry Stones, broken

Place the pulp and stones in a large cask with a good, fixed cover. Let it ferment for 2 or 3 months. Add enough water to prevent its burning when distilled. Distill over to the strength of 55% (10 above proof) and fill it in demijohns or bottles.

EAU DE CHASSEURS (HUNTER'S DEW)

- 145 drops Peppermint Oil
- 48 drops Mace Oil
- 3 gallons Neutral Spirits
- 8 lbs. Sugar
- 6.5 gallons water

Dissolve the oils into the alcohol. Dissolve the Sugar into the water. Combine the two mixtures, then filter.

EAU DE COLOGNE, PURE (COLOGNE WATER)

- 21 oz Orange Oil
- 21 oz Bergamot Oil
- 5 ⅝ oz Neroli Oil
- 6 9/16 oz Lavender Oil
- 3 15/16 oz Rosemary Oil
- 63 drops Rose Oil
- 126 drops Clove Oil
- 10 gallons Neutral Spirits

Dissolve the oils into the alcohol.

EAU DE COLOGNE, A L'AMBREGRIS (AMBERGRIS COLOGNE WATER)

- 21 oz Orange Oil
- 21 oz Bergamot Oil
- 2 ⅝ oz Neroli Oil
- 6 9/16 oz Lavender Oil
- 3 15/16 oz Rosemary Oil
- 63 drops Rose Oil
- 126 drops Clove Oil
- 200 drops Ambergris Essence
- 10 gallons Neutral Spirits

Dissolve the oils and essence into the alcohol.

EAU DE COLOGNE AU MUSC (MUSK COLOGNE WATER)

- 21 oz Orange Oil
- 21 oz Bergamot Oil
- 2 ⅝ oz Neroli Oil
- 6 9/16 oz Lavender Oil
- 3 15/16 oz Rosemary Oil
- 63 drops Rose Oil
- 126 drops Clove Oil
- .5 oz Musk Essence
- 10 gallons Neutral Spirits

Dissolve the oils and essence into the alcohol.

EAU CORDIALE (CORDIAL WATER) [D]

Distilling	Mixing
1 oz Myrrh, ground	8 lbs. Sugar
4 oz Cinnamon, ground	6.5 gallons water
4 oz Cardamom, ground	
3 gallons Neutral Spirits	
3.5 gallons water	

Macerate the distilling ingredients for 24 hours. Distill over 3 gallons of flavored spirit. Dissolve the Sugar into the mixing water and add to the flavored alcohol. Filter.

EAU DE CUMIN

- 1 oz Caraway Seed Oil
- 3 gallons Neutral Spirits
- 8 lbs. Sugar
- 6.5 gallons water

Dissolve the oil into the alcohol. Dissolve the Sugar into the water. Combine the two mixtures and filter.

EAU DIVINE [D]

Distilling	Mixing
1.5 lbs. fresh Lemon Peel, yellow only	2 drachms Neroli Oil
4 oz Coriander Seed	1.5 drachm Bergamot Oil
1 oz Mace	24 lbs. Sugar
1 oz Cardamom	5.5 gallons water
3 gallons Neutral Spirits	
3.5 gallons water	

Grind the dry distilling ingredients. Combine with the distilling alcohol and water, then macerate for 24 hours. Distill from off the water 3 gallons of fine flavored alcohol. Dissolve the oils into the flavored alcohol. Dissolve the Sugar into the mixing water, then combine with the flavored alcohol. Filter.

EAU DE FLEURS D'ORANGES

- 162 drops Neroli Oil
- 3 gallons Neutral Spirits
- 8 lbs. Sugar
- 6.5 gallons water

Dissolve the oil into the alcohol. Dissolve the Sugar into the water. Combine the two mixtures, then filter.

EAU DE FRAISES (STRAWBERRY WATER)

- 6 lbs. Strawberries, pulped
- 8 lbs. Sugar
- 6.5 gallons water
- 3 gallons Neutral Spirits

Combine the Strawberries, Sugar and water.   Bring to a boil for 5 minutes. Strain and press. Add the alcohol then filter.

EAU DE FRAMBOISES (RASPBERRY WATER)

- 6 lbs. Raspberries, pulped
- 8 lbs. Sugar
- 6.5 gallons water
- 3 gallons Neutral Spirits

Combine the Raspberries, Sugar and water. Bring to a boil for 5 minutes. Strain and press. Add the alcohol, then filter.

EAU DE GENIEVRE (JUNIPER WATER)

- 3 drachms Juniper Oil
- 3 gallons Neutral Spirits
- 8 lbs. Sugar
- 6.5 gallons water

Dissolve the oil into the alcohol. Dissolve the Sugar into the water. Combine the two mixtures, then filter.

EAU DE GIROFLE (CLOVE WATER) [D]

Distilling	Mixing
10 oz Cloves, ground	20 lbs. Sugar
1.25 oz Mace, ground	6.75 gallons water
3 gallons Neutral Spirits	
3.5 gallons water	

Combine the distilling ingredients and macerate for 24 hours. Distill from off the water 3 gallons of flavored alcohol. Dissolve the Sugar into the mixing water, then add to the flavored alcohol.

Color the mixture brown with Base Coloring (on page 127), then filter.

EAU DE GROSEILLES (CURRANT WATER)

- 6 lbs. Red Currants, pulped
- 8 lbs. Sugar
- 6.5 gallons water
- 3 gallons Neutral Spirits

Combine the Currants, Sugar and water and bring to a boil for 5 minutes. Strain and press. Add the alcohol, then filter.

EAU DE LA COTE, ST. ANDRE [D]

Distilling	Mixing
4 lbs. Peach Kernels	20 lbs. Sugar
4 oz Ceylon Cinnamon	5.75 gallons water
27 Oranges, rinds only, no pith	
3 gallons Neutral Spirits	
3.5 gallons water	

Cut and macerate the distilling ingredients for 24 hours. Distill from off the water 3 gallons of fine flavored alcohol. Dissolve the Sugar into the mixing water, then combine with the flavored alcohol. Filter.

EAU DE LUCRECE

- 64 drops Cinnamon Oil
- 32 drops Clove Oil
- 146 drops Cedrat Oil
- 3 gallons Neutral Spirits
- 20 lbs. Sugar
- 5.75 gallons water

Dissolve the oils into the alcohol. Dissolve the Sugar into the water. Combine the two mixtures, then filter.

EAU DE MALTE (WATER OF MALTA) [D]

Distilling	Mixing
4 oz Ceylon Cinnamon	20 lbs. Sugar
.5 oz Castoreum	5.75 gallons water
1 oz Mace	
3 gallons Neutral Spirits	
3.5 gallons water	

Cut and grind the dry distilling ingredients. Combine with the distilling alcohol and water, then macerate for 24 hours. Distill from off the water 3 gallons of flavored alcohol. Dissolve the Sugar into the mixing water, then add to the flavored alcohol. Filter.

EAU DE MENTHE (MINT WATER)

- .5 oz Peppermint Oil
- 3 gallons Neutral Spirits
- 8 lbs. Sugar
- 6.5 gallons water

Dissolve the oil into the alcohol. Dissolve the Sugar into the water. Combine the two mixtures, then filter.

EAU DE MERE

- 1 lb. Angelica Root
- 1 lb. Juniper Berries
- 3 gallons Neutral Spirits
- 6.5 gallons water
- 8 lbs. Sugar

Grind the Angelica and Juniper, then combine with the alcohol and water. Macerate for 24 hours then strain and press. Mix in the Sugar until dissolved, then filter.

EAU DE MILLEFLEUR (ALL FLOWER WATER) [D]

Distilling	Mixing
12 oz Orange Flowers	20 lbs. Sugar
9 oz Quince Blossoms	5.75 gallons water
6 oz Lavender Flowers	
5 oz Orris Root	
5 oz Peppermint	
4 oz Lemon Balm	
4 oz Cinnamon	
2 oz Thyme	
1.5 oz Cloves	
3 gallons Neutral Spirits	
3.5 gallons water	

Grind the dry distilling ingredients. Combine with the distilling alcohol and water then macerate for 24 hours. Distill from off the water 3 gallons of flavored alcohol. Dissolve the Sugar into the mixing water, then add to the flavored alcohol. Color the mixture green (on page 128), then filter.

EAU DE NOIX (WALNUT WATER)

- 54 unripe Walnuts, pounded to a pulp
- 8 oz Cinnamon
- 4 oz Cloves
- 3 gallons Neutral Spirits
- 8 lbs. Sugar
- 6.5 gallons water

Grind the dry ingredients and macerate for 8 days with the alcohol. Strain, press and filter. Dissolve the Sugar into the water, then add to the flavored alcohol. Color (on page 126) the mixture dark brown.

EAU DE NOYAUX DE PFALZBURG [D]

Distilling	Mixing
.5 lb. Bitter Almonds	20 lbs. Sugar
⅓ lb. Apricot Kernels	5.75 gallons water
.25 lb. Peach Kernels	
.5 lb. Cherry Kernels	
3 gallons Neutral Spirits	
3.5 gallons water	

Grind the dry distilling ingredients. Combine with the distilling alcohol and water, then macerate for 24 hours. Distill from off the water 3 gallons of fine flavored alcohol. Dissolve the Sugar into the mixing water, then add to the flavored alcohol. Filter.

NOTE: SOME OF THE INGREDIENTS IN THIS RECIPE ARE KNOWN TO CAUSE CYANIDE POISONING WHEN INGESTED IN CERTAIN AMOUNTS. I HAVE ALSO READ THAT THE AMOUNT OF CYANIDE IN THIS DISTILLATE IS NEGLIGIBLE UNLESS IT HAS BEEN SITTING FOR MANY YEARS, IN WHICH CASE THE TOXINS RISE TO THE TOP, AND THE FIRST PERSON TO CRACK THE BOTTLE WILL BE THE UNFORTUNATE ONE TO GET ALL THE TOXIC EFFECTS. IN OTHER WORDS, DO NOT MAKE THIS RECIPE UNLESS YOU **REALLY** KNOW WHAT YOU ARE DOING AND HAVE LEARNED HOW TO PRODUCE IT SAFELY!

EAU D'OILETS (WATER OF PINKS) [D]

Distilling	Mixing
2 lbs. Red-Pink Flowers, cut small	20 lbs. Sugar
1 drachm Cloves, ground	5.75 gallons water
3 gallons Neutral Spirits	
3.5 gallons water	

Combine the distilling ingredients and macerate for 24 hours. Distill from off the water 3 gallons of fine flavored alcohol. Dissolve the Sugar into the mixing water, then add to the flavored alcohol. Color the mixture red (on page 129).

EAU D'OR (GOLDEN WATER) [D]

Distilling	Mixing
12 Oranges, rinds only, no pith	20 lbs. Sugar
12 Lemons, rinds only, no pith	5.75 gallons water
1.5 drachms Mace	2 sheets pure Gold Leaf per bottle
3 oz Cardamom	
3 oz Ambrette seeds	
3 gallons Neutral Spirits	
3.75 gallons water	

Grind dry distilling ingredients. Combine the distilling ingredients and macerate for 24 hours. Distill from off the water 3 gallons of flavored alcohol. Dissolve the Sugar into the mixing water, then combine with the flavored alcohol. Filter. Mix in 2 sheets of pure Gold Leaf to each demijohn.

EAU DES PACIFICATEURS DE GRECE [D]

Distilling	Mixing
24 Lemons, rinds only	20 lbs. Sugar
3 gallons Neutral Spirits	5.25 gallons water
3.5 gallons water	4 pints Orange Flower Water

Cut the Lemon rinds. Combine the distilling ingredients and macerate for 24 hours. Distill from off the water 3 gallons of flavored alcohol. Dissolve the Sugar into the mixing water. Add the Orange Flower Water, then combine with the flavored alcohol. Filter. Color the mixture red (on page 129).

EAU DE QUATRE GRAINES (WATER OF FOUR SEEDS) [D]

Distilling	Mixing
4 oz Fennel Seed	20 lbs. Sugar
4 oz Celery Seed	5.75 gallons water
4 oz Star Anise Seed	
4 oz Dill Seed	
3 gallons Neutral Spirits	
3.5 gallons water	

Grind the dry distilling ingredients. Combine with the distilling alcohol and water, then macerate for 24 hours. Distill from off the water 3 gallons of fine flavored alcohol. Dissolve the Sugar into the mixing water, then add to the flavored alcohol. Filter.

EAU DE THE (TEA WATER)

- 1 lb. Hyson Tea
- .5 lb. Souchong Tea
- 3 gallons Neutral Spirits
- 4.5 gallons water
- 2.5 gallons Plain White Syrup (on page 136)

Grind the teas. Combine with the alcohol and water, then macerate for 8 days. Strain, press and filter. Add in the syrup.

EAU VERTE STOMACHIQUE [D]

Distilling	Mixing
3 oz Coriander Seed	20 lbs. Sugar
1.5 oz Star Anise Seed	5.75 gallons water
3 oz Angelica Seed	
1.5 oz Cloves	
3 drachms Spanish Saffron	
6 drachms Peruvian Balsam	
3 drachms Mace	
1.5 oz Ceylon Cinnamon	
6 drachms Carrot Seed	
18 Acajou Nuts (Cashew)	
6 drachms Rosemary	
6 Oranges, rinds only, no pith	
6 Lemons, rinds only, no pith	
3 gallons Neutral Spirits	
3.5 gallons water	

Grind the dry distilling ingredients. Combine with the distilling alcohol and water, then macerate for 2 weeks. Distill from off the water 3 gallons high-flavored alcohol. Dissolve the Sugar into the mixing water, then add to the flavored alcohol. Filter. Color the mixture green (on page 128).

EAU DE VIE D'ANDAYE [D]

Distilling	Mixing
4 oz Star Anise Seed	40 lbs. Sugar
8 oz Coriander Seed	3.75 gallons water
4 oz Green Anise Seed	
4 oz Orris Root	
18 Oranges, rinds only, no pith	
3.75 gallons Neutral Spirits	
4 gallons water	

Grind and cut the dry distilling ingredients. Combine with the distilling alcohol and water, then macerate for 24 hours. Distill from off the water 3.75 gallons of flavored alcohol. Dissolve the Sugar into the mixing water, then add to the flavored alcohol. Filter.

EAU DE VIE DE DANZIG [D]

Distilling	Mixing
1 lb. Roasted Cacao	40 lbs. Sugar
4 oz Ceylon Cinnamon	3.75 gallons water
8 oz Mace	
13 Lemons, rinds only, no pith	
3.75 gallons Neutral Spirits	
4 gallons water	

Grind and cut the dry distilling ingredients. Combine with the distilling alcohol and water, then macerate for 24 hours. Distill from off the water 3.75 gallons flavored alcohol. Dissolve the Sugar into the mixing water, then add to the flavored alcohol. Filter. Color the mixture yellow (on page 128), mixed with 2 sheets of pure Gold Leaf for each demijohn.

Eau de Vie de Languedoc

Flavored Alcohol	Tincture
4 oz Pearl Barley	15 grains crude (unprocessed) Cassia
4 gallons water	30 grains Turkish Rhubarb
1 oz Linden Flowers	.75 grain Aloe Socotrina
1 oz Alder Flowers	.5 oz Oak Bark
.5 oz Black Tea	3 pints Neutral Spirits
45 pints Neutral Spirits	

Boil the Pearl Barley in the water for 2 hours. Add the Linden Flowers, Alder Flowers and Black Tea and boil for only 2 additional minutes. Add the alcohol. Combine the tincture ingredients and macerate for 48 hours. Combine the tincture and flavored alcohol. Color the mixture pale or dark yellow (on page 128).

LIQUEURS

Life of Man • Culotte du Pape (Pope's Breeches) • Curaçao de Hollande (Holland Curaçao)
Liqueur a la Cambron [D] • Liqueur des Amis Réunis [D] • Liqueur des Braves (Spirit of Mars) [D]
Liqueur de Café (Spirit of Coffee) • Liqueur de Cannelle (Spirit of Cinnamon) [D]
Liqueur de Citron (Spirit of Lemon) [D] • Liqueur de Fleurs d'Oranges (Spirit of Orange Flowers)
Liqueur de Fraises (Spirit of Strawberries) • Liqueur de Framboises (Spirit of Raspberries)
Liqueur de Groseilles (Spirit of Currants) • Liqueur de Mélisse (Spirit of Lemon Balm)
Liqueur d'Orange (Spirit of Oranges) [D] • Liqueur d'Orgeat (Spirit of Orgeat)
Liqueur de Roses (Spirit of Roses) [D] • Liqueur Stomachique [D]
Liqueur de The (Spirit of Tea) • Lovage • Macaroni [D] • Marasquin de Coings [D]
Marasquin de Fraises [D] • Marasquin de Framboises [D] • Marasquin de Groseilles [D]
Marasquin de Peches [D] • Marasquino di Zara [D] (Maraschino Liqueur) • Mirabolanti, Italian [D]
Nectar des Dieux (Nectar of Olympus) [D] • Nordhaeuser Korn Branntwein
Oglio di Venere (Oil of Venus) [D] • Orange Nectar • Parfait Amour (Perfect Love) [D] • Quatia

LIQUEURS ARE SWEETENED, FLAVORED SPIRITS CRAFTED BY INFUSING OR DISTILLING
NEUTRAL ALCOHOL WITH FRUITS, HERBS, SPICES, AND OCCASIONALLY FLORAL ESSENCES.
RECIPES OF THE PERIOD OFTEN PAIRED HIGH-PROOF BASES WITH GENEROUS AMOUNTS
OF SUGAR, RELYING ON EXTENDED MACERATION OR CAREFUL DISTILLATION TO
PRESERVE DELICATE OILS AND AROMATIC COMPOUNDS. THE ALCOHOL CONTENT IN
THESE RECIPES RANGES FROM 25-45% ABV. IN 1860S AMERICA, LIQUEURS LIKELY
SERVED SEVERAL ROLES: AN AFTER-DINNER DIGESTIF, A FLAVORING AGENT FOR PUNCH
BOWLS AT SOCIAL GATHERINGS, AND EVEN A HOUSEHOLD REMEDY, PRIZED BY MANY
HOUSEWIVES FOR THEIR PURPORTED "TONIC" EFFECTS.

LIFE OF MAN

- 2 drachms Lemon Oil
- 1.5 drachms Clove Oil
- 27 drops Mace Oil
- 3 gallons Neutral Spirits
- 24 lbs. Sugar
- 5.5 gallons water

Dissolve the oils into the alcohol. Dissolve the Sugar into the water, then add to the flavored alcohol. Filter.

Color the mixture dark rose with Red Coloring (on page 129).

CULOTTE DU PAPE (POPE'S BREECHES) [D]

Distilling	Mixing
1 oz Nutmeg	42 lbs. Sugar
.5 oz Ceylon Cinnamon	4.5 gallons water
.5 oz Cloves	
.25 oz Vanilla	
3 1/3 gallons Neutral Spirits	
3.5 gallons water	

Combine the distilling ingredients and macerate for 24. Distill from off the water 3 gallons of flavored spirit. Bring the mixing water to a boil, then add the Sugar to make a syrup. Mix the syrup into the flavored alcohol.

Color the mixture pale yellow (on page 128).

CURAÇAO DE HOLLANDE (HOLLAND CURAÇAO)

- 1 lb. Curaçao Orange Peel
- .5 lb. Ceylon Cinnamon
- 16 Oranges, juiced
- 7 gallons Plain White Syrup (on page 136)
- 3 gallons Neutral Spirits

Soak the Orange peels and Cinnamon in water. Combine with the syrup and Orange Juice and bring to a boil for 5 minutes. Add the alcohol, then strain and filter. Color the mixture dark yellow (on page 128).

LIQUEUR A LA CAMBRON [D]

Distilling	Mixing
64 grains ground Vanilla	24 lbs. Sugar
4 oz ground Cinnamon	5.5 gallons water
4 oz ground Orris Root	
3 gallons Neutral Spirits	
3.5 gallons water	

Combine the distilling ingredients, then macerate for 24 hours. Distill from off the water 3 gallons of flavored spirit. Dissolve the Sugar into the mixing water, then add to the flavored alcohol. Filter. Color the mixture red (on page 129).

LIQUEUR DES AMIS RÉUNIS [D]

Distilling	Mixing
8 oz ground Orris Root	24 lbs. Sugar
1 oz ground Myrrh	5.5 gallons water
4 oz ground Cinnamon	
64 grains Vanilla, ground	
3 gallons Neutral Spirits	
3.5 gallons water	

Combine the distilling ingredients and macerate for 24 hours. Distill from off the water 3 gallons of flavored alcohol. Dissolve the Sugar into the mixing water, then add to the flavored alcohol. Filter.

LIQUEUR DES BRAVES (LIQUEUR OF THE BRAVE) [D]

Distilling	Mixing
4 oz Carrot Seed	24 lbs. Sugar
4 oz Cardamom seed	5.5 gallons water
8 oz Roasted Cacao	
4 oz Ceylon Cinnamon	
3 gallons Neutral Spirits	
3.5 gallons water	

Grind the dry distilling ingredients. Combine the distilling ingredients and macerate for 24 hours. Distill from off the water 3 gallons of flavored spirit. Dissolve the Sugar into the mixing water, then add to the flavored alcohol. Filter.

LIQUEUR DE CAFE (COFFEE)

- 3 lbs. Light-Brown Roasted Coffee, ground
- 5.5 gallons water
- 24 lbs. Sugar
- 3 gallons Neutral Spirits

Boil the Coffee for 2 minutes with 2 gallons of the water. Strain. When the Coffee is cool, dissolve the Sugar into the remaining 3.5 gallons of water and add to the Coffee. Mix in the alcohol, then filter.

LIQUEUR DE CANNELLE (CINNAMON) [D]

Distilling	Mixing
2 lbs. Cinnamon, ground	24 lbs. Sugar
3 gallons Neutral Spirits	5.5 gallons water
3.5 gallons water	

Combine the distilling ingredients and macerate for 24 hours. Distill from off the water 3 gallons of flavored alcohol. Dissolve the Sugar into the mixing water, then add to the flavored alcohol. Filter. Color the mixture red (on page 129).

LIQUEUR DE CITRON (LEMON) [D]

Distilling	Mixing
3 lbs. Lemon Rinds, yellow part only	24 lbs. Sugar
3 gallons Neutral Spirits	5.5 gallons water
3.5 gallons water	

Cut the rinds and macerate for 24 hours with the distilling ingredients. Distill from off the water 3 gallons of flavored alcohol. Dissolve the Sugar into the mixing water, then add to the flavored alcohol. Filter. Color the mixture yellow (on page 128).

LIQUEUR DE FLEURS D'ORANGES (ORANGE FLOWERS)

- 1 gallon Orange Flower Water
- 24 lbs. Sugar
- 4.5 gallons water
- 3 gallons Neutral Spirits

Make a syrup from the Sugar and water, then add the Orange Flower Water. Mix with the alcohol, then filter.

LIQUEUR DE FRAISES (STRAWBERRIES)

- 10 lbs. Strawberries
- 24 lbs. Sugar
- 5.5 gallons water
- 3 gallons Neutral Spirits

Make a syrup from the Sugar and water, then add the Strawberries and boil for 5 minus. Strain and add the alcohol. Filter.

LIQUEUR DE FRAMBOISES (RASPBERRIES)

- 10 lbs. Raspberries
- 24 lbs. Sugar
- 5.5 gallons water
- 3 gallons Neutral Spirits

Make a syrup from the Sugar and water, then add the Raspberries and boil for 5 minutes. Strain and add the alcohol. Filter.

LIQUEUR DE GROSEILLES (CURRANTS)

- 10 lbs. Red Currants
- 24 lbs. Sugar
- 5.5 gallons water
- 3 gallons Neutral Spirits

Make a syrup from the Sugar and water, then add the Red Currants and boil for 5 minus. Strain and add the alcohol. Filter.

LIQUEUR DE MÉLISSE (LEMON BALM)

- .5 oz Lemon Balm Oil
- 24 lbs. Sugar
- 5.5 gallons water
- 3 gallons Neutral Spirits

Make a syrup from the Sugar and water. Dissolve the Lemon Balm Oil into the alcohol, then combine with the syrup. Filter. Color the mixture deep green (on page 128).

LIQUEUR D'ORANGE (ORANGES) [D]

Distilling	Mixing
2 lbs. Curaçao Orange Peels, ground	24 lbs. Sugar
3 gallons Neutral Spirits	4.75 gallons water
3.5 gallons water	1 gallons Orange Flower Water

Macerate the distilling ingredients for 24 hours. Distill from off the water 3 gallons of flavored spirit. Dissolve the Sugar into the mixing water, then add to the flavored alcohol. Add the Orange Flower Water, then filter. Color the mixture green (on page 128).

LIQUEUR D'ORGEAT

- 3 lbs. Sweet Almonds
- 1 lb. Bitter Almonds
- 6 gallons water
- 3 gallons Neutral Spirits
- 4 pints Orange Flower Water
- 24 lbs. Sugar

Boil 1 gallon of the water and add the Almonds. Take off the heat and sit until nearly cold. Remove the Almond skins by pressing with the fingers. Grind the Almonds and macerate for 10 days with the alcohol. Strain and press. Dissolve the Sugar into the remaining 5 gallons of water, then add the Orange Flower Water. Combine with the flavored alcohol. Filter.

LIQUEUR DE ROSES [D]

Distilling	Mixing
5 lbs. Rose Petals	24 lbs. Sugar
3 oz Cinnamon, ground	5.5 gallons water
1 oz Fennel Seed, ground	
3 gallons Neutral Spirits	
4 gallons water	

Combine the distilling ingredients and macerate for 24 hours. Distill over 3 gallons of flavored alcohol. Dissolve the Sugar into the mixing water, then add to the flavored alcohol. Filter. Color the mixture Rose with Red Coloring (on page 129).

LIQUEUR STOMACHIQUE [D]

Distilling	Mixing
6 oz Orange Peels	24 lbs. Sugar
4 oz Lemon Peels	5.5 gallons water
2 oz Anise Seed	
1.5 oz Galangal Root	
1.5 oz Cinnamon	
1.5 oz Orris Root	
1.5 oz Basil	
1.5 oz large Chamomile Flowers	
1 oz Lavender Flowers	
1 oz Rosemary	
.5 oz Vanilla	
.5 oz Nutmeg	
.5 oz Cubebs	
.5 oz Cardamom	
3 gallons Neutral Spirits	
4 gallons water	

Grind the dry distilling ingredients, then macerate with the distilling alcohol land water for 24 hours. Distill from off the water 3 gallons of flavored alcohol. Dissolve the Sugar into the mixing water, then add to the flavored alcohol. Color the mixture red-yellow, with a tincture of Saffron (on page 128) and Cochineal (on page 129). Filter.

LIQUEUR DE THE (TEA)

- 24 lbs. Sugar
- 5.5 gallons water
- 8 oz best Hyson Tea
- 3 gallons Neutral Spirits

Make a syrup from the Sugar and water, then add the Tea. Let it stand until nearly cool, then strain and press. Mix with the alcohol, then filter. (One oz Spanish Saffron may do well).

LOVAGE

- 8 gallons Holland Gin
- 1 gallon Plain White Syrup (on page 136)
- 4 lbs. finely cut Celery Root
- 1 gallon Neutral Spirits
- 6 drachms Cinnamon Oil
- 2 drachms Caraway Seed Oil

Create a tincture by macerating the Celery root with the Neutral Spirits for 24 hours. Strain and press very well. Combine with the Gin and syrup. Dissolve the oils into the mixture, then filter.

MACARONI [D]

Distilling	Mixing
4 lbs. Bitter Almonds, ground	24 lbs. Sugar
8 oz Cinnamon, ground	3.5 gallons water
8 oz Nutmeg, ground	
3 gallons Neutral Spirits	
3.5 gallons water	

Combine the distilling ingredients and macerate with the distilling alcohol and water for 24 hours. Distill from off the water 3 gallons of flavored alcohol. Dissolve the Sugar into the mixing water, then add to the flavored alcohol. Filter.

MARASQUIN DE COINGS [D]

- 48 Quinces, grated
- 1 oz Peach Kernels, broken
- 3.5 gallons Neutral Spirits
- 3.5 gallons water
- 7 gallons Plain Extra-White Syrup (on page 136)

Macerate the quinces and Peach Kernels for 24 hours with the alcohol and water. Distill over 3 gallons of flavored alcohol. Add the syrup.

MARASQUIN DE FRAISES (STRAWBERRY) [D]

- 10 lbs. Strawberries, pulped
- 3.5 gallons Neutral Spirits
- 3.5 gallons water
- 7 gallons Plain Extra-White Syrup (on page 136)

Macerate the Strawberries with the alcohol and water for 24 hours. Distill from off the water 3 gallons of flavored alcohol. Add the syrup.

MARASQUIN DE FRAMBOISES (RASPBERRY) [D]

- 10 lbs. Raspberries, pulped
- 3.5 gallons Neutral Spirits
- 3.5 gallons water
- 7 gallons Plain Extra-White Syrup (on page 136)

Macerate the Raspberries with the alcohol and water for 24 hours. Distill from off the water 3 gallons of flavored alcohol. Add the syrup.

MARASQUIN DE GROSEILLES (CURRANT) [D]

- 10 lbs. Red Currants, pulped
- 3.5 gallons Neutral Spirits
- 3.5 gallons water
- 7 gallons Plain Extra-White Syrup   (on page 136)

Macerate the Currants with the alcohol and water for 24 hours. Distill from off the water 3 gallons of flavored alcohol. Add the syrup.

MARASQUIN DE PECHES (PEACH) [D]

- 12 lbs. Peaches, pulped
- A few Peach Stones broken
- 3.5 gallons Neutral Spirits
- 3.5 gallons water
- 7 gallons Plain Extra-White Syrup (on page 136)

Macerate the Peaches and stones with the alcohol and water for 24 hours. Distill from off the water 3 gallons of flavored alcohol. Add the syrup.

MARASQUINO DI ZARA [D] (MARASCHINO LIQUEUR)

- 9 lbs. Raspberries, pulped
- 6 lbs. Sour Red Cherries, pulped, with stones
- 3 lbs. Orange Flowers
- 3.5 gallons Neutral Spirits
- 3.5 gallons water
- 7 gallons Plain Extra-White Syrup (on page 136)

Macerate the Raspberries, Cherries and flowers with the alcohol and water for 24 hours. Distill from off the water 3 gallons of flavored alcohol. Add the syrup.

MIRABOLANTI, ITALIAN [D]

Distilling	Mixing
1 lb. ground Mirabolanti	24 lbs. Sugar
8 oz ground Cardamom	5.5 gallons water
3.5 gallons Neutral Spirits	
3 gallons water	

Combine the distilling ingredients and macerate for 24 hours. Distill from off the water 3 gallons of flavored alcohol. Dissolve the Sugar into the mixing water, then add to the flavored alcohol. Filter.

NECTAR DES DIEUX (NECTAR OF OLYMPUS) [D]

Distilling	Mixing
2 lbs. Honey	8 oz Orange Water
1 lb. Coriander Seed	1.5 drachm Vanilla Tincture
8 oz fresh Lemon Peel	30 lbs. Sugar
2 oz Cloves	5.5 gallons water
4 oz Styrax Calamitus	
4 oz Benzoin	
3.5 gallons Neutral Spirits	
3.5 gallons water	

Grind and cut the dry distilling ingredients, then macerate for two weeks with the distilling alcohol and water. Distill from off the water 3 gallons of flavored alcohol. Dissolve the Sugar, Orange water and Vanilla tincture into the mixing water, then combine with the flavored alcohol. Filter. Color the mixture deep red (on page 129).

NORDHAEUSER KORN BRANNTWEIN

- 22.5 grains Tartaric Acid
- 5 gallons water
- 45 drops Star Anise Seed Oil
- 6 ⅔ drachms Acetic Ether
- 7 oz Carob
- .5 drachms Spanish Saffron
- 1 drachm Gunpowder Tea
- 6 drachms Cinnamon
- 5 gallons Neutral Spirits

Dissolve the Tartaric Acid into the water. Cut, dissolve and macerate the remaining ingredients for 24 hours. Combine the two mixtures. Color the mixture yellow (on page 128), then filter.

OGLIO DI VENERE (OIL OF VENUS) [D]

Distilling	Mixing
1.5 lbs. Cardamom, ground	24 lbs. Sugar
4 oz drained d'Ambrettes	5.5 gallons water
4 oz Cinnamon, ground	
8 oz Myrrh, ground	
16 Oranges, yellow rinds only	
3 gallons Neutral Spirits	
3.5 gallons water	

Combine the distilling ingredients and macerate for 24 hours. Distill from off the water 3 gallons of flavored alcohol. Dissolve the Sugar into the mixing water and add to the flavored alcohol. Color the mixture Sweet Oil color, then filter.

ORANGE NECTAR

- 1 oz Neroli Oil
- 40 Oranges, yellow rinds only
- 3 gallons Neutral Spirits
- 24 lbs. Sugar
- 5.5 gallons water

Dissolve the oil in the alcohol. Add the Orange rinds and macerate for 8 days. Dissolve the Sugar into the water, then add to the flavored alcohol. Filter. Color the mixture yellow (on page 128).

PARFAIT AMOUR (PERFECT LOVE) [D]

Distilling	Mixing
8 oz Cedrat Rinds	30 lbs. Sugar
4 oz Lemon Peels	5.5 gallons water
.5 oz Cloves, ground	
3 gallons Neutral Spirits	
3.5 gallons water	

Combine the distilling ingredients and macerate for 24 hours. Distill from off the water 3 gallons of flavored alcohol. Dissolve the Sugar into the mixing water and add to the flavored alcohol. Color the mixture deep red (on page 129), then filter.

QUATIA

- 1 lb. Quassia Root
- 1 lb. Orange Peel
- 3 gallons Neutral Spirits
- 32 lbs. Sugar
- 5 gallons water

Grind the dry ingredients, then macerate for 24 hours with the alcohol. Strain and press. Dissolve the Sugar into the water, then add to the flavored alcohol. Filter.

HUILE'S (OILS LIQUEURS)

Huile d'Absinthe (Oil of Absinthe) [D] • Huile d'Amour (Oil of Love) [D]
Huile d'Ananas (Oil of Pineapple) • Huile d'Angelique (Oil of Angelica) [D]
Huile d'Anis (Oil of Anis Seed) • Huile de Bergamot (Oil of Bergamot)
Huile de Cannelle (Oil of Cinnamon) • Huile de Celery (Oil of Celery) [D]
Huile des Chasseurs (Hunter's Oil) • Huile de Citron (Oil of Lemon)
Huile de Fleurs d'Orange (Oil of Orange Flowers)
Huile de Gerofie (Oil of Cloves) • Huile de Jasmin (Oil of Jasmin)
Huile de Jupiter (Oil of Jove) [D] • Huile de Kirsschwasser (Oil of Kirschwasser)
Huile de Menthe (Oil of Mint) • Huile de Muscade (Oil of Mace)
Huile de Myrrhe (Oil of Myrrh) • Huile de Sept Grains (Oil of Seven Seeds) [D]
Huile de Rose (Oil of Roses) • Huile Royale (Royal Oil) [D]
Huile de Rhum (Oil of Rum) • Huile de The (Oil of Tea)
Huile de Vanille (Oil of Vanilla) • Huile de Venus (Oil of Venus) [D]
Huile de Violettes (Oil of Violets)

HUILES OCCUPY A SPECIALIZED NICHE IN MID-19TH-CENTURY CORDIAL MAKING, PAIRING NEUTRAL SPIRITS WITH BOTANICAL OILS, FLOWER INFUSIONS, AND DENSE SUGAR SYRUP TO PRESERVE DELICATE AROMATICS. UNLIKE FRUIT LIQUEURS, THESE HIGH-PROOF ELIXIRS SHOWCASED CONCENTRATED FLORAL AND HERBAL CHARACTER, MOST SITTING IN THE 49-52% ABV RANGE. SERVED AS DIGESTIFS OR STIRRED INTO PUNCHES AND SWEETS, *HUILES* EMBODIED A UNIQUE INTERSECTION OF APOTHECARY CRAFT AND CULINARY REFINEMENT.

HUILE D'ABSINTHE (OIL OF ABSINTHE) [D]

Distilling	Mixing
1.5 lbs. Wormwood	48 lbs. Sugar
1 lb. Green Anise Seed	3 gallons water
1 lb. Fennel Seed	
4 gallons Neutral Spirits	
5 gallons water	

Grind the dry distilling ingredients. Macerate for 10 days with the alcohol. Add the distilling water. Distill from off the water 4 gallons of flavored alcohol. Make a 2:1 syrup by combining the mixing Sugar and water and boiling for 3 hours, adding more water as it evaporates. Skim, mix, and filter, while warm. Color the mixture Sweet Oil color.

HUILE D'AMOUR (OIL OF LOVE) [D]

Distilling	Mixing
8 oz Moldavique Seed (Moldavian Dragonhead?)	48 lbs. Sugar
4 oz sprouts of Rosemary with flowers	3 gallons water
16 oz Lemon Balm	
4 gallons Neutral Spirits	
5 gallons water	

Grind the dry distilling ingredients. Combine with the alcohol, then macerate for 10 days. Add the distilling water. Distill from off the water 4 gallons of flavored alcohol. Make a 2:1 syrup by combining the mixing Sugar and water and boiling for 3 hours, adding more water as it evaporates. Skim, mix, and filter while warm. Color the mixture green (on page 128).

HUILE D'ANANAS (OIL OF PINEAPPLE)

- 4 lbs. Pineapple, grated
- 4 gallons Neutral Spirits
- 48 lbs. Sugar
- 3 gallons water

Combine the Pineapple and alcohol, then macerate for 7 days. Strain, press and filter. Make a 2:1 syrup by combining the Sugar and water and boiling for 3 hours, adding more water as it evaporates. Skim, mix and filter if necessary.

HUILE D'ANGELIQUE (OIL OF ANGELICA) [D]

Distilling	Mixing
12 oz Angelica Root	48 lbs. Sugar
2 oz Ceylon Cinnamon	3 gallons water
4 gallons Neutral Spirits	
5 gallons water	

Grind the Angelica and Cinnamon. Combine with the alcohol and water, then macerate for 10 days. Distill from off the water 4 gallons of flavored alcohol. Make a 2:1 syrup by combining the mixing Sugar and water and boiling for 3 hours, adding more water as it evaporates. Skim, mix and filter while warm.

HUILE D'ANIS (OIL OF ANISE SEED)

- 3 drachms of Anise Seed Oil
- .5 oz Vanilla Tincture
- 4 gallons Neutral Spirits
- 48 lbs. Sugar
- 3 gallons water

Dissolve the oil and tincture into the alcohol. Make a 2:1 syrup by combining the Sugar and water and boiling for 3 hours, adding more water as it evaporates. Skim, mix, and filter (if necessary) while warm.

HUILE DE BERGAMOT (OIL OF BERGAMOT)

- .5 oz Bergamot Oil
- 1 drachm Orange Oil
- 4 gallons Neutral Spirits
- 48 lbs. Sugar
- 3 gallons water

Dissolve the oils into the alcohol. Make a 2:1 syrup by combining the Sugar and water and boiling for 3 hours, adding more water as it evaporates. Skim, mix, filter (if necessary) while warm.

HUILE DE CANNELLE (OIL OF CINNAMON)

- .25 oz Cinnamon Oil
- 4 gallons Neutral Spirits
- 48 lbs. Sugar
- 3 gallons water

Dissolve the oil into the alcohol. Make a 2:1 syrup by combining the Sugar and water and boiling for 3 hours, adding more water as it evaporates. Skim, mix, filter (if necessary) while warm.

HUILE DE CELERY (OIL OF CELERY) [D]

Distilling	Mixing
.75 lb. Celery Seed, ground	48 lbs. Sugar
4 gallons Neutral Spirits	3 gallons water
5 gallons water	

Combine the distilling ingredients and macerate for 10 days. Distill from off the water 4 gallons of flavored alcohol. Make a 2:1 syrup by combining the mixing Sugar and water and boiling for 3 hours, adding more water as it evaporates. Skim, mix and filter (if necessary) while warm.

HUILE DES CHASSEURS (HUNTER'S OIL)

- 20 drops Mace Oil
- 12 drops Spearmint Oil
- 8 drops Neroli Oil
- 120 drops Peppermint Oil
- 4 gallons Neutral Spirits
- 48 lbs. Sugar
- 3 gallons water

Dissolve the oils into the alcohol. Make a 2:1 syrup by combining the Sugar and water and boiling for 3 hours, adding more water as it evaporates. Skim, mix, filter (if necessary) while warm. Color the mixture green (on page 128).

HUILE DE CITRON (OIL OF LEMON)

- .5 oz Lemon Oil
- 4 gallons Neutral Spirits
- 48 lbs. Sugar
- 3 gallons water

Dissolve the oil into the alcohol. Make a 2:1 syrup by combining the Sugar and water and boiling for 3 hours, adding more water as it evaporates. Skim, mix, filter (if necessary) while warm. Color the mixture yellow (on page 128).

HUILE DE FLEURS D'ORANGE (OIL OF ORANGE FLOWERS)

- 50 drops Neroli Oil
- 4 gallons Neutral Spirits
- 48 lbs. Sugar
- 3 gallons water

Dissolve the oil into the alcohol. Make a 2:1 syrup by combining the Sugar and water and boiling for 3 hours, adding more water as it evaporates. Skim, mix, filter (if necessary) while warm.

HUILE DE GEROFIE (OIL OF CLOVES)

- 3 drachms Clove Oil
- 4 gallons Neutral Spirits
- 48 lbs. Sugar
- 3 gallons water

Dissolve the oil into the alcohol. Make a 2:1 syrup by combining the Sugar and water and boiling for 3 hours, adding more water as it evaporates. Skim, mix, filter (if necessary) while warm. Color dark yellow (on page 128).

HUILE DE JASMIN (OIL OF JASMIN)

- 4 lbs. Jasmine Flowers
- 4 gallons Neutral Spirits
- 48 lbs. Sugar
- 3 gallons water

Macerate the Jasmine Flowers in the alcohol for 2 weeks. Strain and press. Make a 2:1 syrup by combining the Sugar and water and boiling for 3 hours, adding more water as it evaporates. Skim, mix, filter (if necessary) while warm.

HUILE DE JUPITER (OIL OF JOVE) [D]
Distilling   Mixing

Distilling	Mixing
8 oz Italian Fennel Seed	48 lbs. Sugar
8 oz Cinnamon	3 gallons water
8 oz Roasted Cacao	
4 oz Orris Root	

Grind the dry distilling ingredients. Combine with the alcohol, then macerate for 10 days. Distill from off the water 4 gallons of flavored alcohol. Make a 2:1 syrup by combining the mixing Sugar and water and boiling for 3 hours, adding more water as it evaporates. Skim, mix and filter (if necessary) while warm.

HUILE DE KIRSCHWASSER (OIL OF KIRSCHWASSER)

- 4 gallons Kirschwasser
- 48 lbs. Sugar
- 3 gallons water

Make a 2:1 syrup by combining the Sugar and water, and boiling for 3 hours, adding more water as it evaporates. Skim, mix in the Kirschwasser and filter (if necessary) while warm.

HUILE DE MENTHE (OIL OF MINT)

- .5 oz Peppermint Oil
- 4 gallons Neutral Spirits
- 48 lbs. Sugar
- 3 gallons water

Dissolve the oil into the alcohol. Make a 2:1 syrup by combining the Sugar and water and boiling for 3 hours, adding more water as it evaporates. Skim, mix, filter (if necessary) while warm.

HUILE DE MUSCADE (OIL OF MACE)

- .5 oz Mace Oil
- 4 gallons Neutral Spirits
- 48 lbs. Sugar
- 3 gallons water

Dissolve the oil into the alcohol. Make a 2:1 syrup by combining the Sugar and water and boiling for 3 hours, adding more water as it evaporates. Skim, mix, filter (if necessary) while warm.

HUILE DE MYRRHE (OIL OF MYRRH)

- 2 oz Myrrh, ground
- 4 oz Cinnamon, ground
- 4 gallons Neutral Spirits
- 48 lbs. Sugar
- 3 gallons water

Combine the Myrrh, Cinnamon and alcohol. Macerate for 10 days, then strain and press. Make a 2:1 syrup by combining the Sugar and water and boiling for 3 hours, adding more water as it evaporates. Skim, mix, filter (if necessary) while warm.

HUILE DE SEPT GRAINS (OIL OF SEVEN SEEDS) [D]

Distilling	Mixing
6 oz Green Anise Seed	48 lbs. Sugar
3 oz Dill Seed	3 gallons water
3 oz Coriander Seed	
3 oz Fennel Seed	
3 oz Star Anise Seed	
3 oz Caraway Seed	
1.5 oz Celery Seed	
4 gallons Neutral Spirits	
5 gallons water	

Grind the dry distilling ingredients. Combine with the distilling alcohol and water, then macerate for 10 days. Distill from off the water 4 gallons of flavored alcohol. Make a 2:1 syrup by combining the mixing Sugar and water and boiling for 3 hours, adding more water as it evaporates. Skim, mix and filter (if necessary) while warm.

HUILE DE ROSE (OIL OF ROSES)

- 50 drops Rose Oil
- 4 gallons Neutral Spirits
- 48 lbs. Sugar
- 3 gallons water

Dissolve the oil into the alcohol. Make a 2:1 syrup by combining the Sugar and water and boiling for 3 hours, adding more water as it evaporates. Skim, mix, filter (if necessary) while warm. Color the mixture rose with Red Coloring (on page 129).

HUILE ROYALE (ROYAL OIL) [D]

Distilling	Mixing
4 oz ground Cloves	48 lbs. Sugar
4 oz ground Cinnamon	3 gallons water
4 oz ground Myrrh	
8 oz ground Carrot Seed	
10 Oranges, rinds only, no pith	
4 gallons Neutral Spirits	
5 gallons water	

Combine the distilling ingredients and macerate for 10 days. Distill from off the water 4 gallons of flavored alcohol. Make a 2:1 syrup by combining the mixing Sugar and water and boiling for 3 hours, adding more water as it evaporates. Skim, mix and filter (if necessary) while warm.

HUILE DE RHUM (OIL OF RUM)

- 2.75 oz Maidenhair Fern, cut
- 2.75 oz Ceylon Cinnamon, ground
- 48 lbs. Sugar
- 3 gallons water
- 4 gallons good Jamaican Rum

Make a 2:1 syrup by combining the Sugar and water and boiling for 3 hours, adding more water as it evaporates. Before the boiling is finished, add the Maidenhair and Cinnamon. Skim, press and filter, then add the rum.

HUILE DE THE (OIL OF TEA)

- 8 oz Imperial Tea
- 48 lbs. Sugar
- 3 gallons water
- 4 gallons Neutral Spirits

Make a 2:1 syrup by combining the Sugar and water and boiling for 3 hours, adding more water as it evaporates. Add the Tea, then strain and press. Add the alcohol, then filter while warm.

HUILE DE VANILLE (OIL OF VANILLA)

- 2 drachms Vanilla
- 13 drops Rose Oil
- 4 gallons Neutral Spirits
- 48 lbs. + 1 oz Sugar
- 3 gallons water

Cut the Vanilla and muddle with 1 oz of Sugar. Add the Rose Oil then dissolve into the alcohol. Make a 2:1 syrup by combining the Sugar and water and boiling for 3 hours, adding more water as it evaporates. Skim, mix, filter (if necessary) while warm.

HUILE DE VENUS (OIL OF VENUS) [D]

Distilling	Mixing
5 oz Carrot Flowers	48 lbs. Sugar
5 oz Green Anise Seed	3 gallons water
5 oz Caraway Seed	
15 Oranges, yellow rind only	
4 gallons Neutral Spirits	
5 gallons water	

Cut and grind the dry distilling ingredients. Add to the distilling alcohol and water, then macerate for 10 days. Distill from off the water 4 gallons of flavored alcohol. Make a 2:1 syrup by combining the mixing Sugar and water and boiling for 3 hours, adding more water as it evaporates. Skim, mix and filter (if necessary) while warm.

HUILE DE VIOLETTES (OIL OF VIOLETS)

- 48 lbs. Sugar
- 3 gallons water
- 8 oz Violet Flowers
- 4 gallons Neutral Spirits

Make a 2:1 syrup by combining the Sugar and water and boiling for 3 hours, adding more water as it evaporates. Remove from the heat and add the violets. When nearly cool, add the alcohol. Strain and filter. Color the mixture violet (on page 129).

RATAFIAS

Ratafia d'Abricots (Apricots) • Ratafia d'Angelique (Angelica)
Ratafia d'Anis (Anise Seed) • Ratafia de Café (Coffee)
Ratafia de Cassis (Black Currants) • Ratafia de Coings (Quinces)
Ratafia de Fleurs d'Oranges (Orange Flowers)
Ratafia de Framboise (Raspberries) • Ratafia de Genievre (Juniper)
Ratafia de Grenades (Ratafia of Pomegranates) • Ratafia de Grenoble
Ratafia de Groseilles (Currants) • Ratafia de Mares (Blackberries)
Ratafia de Neuilly • Ratafia de Noix (Walnuts) • Ratafia de Noyaux (Noyau)
Ratafia de Oillets (Pinks) • Ratafia de Peaches (Peaches)
Ratafia de Quatre Fruits (Four Fruits) • Ratafia de Sept Graines (Seven Seeds)
Rosa Blanca (White Rose) • Rose Rouge (Red Rose
Rosolio • Rosolio de Breslau • Ruga (Rue)

Every liqueur made by infusions is called ratafia. That is, when the spirit is made to imbibe thoroughly the aromatic flavor and color of the fruit steeped in it. When this has taken place, the liquor is drawn off, and Sugar added to it. It is then filtered and bottled.

IN MID-19TH-CENTURY AMERICA, **RATAFIA** REFERRED TO A FAMILY OF FRUIT-BASED LIQUEURS MADE BY STEEPING OR BOILING FRESH FRUIT, KERNELS, SPICES, AND SUGAR WITH A NEUTRAL SPIRIT. WITH SUGAR LEVELS OFTEN EXCEEDING 20–30 PERCENT BY WEIGHT, RATAFIAS STRADDLED THE LINE BETWEEN SIMPLE FRUIT WINES AND HEAVIER, SPIRIT-FORWARD CORDIALS. THEIR ALCOHOL CONTENT RANGED WIDELY FROM 14-43% ABV. GIVEN THE SEASONAL NATURE OF FRESH FRUIT, MANY RATAFIAS WERE LIKELY PRODUCED IN LATE SUMMER AND EARLY AUTUMN, WHEN THE SUMMER HARVEST WAS PRESERVED FOR USE THROUGH THE WINTER MONTHS. IN PARLORS AND BACK-PORCH GATHERINGS, RATAFIAS PROBABLY SERVED BOTH AS A CORDIAL AFTER SUPPER AND AS A GENTLE MEDICINAL TONIC—VALUED FOR THEIR BRIGHT FRUIT FLAVORS, WARMING ALCOHOL, AND PERCEIVED RESTORATIVE QUALITIES. RATAFIAS SERVED NOT ONLY AS BEVERAGES BUT AS BUILDING BLOCKS — FOLDED INTO MORE ELABORATE CORDIALS AND LIQUEURS, OR MEASURED INTO MIXED DRINKS AND PUNCHES WHERE THEIR BRIGHT FRUIT CHARACTER SHAPED THE FINAL FLAVOR.

RATAFIA D'ABRICOTS (APRICOTS)

- 8.5 lbs. Apricots (juiced)
- 20 lbs. Sugar
- 4.25 gallons water
- 4 gallons Neutral Spirits

Combine the Apricot Juice, Sugar and water, then boil for 5 minutes. Add the alcohol, then filter.

RATAFIA D'ANGELIQUE (ANGELICA)

- 12 oz Angelica Root, cut
- 8 oz Juniper Berries, ground
- 4 gallons Neutral Spirits
- 20 lbs. Sugar
- 4.75 gallons water

Dissolve the Sugar into the water. Combine all the ingredients and macerate for 8 days. Filter.

RATAFIA D'ANIS (ANISE SEED)

- 6.75 oz Green Anise Seed, ground
- 13.5 oz Star Anise Seed, ground
- 4 gallons Neutral Spirits
- 20 lbs. Sugar
- 4.75 gallons water

Combine the spices and alcohol, then macerate for 8 days. Strain and press. Dissolve the Sugar into the water, then add to the flavored alcohol. Filter.

RATAFIA DE CAFE (COFFEE)

- 10 lbs. roasted Mocha Coffee, ground
- 4 gallons Neutral Spirits
- 20 lbs. Sugar
- 4.75 gallons water

Combine the Coffee and alcohol, then macerate for 8 days. Strain. Dissolve the Sugar into the water, then add to the flavored alcohol. Filter.

RATAFIA DE CASSIS (BLACK CURRANTS)

- 12 lbs. Black Currants, juiced
- 20 lbs. Sugar
- 4.5 gallons water
- 4 gallons Neutral Spirits

Combine the Currant juice, Sugar and water, then boil for 5 minutes. Add the alcohol, then filter.

RATAFIA DE COINGS (QUINCES)

- 49 Quinces, grated
- 4 gallons Neutral Spirits
- 20 lbs. Sugar
- 4.75 gallons water

Combine the quinces and alcohol, then macerate for 8 days. Press. Dissolve the Sugar in the water, then add to the flavored alcohol. Filter.

RATAFIA DE FLEURS D'ORANGES (ORANGE FLOWERS)

- 4.5 lbs. fresh Orange Flowers
- 4 gallons Neutral Spirits
- 6 pints Double Orange Flower Water
- 20 lbs. Sugar
- 4 gallons water

Combine the Orange Flowers with the alcohol, then macerate for 8 days. Strain and press. Dissolve the Sugar into the water, then add the Double Orange Flower Water. Combine with the flavored alcohol, then filter.

NOTE: DOUBLE ORANGE FLOWER WATER REFERS TO THE RATIO OF FLOWERS TO WATER DURING DISTILLATION. WHEN TWO POUNDS OF ORANGE FLOWER WATER ARE OBTAINED FROM EACH POUND OF FLOWERS, IT IS CALLED DOUBLE ORANGE FLOWER WATER.

RATAFIA DE FRAMBOISE (RASPBERRIES)

- 12 lbs. Raspberries, juiced
- 20 lbs. Sugar
- 4.5 gallons water
- 4 gallons Neutral Spirits

Combine the Raspberry Juice, Sugar and water, then boil for 5 minutes. Strain, then add the alcohol and filter.

RATAFIA DE GENIEVRE (JUNIPER)

- 2 lbs. Juniper Berries
- .5 oz Cinnamon, ground
- 1 oz Coriander Seed, ground
- .25 oz Mace, ground
- 4 gallons Neutral Spirits
- 20 lbs. Sugar
- 4.75 gallons water

Combine the berries, spices and alcohol, then macerate for 8 days. Strain. Dissolve the Sugar into the water, then add to the flavored alcohol. Filter.

RATAFIA DE GRENADES (POMEGRANATES)

- 105 Pomegranates, ripe, cut
- 4 gallons Neutral Spirits
- 20 lbs. Sugar
- 4.75 gallons water

Combine the pomegranates and alcohol, then macerate for 8 days. Strain and press. Dissolve the Sugar into the water, then add to the flavored alcohol and filter.

RATAFIA DE GRENOBLE

- .5 oz Ceylon Cinnamon, ground
- .25 oz Cloves, ground
- .25 oz Mace, ground
- 1.25 lbs. Cherry Leaves
- 8 lbs. Black Cherries
- 20 lbs. Sugar
- 5 gallons Wild Black Cherry Juice

Combine the spices, leaves, Cherries and alcohol, then macerate for 8 days. Dissolve the Sugar into the Cherry Juice then add to the flavored alcohol. Filter.

RATAFIA DE GROSEILLES (CURRANTS)

- 12 lbs. Red Currants, juiced
- 20 lbs. Sugar
- 4.25 gallons water
- 4 gallons Neutral Spirits

Combine the Currant Juice, Sugar and water, then boil for 5 minutes. Strain. Add the alcohol, then filter.

RATAFIA DE MARES (BLACKBERRIES)

- 12 lbs. Blackberries, juiced
- 20 lbs. Sugar
- 4.25 gallons water
- 4 gallons Neutral Spirits

Combine the Blackberry Juice, Sugar and water, then boil for 5 minutes. Strain. Add the alcohol, then filter.

RATAFIA DE NEUILLY

- 25 lbs. Sour Red Cherries (with small stems)
- 10 lbs. Black Cherries
- 5 lbs. Red-Pink Flowers
- 4.25 gallons Neutral Spirits
- 1 gallon Plain White Syrup (on page 136)
- water

Make a pulp of the Cherries and pinks without breaking the stones. Combine with the alcohol and macerate for 2 weeks. Strain and press. Add the syrup, and enough water to make 10 gallons.

RATAFIA DE NOIX (WALNUTS)

- 420 unripe Walnuts (in month of August), mashed
- 4 ⅓ drachms Cloves, ground
- 4 ⅓ drachms Mace, ground
- 4 ⅓ drachms Ceylon Cinnamon, ground
- 4 gallons Neutral Spirits
- 3.5 gallons water
- 2.5 gallons Plain White Syrup (on page 136)

Combine the dry ingredients with the alcohol and water, then macerate for 2 weeks. Strain and press. Add the syrup, then filter.

RATAFIA DE NOYAUX (NOYAU)

- 3.25 lbs. Apricot Kernels, ground
- 4 gallons Neutral Spirits
- 20 lbs. Sugar
- 4.75 gallons water

Combine the Apricot Kernels and alcohol, then macerate for 2 weeks. Strain and press. Dissolve the Sugar into the water, then add to the flavored alcohol. Filter.

RATAFIA DE OILLETS (PINKS)

- 16 lbs. Red-Pink Flowers, flower leaves only (petals)
- 1 oz Ceylon Cinnamon, ground
- 1 oz Cloves, ground
- 4 gallons Neutral Spirits
- 3.5 gallons water
- 2.5 gallons Plain White Syrup (on page 136)

Combine the dry ingredients, alcohol and water, then macerate for 2 weeks. Strain and press. Add the syrup, then filter.

RATAFIA DE PEACHES (PEACHES)

- 12 lbs. Peaches
- 20 lbs. Sugar
- 4.25 gallons water
- 4 gallons Neutral Spirits

Juice the Peaches and reserve the stones. Let the liquid ferment for 8 days. Break the stones. Boil the Sugar with the water for 5 minutes, then combine with the stones and juice. Add the alcohol, then filter.

RATAFIA DE QUATRE FRUITS (FOUR FRUITS)

- 1 gallon Black Cherry Juice
- 1 gallon Red Currant Juice
- 1 gallon Black Currant Juice
- 1 gallon Raspberry Juice
- .5 oz ground Cloves
- .5 oz Coriander Seed
- 4 gallons Neutral Spirits
- 24 lbs. Sugar
- 4 pints water

Combine the juices, Cloves and Coriander with the alcohol, then macerate for 1 week. Combine the Sugar and water and bring to a boil, and while still boiling hot, combine the two mixtures. Filter.

Ratafia de Sept Graines (Seven Seeds)

- 3 oz Dill Seed, ground
- 3 oz Angelica Seed, ground
- 3 oz Fennel Seed, ground
- 3 oz Coriander Seed, ground
- 3 oz Carrot Seed, ground
- 3 oz Caraway Seed, ground
- 3 oz Green Anise Seed, ground
- 4 gallons Neutral Spirits
- 3.5 gallons water
- 2.5 gallons Plain White Syrup (on page 136)

Combine all ingredients except the syrup and macerate for 8 days. Add the syrup, then filter.

Rosa Blanca (White Rose)

- 40 drops Rose Oil
- 65 drops Tincture of Musk
- 3 gallons Neutral Spirits
- 20 lbs. Sugar
- 5.75 gallons water

Dissolve the oil and tincture into the alcohol. Dissolve the Sugar into the water. Combine the two mixtures, then filter.

Rose Rouge (Red Rose)

- 40 drops Rose Oil
- 40 drops Tincture of Musk
- 24 drops Orange Oil
- 3 gallons Neutral Spirits
- 20 lbs. Sugar
- 5.75 gallons water

Dissolve the oils and tincture into the alcohol. Dissolve the Sugar into the water. Combine the two mixtures. Color the mixture rose with Red Coloring (on page 129), then filter.

ROSOLIO

- 2 drachms Vanilla Essence
- 13 drops Rose Oil
- 57 drops Ambergris Essence
- 3 gallons Neutral Spirits
- 20 lbs. Sugar
- 5.75 gallons water

Dissolve the Vanilla, Rose Oil, Ambergris Essence into the Neutral Spirits. Dissolve the Sugar into the water. Combine the two mixtures. Color the mixture rose with Red Coloring (on page 129), then filter.

ROSOLIO DE BRESLAU

- 9 Oranges, juiced
- 4 lbs. dried Figs, cut
- 20 lbs. Sugar
- 5.75 gallons Water
- 2 drachms Vanilla Essence
- 16 drops Rose Oil
- 24 drops Neroli Oil
- 3 gallons Neutral Spirits

Combine the Orange Juice, Figs, Sugar and water, then boil together for 5 minutes. Strain and Press. Dissolve oils and essences into the Neutral Spirits. Combine the two mixtures. Color the mixture rose with Red Coloring (on page 129), then filter.

RUGA (RUE)

- 2 lbs. Ruga or Rue
- 3 gallons Neutral Spirits
- 20 lbs. Sugar
- 5.75 gallons water

Combine the ruga and alcohol, then macerate for 24 hours. Strain and press. Dissolve the Sugar into the water, then combine with the flavored alcohol. Filter.

RATAFIAS (SMALL BATCH)

*Badiane • Balm of Molucca • Ratafia of Angelica • Ratafia of Cherries
Another Ratafia of Cherries • Ratafia of Four Fruits
Ratafia of Green Walnut Shells • Ratafia of Black Currants
Ratafia of Currants • Ratafia of Mulberries • Ratafia of Orange
Ratafia of Orange Flowers • Ratafia of Raspberries
Ratafia of Red Pinks • Tears of the Widow of Malabar • Vespitro
Yellow Escubao*

BADIANE

- 3 pints Brandy
- 3 pints water
- 1 lb. Bitter Almonds
- 1 lb. Sugar
- 1 Lemon Peel, rasped
- 6 Cloves
- 1 oz Cinnamon

Break up the Almonds, Cloves and Cinnamon. Melt the Sugar in the water. Combine all ingredients in a jar and infuse for 1 month. Strain through a flannel bag. Filter the liquor and bottle it.

BALM OF MOLUCCA

- 1 drachm Mace shredded
- 1 oz Cloves, bruised
- 1 gallon Clean Spirit, 22 under Proof (39% ABV)
- 4.5 lbs. Sugar
- 4 pints pure soft water

Macerate the Mace and Cloves for a week in a well-corked demijohn or jar, frequently shaking. Color the mixture with Base Coloring (on page 127). Dissolve the Sugar into the water, then mix with the flavored alcohol.

RATAFIA OF ANGELICA

- 4 oz Angelica Seed
- 2 oz Angelica Root
- 10 pints Brandy
- 1 drachm Cloves
- 1 drachm Cinnamon
- 4 lbs. Sugar

Pound the ingredients coarsely. Dissolve the Sugar in water and add it to the mixture. Infuse it in the Brandy for a month. Strain through a bag and filter.

RATAFIA OF CHERRIES

- 10 lbs. Wild Cherries
- 10 lbs. Morello Cherries
- 2 drachms Cinnamon
- 2 drachms Mace
- 4 oz Coriander Seed
- 1 gallon Brandy
- 2 lbs. Strawberries
- 2 lbs. Raspberries
- 4 oz Sugar for every pint of juice

Crush the fruit. Strain the juice through a sieve and reserve the Cherry stones. Pound the stones, Coriander, Cinnamon, and Mace separately and add to the juice. To every pint of juice add 4 oz Sugar. Add the Brandy. Let it steep in a jar for a month. Filter and bottle.

ANOTHER RATAFIA OF CHERRIES

- 30-40 lbs. Morello Cherries (to make 15 pints Morello Cherry Juice)
- 1 lb. Peach Leaves
- 14 pints Brandy
- 3 drachms Cinnamon
- 1 drachm Cloves
- 8 lbs. Sugar

Crush cherries and strain through a sieve to separate the pulp of your Cherries from the stones. Pound the Cherry stones. Put them all together in a pan on the fire, and give them one boil. When cold, measure the juice out to 15 pints. Bruise Peach leaves, Cinnamon and Cloves in a mortar, and add to the juice. Add the Sugar and Brandy. Put everything together in a jar. Leave it for a month. Draw it off and bottle it.

RATAFIA OF FOUR FRUITS

- 8 lbs. Morello Cherries
- 6 lbs. Wild Cherries
- 4 lbs. Raspberries
- 8 lbs. Red Currants
- 4 lbs. Black Currants
- 1 drachm Mace
- 1 drachm Cloves
- 1 gallon Brandy
- 4 oz Sugar for every pint of juice

Crush the fruit. Strain the juice through a sieve and reserve the Cherry stones. Pound the Cherry stones, Cloves, and Mace separately and add to the juice. To every pint of juice add 4 oz Sugar. Add the Brandy. Let it steep in a jar for a month. Filter and bottle.

RATAFIA OF GREEN WALNUT SHELLS

- 200 Walnuts
- 10 pints Brandy
- 4 lbs. Sugar
- 1 drachm Nutmeg
- 1 drachm Cloves

Choose 200 Walnuts so young that a pin may easily go through them. Pound them in a mortar. Infuse in Brandy with the Nutmeg and Cloves for a month. Strain the mixture through a flannel bag. Filter and bottle.

RATAFIA OF BLACK CURRANTS

- 4 lbs. Black Currants
- 1 lb. Black Currant Leaves
- 2 lbs. Morello Cherries
- 1 drachm Cloves
- 10 pints Brandy
- 10 lbs. Sugar

Crush the fruit. Strain the juice through a sieve and reserve the Cherry stones. Pound the Cherry stones and Cloves separately and add to the juice. Add the Sugar. Let it steep in a jar for a month. Filter and bottle.

RATAFIA OF CURRANTS

- 10 lbs. Currants
- 10 pints Brandy
- 4 lbs. Sugar
- 2 drachms Cinnamon
- 2 drachms Cloves

Infuse all ingredients for 15 days. Stir the mixture every day. Strain through a bag and filter it.

RATAFIA OF MULBERRIES

- 10 lbs. Mulberries
- 10 pints Brandy
- 4 lbs. Sugar
- 2 drachms Mace

Infuse all ingredients for 15 days. Stir the mixture every day. Strain through a bag and filter it.

RATAFIA OF ORANGE

- 6 Mandarin Oranges
- 4 pints Brandy
- 2 lbs. Sugar
- 1 pint water

Peel the oranges. Infuse the rind in the Brandy for 15 days. Melt your Sugar in the cold water. Strain and filter.

RATAFIA OF ORANGE FLOWERS

- 3 pints Brandy
- 2 pints water
- 1 lb. Orange Flowers
- 1 lb. Sugar

Put all ingredients in a jar, well stopped. Place in a water bath that is almost boiling hot, for a day. The next day, filter and bottle it.

RATAFIA OF RASPBERRIES

- 10 lbs. Raspberries
- 4 lbs. Sugar
- 10 pints Brandy
- 2 drachms Cinnamon
- 1 drachm Cloves

Infuse all ingredients for 15 days. Stir the mixture every day. Strain through a bag and filter it.

RATAFIA OF RED PINKS

- 3 lbs. Red-Pink Flowers
- 10 pints of Brandy
- 4 lbs. Sugar
- 1 drachm of Cloves
- 1 drachm Cinnamon

Pick off the green from your pinks. Pound the leaves and infuse them for a month in the Brandy along with the Cloves and Cinnamon. Draw off the liquor and filter it.

TEARS OF THE WIDOW OF MALABAR

- 1 drachm Mace shredded
- .5 oz Cloves, bruised
- 1 teaspoon Vanilla Essence
- 4 oz Orange Flower Water (optional)
- 1 gallon Clean Spirit, 22 under Proof (39% ABV)
- 4.5 lbs. Sugar
- 4 pints pure soft water

Combine the Mace, Cloves, Vanilla, and Orange Flower Water (if using) with the alcohol. Macerate for a week in a well-corked demijohn or jar, frequently shaking. Color the mixture slightly with Base Coloring (on page 127). Dissolve the Sugar into the water, then mix with the flavored alcohol.

VESPITRO

- 2 pints Brandy
- 1 oz Anise Seed
- 2 Lemons
- 1 lb. Sugar
- 2 oz Coriander Seed
- 1 oz Fennel
- 2 drachms Angelica

Break up solids and put them in a jar with the Brandy. Peel the 2 Lemons and add the peels to the mixture. Squeeze in the juice. Break the Sugar, dissolve it in water and put it into the jar. Let it stand for two weeks. Strain it through a flannel bag. Filter and bottle it.

YELLOW ESCUBAO

- 1 oz Saffron
- 1 oz Damascus Raisins
- 1 oz Cinnamon
- 3 lbs. Sugar
- 1 oz Licorice
- 1 oz Coriander Seed
- 3 pints Brandy
- 2 pints water

Pound ingredients and dissolve the Sugar in 2 pints water. Put the whole in a jar to infuse for a month, taking care to stir it up every second day, or the third at most.

HYPOCRAS

HYPOCRAS IS A SWEETENED, SPICED WINE CORDIAL IN WHICH WHOLE OR GROUND SPICES—CINNAMON, CLOVES, MACE, CITRUS PEELS—ARE MACERATED IN A BLEND OF WINE AND NEUTRAL SPIRITS BEFORE BEING STRAINED AND SWEETENED, RESULTING IN AN ALCOHOL CONTENT OF APPROXIMATELY 13.5% ABV. THE RECIPE FIRST APPEARED IN LATE MEDIEVAL EUROPE AND WAS POPULARIZED IN ENGLAND BEFORE APPEARING IN AMERICAN COOKERY AND MEDICINAL MANUALS BY THE MID-19TH CENTURY. BY 1862, HYPOCRAS HAD LARGELY FADED FROM COMMERCIAL POPULARITY, BUT IT PERSISTED IN HOUSEHOLD AND APOTHECARY CIRCLES—SERVED NEAT IN THIMBLE-SIZED GLASSES OR FOLDED INTO PUNCHES AND DESSERTS. ITS BITTERSWEET WARMTH AND AROMATIC COMPLEXITY MADE IT BOTH AN ELEGANT DIGESTIF AND A PERCEIVED TONIC IN DOMESTIC SETTINGS.

HYPOCRAS A L'ANGELIQUE (ANGELICA)

- 10 oz Angelica Root, ground
- 1 oz Nutmeg, ground
- 9 gallons Claret Wine
- 8 lbs. Powdered Sugar
- 4 pints Neutral Spirits

Combine the Angelica, Nutmeg and Claret, then macerate for 2 days. Add the Powdered Sugar and alcohol. Filter.

HYPOCRAS AN CEDRAT (CEDRAT)

- 40 Cedrats, rinds cut
- 4 pints Neutral Spirits
- 9 gallons good Claret Wine
- 8 lbs. Powdered Sugar

Combine the Cedrats, wine, and alcohol, then macerate for 2 days. Dissolve the Powdered Sugar into the mixture, then filter.

HYPOCRAS AU GENIEVRE (JUNIPER)

- 2.5 lbs. ground Juniper Berries
- 9 gallons Claret Wine
- 4 pints Neutral Spirits
- 8 lbs. Powdered Sugar

Combine the Juniper, wine, and alcohol, then macerate for 2 days. Dissolve the Powdered Sugar into the mixture. Strain and filter.

HYPOCRAS AUX NOYAUX (NOYAU)

- 480 Apricot Kernels
- 240 Peach Kernels
- 9 gallons white French Wine
- 4 pints Neutral Spirits
- 8 lbs. Powdered Sugar

Break the stones without touching the kernels. Macerate stones and kernels together with the wine and alcohol for 2 days. Dissolve the Powdered Sugar into the mixture. Strain and Filter.

HYPOCRAS SIMPLE

- 5 oz Cinnamon, ground
- 2 drachms Cloves, ground
- 1 drachm Mace, ground
- 4 pints Neutral Spirits
- 1 drachm Ambergris Essence
- 8 lbs. Powdered Sugar
- 9 gallons Claret Wine

Combine the Cinnamon, Cloves, Mace with the alcohol and macerate for 2 days. Add the Ambergris Essence. Dissolve the Powdered Sugar into the mixture, then add the wine. Strain and filter.

HYPOCRAS A LA VANILLE (VANILLA)

- 1 oz Vanilla, powdered
- 8 lbs. Powdered Sugar
- 9 gallons Claret Wine
- 4 pints Neutral Spirits

Dissolve the Vanilla and Powdered Sugar into the wine. Add the alcohol, then filter.

HYPOCRAS AU VIN D'ABSINTHE (ABSINTHE)

- 2.5 lbs. fresh Wormwood
- 9 gallons White Wine
- 40 Lemons, thin rinds only
- 40 Cedrats, thin rinds only
- 5 oz Anise Seed, ground
- .5 oz Cloves, ground
- 4 pints Neutral Spirits
- 8 lbs. Powdered Sugar

Combine the Wormwood and wine. Macerate for 12 hours, then filter. Add the citrus peels, Anise, Cloves and alcohol, then let the mixture macerate. Dissolve the Powdered Sugar into the mixture. Strain and filter.

HYPOCRAS A LA VIOLETTE (VIOLET)

- 7.5 oz Orris Root
- 1 oz Cloves, ground
- 9 gallons Claret Wine
- 4 pints Neutral Spirits
- 8 lbs. Powdered Sugar
- 40 drops Ambergris Essence
- 40 drops Musk Essence

Combine the Cloves, wine and alcohol, then macerate for 2 days. Dissolve the Powdered Sugar into the mixture, then strain and filter. Mix in the essences of Ambergris and Musk.

PUNCHES

Arrack Punch (Syrup) • *D'Orsay Punch*
Imperial Raspberry Whiskey Punch • *Kirschwasser Punch (Syrup)*
Regent Punch • *Roman Punch* • *Rum Punch (Syrup)*

ARRACK PUNCH (SYRUP)

- 53 ⅓ lbs. Sugar
- 3 ⅓ gallons water
- 1 2/3 gallons Lemon Juice
- 5 gallons Batavia Arrack

Combine the Sugar and water, then boil to the crack. Add the Lemon Juice and stir until the liquid is clear. Pour it in a clean tub, and when nearly cool, add the Arrack. Filter.

D'ORSAY PUNCH

- 24 Lemons
- 24 Oranges
- 4 gallons 12.5% Brandy
- 12 lbs. Sugar
- 6 gallons water

Peel the Lemons and juice 12 of them. Peel and juice the oranges. Cut the peels and macerate for 24 hours with the Brandy. Make a syrup from the Sugar, water, Lemon Juice and Orange Juice. Skim the syrup. Mix all ingredients together, then filter.

IMPERIAL RASPBERRY WHISKEY PUNCH

- 5 oz Sweet Almonds
- 5 oz Bitter Almonds
- 1.25 oz powdered Cinnamon
- .5 oz powdered Cloves
- 5 oz Plain White Syrup (on page 136)
- 7 gallons boiling water
- 2 gallons Whiskey
- 1 gallon Raspberry Syrup (on page 309)

Infuse the Almonds in some boiling water. Then skin the Almonds and add the Cinnamon, Cloves, and plain white syrup. Rub them fine. Add to the 7 gallons of boiling water and let boil for 5 minutes. Strain. When cold, add the whiskey and Raspberry syrup.

KIRSCHWASSER PUNCH (SYRUP)

- 53 ⅓ lbs. White Sugar
- 3 ⅓ gallons water
- 1 2/3 gallons Lemon Juice
- 5 gallons Kirschwasser (on page 212)

Combine the Sugar and water and boil to the crack. Add the Lemon Juice. Stir until getting clear, then put it in a clean tub. When cold, add the Kirschwasser and filter.

REGENT PUNCH

- 60 Lemons (reserve 14 Lemon Rinds)
- 14 Oranges
- 18 ⅔ drachms ground Cinnamon
- ⅔ drachms ground Cloves
- 2 drachms ground Vanilla
- 2 gallons pure Cognac
- 2 gallons pure Jamaican Rum
- 12 lbs. Sugar
- 6 gallons water
- 2 oz Green Tea

Juice the Lemons, reserving the peels from 14 of them. Juice and peel the oranges. Cut the lemn and orange peels and grind the spices, then add to the Cognac and Rum. Macerate for 24 hours then strain, press. Make a syrup from the Sugar and water. Skim the syrup, then add the Green Tea and let it cool. Add the Lemon and Orange juices, then filter.

ROMAN PUNCH

- 84 Lemons, juiced
- 42 Eggs
- 1.5 gallons boiling Plain White Syrup (on page 136)
- 1.5 gallons Cognac
- 1.5 gallons Jamaican Rum
- 2 gallons Maraschino Sherbet (on page 288)
- 1 gallon Maraquino di Zara (on page 235)

Combine the Lemon Juice and Eggs, beating to a froth. Add the remaining ingredients.

RUM PUNCH (SYRUP)

- 53 ⅓ lbs. Sugar
- 3 ⅓ gallons water
- 1 2/3 gallons Lemon Juice
- 5 gallons good Jamaican Rum

Combine the Sugar and water then boil to the crack. Add the Lemon Juice and stir until getting clear. Transfer to a clean tub. When nearly cool, add the Rum and filter.

ELIXIRS

Elixir de Garus [D] • Elixir de Genievre (Elixir of Juniper) • Elixir of Long Life
Elixir de Neroly • Elixir des Troubadours [D] • Elixir de Violettes

---

ELIXIRS IN MID-19TH-CENTURY AMERICA WERE DISTILLED OR STEEPED SPIRITUOUS PREPARATIONS, COMBINING BITTER ROOTS, EXOTIC SPICES, AND AROMATIC FLOWERS, THEN SWEETENED WITH SYRUPS AND OFTEN COLORED FOR VISUAL APPEAL. TYPICAL RECIPES YIELDED LIQUEURS IN THE 30–45% ABV RANGE, SOLD BY DISTILLERS, APOTHECARIES, AND TAVERN-KEEPERS. WHILE ELIXIRS WERE OFTEN SWEETENED AND SERVED LIKE CORDIALS, THEY CARRIED MEDICINAL OR TONIC CONNOTATIONS — MARKETED UNDER NAMES PROMISING EXOTIC BENEFITS LIKE "LONG LIFE" OR "FLOWER OF YOUTH." AT A TIME WHEN PATENT MEDICINES COEXISTED WITH HOME-BREWED GIN, ELIXIRS WOULD EVENTUALLY BECOME ASSOCIATED WITH A LESS SAVORY FIGURE: THE SNAKE OIL SALESMAN.

ELIXIR DE GARUS [D]

Distilling	Mixing
10 drachms Myrrh	4.25 gallons Plain White Syrup (on page 136)
10 drachms Sloe Berries	
15 drachms Cloves	2 gallons water
15 drachms Nutmeg	
5 oz Spanish Saffron	
3.5 oz Ceylon Cinnamon	
3.75 gallons Neutral Spirits	
4 gallons water	

Grind and cut the dry distilling ingredients. Macerate for 8 days with the distilling alcohol and water. Distill from off the water 3.75 gallons of flavored alcohol. Combine the mixing syrup and water, then mix with the flavored alcohol. Color the mixture yellow (on page 128).

ELIXIR DE GENIEVRE (ELIXIR OF JUNIPER)

- 1.5 lbs. Juniper Berries, ground
- 3.75 gallons Neutral Spirits
- 2 gallons water
- 4.25 gallons Plain White Syrup (on page 136)

Combine the Juniper, alcohol and water, then macerate for 8 days. Slowly add the syrup.

ELIXIR OF LONG LIFE

- 2 oz Zedoary Root
- 2 oz Agaric
- 2 oz Gentian Root
- 2 oz Venetian Theriac
- 2 oz Turkish Rhubarb
- 2 oz Angelica Root
- 4 oz Ginger
- 4.75 gallons Neutral Spirits
- 5.25 gallons water

Grind the dry ingredients. Combine with the alcohol and macerate for 2 weeks. Mix in the water, then filter.

ELIXIR DE NEROLY

- 2 oz Myrrh, ground
- 3.75 gallons Neutral Spirits
- 97 drops Neroli Oil
- 20 lbs. Sugar
- 5 gallons water

Combine the Myrrh and alcohol, then macerate for 8 days. Add the Neroli Oil. Dissolve the Sugar into the water, then mix with the flavored alcohol. Filter.

ELIXIR DES TROUBADOURS [D]

Distilling	Mixing
4 lbs. Musk Roses	20 lbs. Sugar
1.5 lbs. Jasmine Flowers	5 gallons water
1 lb. Orange Flowers	
.5 oz Mace	
2 oz Ravenzara Nuts, or Allspice	
3.75 gallons Neutral Spirits	
4 gallons water	

Cut the dry distilling ingredients. Combine with the distilling water and alcohol, then macerate for 2 weeks. Distill from off the water 3.75 gallons of well flavored alcohol. Dissolve the Sugar into the mixing water, then mix with the flavored alcohol. Filter. Color the mixture rose with Red Coloring (on page 129).

ELIXIR DE VIOLETTES

- 3 gallons Violet Syrup (on page 311)
- 2 gallons Raspberry Syrup (on page 309)
- 5 gallons 60% ABV Alcohol

Mix and Filter

ESSENCES

Essence of Ginger • *Essence of Lemon* • *Essence of Peppermint* • *Essence of Wintergreen*

ESSENCE IS A CONCENTRATED ALCOHOLIC EXTRACT OF VOLATILE OILS OR MACERATED BOTANICALS, DILUTED WITH WATER TO ROUGHLY 50–60% ABV FOR A STABLE, LONG-LASTING FLAVORING BASE. PREPARATION METHODS RANGED FROM THE SIMPLE DISSOLUTION OF ESSENTIAL OILS INTO HIGH-PROOF SPIRIT TO MULTI-WEEK MACERATIONS OF GROUND OR SLICED PLANT MATERIAL, ALWAYS FOLLOWED BY CAREFUL FILTRATION TO ENSURE CLARITY. IN THE 1860S, ESSENCES SERVED AS MODULAR COMPONENTS IN COMPOUND CORDIALS AND LIQUEURS, ADDED FLAVOR TO HOUSEHOLD DESSERTS AND BAKED GOODS, AND WERE SOLD IN BULK TO TAVERN-KEEPERS, GROCERS, AND CORDIAL MANUFACTURERS FOR SCALED PRODUCTION.

ESSENCE OF GINGER

- 2 lbs. ground Ginger
- 6 gallons Neutral Spirits
- 4 gallons water

Combine ingredients and macerate for 2 weeks. Strain and filter.

ESSENCE OF LEMON

- 2 oz Lemon Oil
- 6 gallons Neutral Spirits
- 4 gallons water

Dissolve the oil into the alcohol, then add the water. Filter. Color the mixture yellow (on page 128).

ESSENCE OF PEPPERMINT

- 2 oz Peppermint Oil
- 6 gallons Neutral Spirits
- 4 gallons water

Dissolve the oil into the alcohol, then add the water. Color the mixture yellow (on page 128) with Tincture of Turmeric, then filter.

ESSENCE OF WINTERGREEN

- 2 oz Wintergreen Oil
- 6 gallons Neutral Spirits
- 4 gallons water

Dissolve the oil into the alcohol, then add the water. Color the mixture red with Sanders Wood Tincture, then filter.

EXTRACTS AND TINCTURES

Bishop Extract (Tincture) • Extrait d'Absinthe [D] • Fever Drops

---

AN **EXTRACT** IS A CONCENTRATED SOLUTION OBTAINED BY MACERATING BOTANICAL MATERIALS—PEELS, SEEDS, ROOTS, OR HERBS—IN HIGH-PROOF NEUTRAL SPIRITS, THEN PRESSING AND FILTERING TO ISOLATE ESSENTIAL OILS AND AROMATIC COMPOUNDS. MACERATION PERIODS TYPICALLY RANGED FROM ONE TO SIX WEEKS, AND SOME RECIPES EMPLOYED SECONDARY DISTILLATION TO REACH A TARGET STRENGTH (OFTEN AROUND 45% ABV) AND CRYSTALLINE CLARITY. IN 1860S AMERICA, EXTRACTS AND TINCTURES APPEARED IN DISTILLING AND APOTHECARY PRACTICE AS STANDARDIZED BASES FOR COMPOUND BEVERAGES AND TONICS: BISHOP EXTRACT WAS LIKELY DOSED INTO WARM PUNCHES, ABSINTHE EXTRACT USED BY BARTENDERS AND DISTILLERS FOR PRECISION FLAVORING IN MIXED DRINKS OR CORDIALS, AND FEVER DROPS SERVED AS A MEDICINAL PREPARATION, DOSED BY THE TEASPOON FOR AILMENTS. THEIR MODULAR POTENCY ALLOWED FOR FLAVOR LAYERING WITHOUT RELIANCE ON BULKY FRESH INGREDIENTS.

BISHOP EXTRACT (TINCTURE)

- 10 ⅛ lbs. of ground Orange Peel
- 2.5 lbs. ground Cinnamon
- 2.5 lbs. ground Cardamom
- 10 gallons Neutral Spirits

Combine all ingredients and let macerate for 14 days. Press and filter. Color the mixture red (on page 129).

EXTRAIT D'ABSINTHE [D]

- 26 ⅔ oz Italian Fennel Seed
- 5 lbs. Green Anise Seed
- 13 ⅔ oz Licorice Root
- 3 ⅔ drachms Calamus Root
- 7.75 gallons Neutral Spirits
- 6.25 gallons water
- 4.5 oz Peppermint
- 12 oz Pontic Wormwood

Grind the Fennel, Anise, Licorice and Calamus. Combine with the alcohol and water, then macerate for 24 hours. Distill over to 45%. Add the peppermint and Wormwood, then macerate for 48 hours. Press and Filter.

FEVER DROPS

- 5.25 lbs. Calamus Root
- 1.75 lbs. Zedoary
- 1.75 lbs. Ginger
- 3.5 lbs. dried Orange Apples
- 10 gallons 80% ABV Alcohol
- 4-6 oz Peruvian Bark Extract

Grind the dry ingredients. Combine with 5 gallons of the alcohol, then macerate for 8 days. Strain, press and filter. Dissolve 4 to 6 ounces of Peruvian Bark Extract into the remaining 5 gallons of alcohol. Combine the two mixtures, then filter. Dose 3-4 teaspoons per day.

BITTERS

Aromatic Bitters • Bitter Danzinger Drops • Danziger Drops • English Bitters
Essence Bitters • Hamburg Bitters • Orange Bitters • Spanish Bitters
Stomach Bitters • Stoughton Bitters

BITTERS ARE CONCENTRATED INFUSIONS OF BITTER ROOTS, BARKS, AND AROMATIC BOTANICALS STEEPED IN HIGH-PROOF SPIRITS, THEN STRAINED AND BOTTLED FOR USE IN CORDIALS, TONICS, AND MIXED DRINKS. MOST (BUT NOT ALL) OF THESE RECIPES SIT IN THE RANGE OF 40-45% ABV. BY 1862, BITTERS WERE A KEY COMPONENT OF THE EMERGING AMERICAN DRINK CALLED THE COCKTAIL—FIRST DOCUMENTED IN RECIPE FORM WITHIN THESE VOLUMES. ONE NOTABLY MISSING FORMULA IS "BOGART'S BITTERS," CITED IN SEVERAL OF JERRY THOMAS'S RECIPES AND LIKELY A MISSPELLING OF BOKER'S BITTERS. NO KNOWN RECIPE FOR BOKER'S SURVIVES, BUT ITS RECURRENCE UNDERSCORES HOW ESSENTIAL BITTERS WERE TO EARLY MIXOLOGY. THE ONLY SUBSTITUTION I HAVE FOUND FROM THAT ERA IS A SINGLE REFERENCE TO ANGOSTURA AS A STAND-IN, NOTED IN THE 1876 EDITION OF THOMAS'S MANUAL. BITTERS BRIDGED MEDICINAL PRACTICE AND REFINED DRINKING RITUAL, AND THEIR PROMINENCE IN AMERICAN CORDIAL LITERATURE REFLECTS A CULINARY SHIFT: SUGAR HAD BECOME WIDELY AVAILABLE, YET THE REFINED PALATE STILL SOUGHT BALANCE THROUGH THE INTERPLAY OF SWEET AND BITTER.

AROMATIC BITTERS

- 2.75 lbs. ground dried small Orange Apples
- .25 lbs. ground Orange Peel
- 2 oz ground Calamus Root
- 2 oz ground Pimpinella Root
- 1 oz ground cut Hops
- 10 gallons 45% ABV Alcohol
- 2 1/3 pints Brown Sugar Syrup (on page 136)

Combine the Apples, Orange peel, Calamus root, Pimpinella root, Hops and alcohol. Create a tincture by letting macerate for 14 days (see page 124). Press out the dregs, and add the Brown Sugar Syrup. Filter. Color the mixture dark brown with Base Coloring (on page 127).

BITTER DANZIGER DROPS

- 2 oz Centaurium
- 3 oz Angelica Root
- 3.5 drachms of Aloe Socotrina
- 1 oz Myrrh
- 2 oz Cassia Flowers
- 2.5 oz Ginger
- 1.5 oz Nutmeg
- 2 oz Galangal Root
- .75 oz Gentian Root
- 1.5 oz Wormwood
- .75 oz Agaric
- 10 gallons 45% ABV Alcohol

Coarsely grind all dry ingredients and combine with the alcohol. Create a tincture by letting macerate for 14 days. Strain, press out the dregs and filter. Color the mixture dark brown with Base Coloring (on page 127).

DANZIGER DROPS

- 2 oz Centaurium
- 3 oz Angelica Root
- .5 drachm Aloe Socotrina
- .5 oz Myrrh
- 2 oz Cassia Buds
- .75 oz Agaric
- 2.5 oz Ginger
- 1.5 oz Nutmeg
- 2 oz Galangal Root
- .75 oz Gentian Root
- 1.5 oz Wormwood
- 4.75 gallons Neutral Spirits
- 5.25 gallons water

Coarsely grind the dry ingredients and macerate with the alcohol and water. Strain, press and filter. Color the mixture dark yellow (on page 128).

ENGLISH BITTERS

- 12 oz Lemon Peels
- 6.5 oz Orange Peels
- 6.5 oz small Orange Apples
- 1.5 oz Calamus Root
- 1.5 oz Angelica Root
- 1.5 oz Galangal Root
- .75 oz Quassia Wood
- 2.25 oz Gentian Root
- 3 drachms Nutmeg
- 3 drachms Cloves
- 4.5 gallons Neutral Spirits
- 4.25 lbs. Brown Sugar
- 5.5 gallons pure water
- 7.25 ounces Base Coloring (on page 127) the color of dark-brown sugar.

Grind all dry ingredients into a course powder and combine with the alcohol. Create a tincture by either macerating for 2 weeks or displacing. Create a syrup using the Brown Sugar and water. Combine the tincture, the syrup, and coloring. Filter.

ESSENCE BITTERS

- 30 oz Orange Peel
- 30 oz Orange Apples
- 30 oz Gentian Root
- 30 oz Lemon Peel
- 59 pints Neutral Spirits
- 21 pints water

Grind all dry ingredients into a coarse powder and combine with the alcohol and water. Create a tincture by either macerating for 2 weeks or displacing. Filter.

HAMBURG BITTERS

- 2 oz Agaric
- 5 oz Cinnamon
- 4 oz Cassia Buds
- .5 oz Grains of Paradise
- 3 oz Quassia Wood
- .75 oz Cardamom seed
- 3 oz Gentian Root
- 3 oz Orange Apples, dried
- 1.5 oz Orange Peel
- 4.25 gallons Neutral Spirits
- 5.75 gallons water
- 2.75 oz Acetic Ether (Ethyl Acetate)

Grind all dry ingredients into a coarse powder and combine with the alcohol and water. Create a tincture by letting macerate for 2 weeks. Add the Acetic Ether. Color the mixture brown with Base Coloring (on page 127).

ORANGE BITTERS

- 6 lbs. Orange Peel
- 1 gallon water
- 4.75 gallons Neutral Spirits
- 16 lbs. Sugar
- 4.25 gallons water

Combine the Orange peel with 1 gallon water and let macerate for 24 hours. Cut the yellow part of the peel from the white and chop it fine. Create a tincture by either macerating for 2 weeks or displacing. Create a syrup from the Sugar and 4.25 gallons of water. Filter.

SPANISH BITTERS

- 5 oz Polypody
- 6 oz Calamus Root
- 8 oz Orris Root
- 2.5 oz Coriander Seed
- 1 oz Centaurium
- 3 oz Orange Peel
- 2 oz German Chamomile Flowers
- 4.75 gallons Neutral Spirits
- 5.25 gallons water
- 1.5 oz Sugar

Grind all dry ingredients into a coarse powder and combine with the alcohol. Create a tincture by letting macerate for 2 weeks. Add the water and Sugar. Filter. Color the mixture brown with Base Coloring (on page 127).

STOMACH BITTERS

- 8 oz Cardamom seed
- 2 oz Nutmeg
- 12 oz Grains of Paradise
- 8 oz Cinnamon
- 4 oz Cloves
- 4 oz Ginger
- 4 oz Galangal
- 4 oz Orange Peel
- 2 oz Lemon Peel
- 4.75 gallons Neutral Spirits
- 12 lbs. Sugar
- 4.5 gallons water

Grind all dry ingredients into a coarse powder and combine with the alcohol. Create a tincture by letting macerate for 2 weeks. Create a syrup from the Sugar and water. Combine with the tincture, then filter.

STOUGHTON BITTERS

- 8 lbs. Gentian Root
- 6 lbs. Orange Peel
- 1.5 lbs. Snakeroot (Virginia)
- ½ lb. American Saffron
- ½ lb. Red Saunders Wood
- 10 gallons 25% ABV Alcohol

Grind all dry ingredients into a coarse powder and combine with the alcohol. Create a tincture by displacement (on page 123).

SHERBET

Currant Sherbet • Lemon Sherbet • Marasquino Sherbet
Sherbet de Quatre Fruits (Four Fruits) • Raspberry Sherbet • Rum Sherbet

---

SHERBETS ARE CORDIAL BEVERAGES MADE BY COMBINING FRUIT JUICES, CALF'S-FOOT JELLY, SUGAR (OFTEN RUBBED WITH CITRUS RINDS), AND FORTIFIED WINES OR SPIRITS, THEN WARMING TO DISSOLVE AND CLARIFYING BY WARM FILTRATION. THE USE OF CALF'S-FOOT JELLY IMPARTS A SLIGHT VISCOSITY—RETAINED EVEN AFTER FILTERING—TO GIVE SHERBETS A SOFT, VELVETY MOUTHFEEL WITHOUT ANY ICE OR CHILLING APPARATUS DURING PREPARATION. THESE WERE RELATIVELY LOW ON ALCOHOL CONTENT (6-17% ABV). DESPITE SHARING A NAME, THESE GELATIN-CLARIFIED DRINKS ARE ENTIRELY DISTINCT FROM ICED SHERBET DESSERTS, RELYING ON WARM PREPARATION AND ALCOHOL FORTIFICATION RATHER THAN FREEZING. IN JERRY THOMAS' VOLUME, SHERBET REFERS TO A SYRUP MADE FROM COMBINING FRUIT OR HERBS WITH SUGAR AND WATER. IN MID-19TH-CENTURY AMERICA, SHERBETS WERE SERVED AS ELEGANT PUNCH BASES OR STANDALONE CORDIAL DRINKS—OFTEN ENJOYED WARM IN SOCIAL SETTINGS OR DILUTED INTO MIXED BEVERAGES.

CURRANT SHERBET

- 2.5 gallons Currant Juice
- 2 gallons fresh Calf's Foot Jelly
- 2 gallons Currant Wine (on page 150)
- 2 gallons Currant Ratafia (on page 252)
- 24 lbs. Sugar

Combine all the ingredients and mix until Sugar is dissolved. Filter warm.

LEMON SHERBET

- 2.5 gallons Lemon Juice
- 2 gallons fresh Calf's Foot Jelly
- 2 gallons Madeira Wine
- 2 gallons French Brandy
- 24 lbs. Sugar rubbed with the rinds of the Lemons

Dissolve ingredients together. Filter warm.

MARASQUINO SHERBET

- 2.5 gallons Orange Juice
- 2 gallons fresh Calf's Foot Jelly
- 5.5 gallons Marasquino di Zara (on page 235)

Combine, and filter warm.

SHERBET DE QUATRE FRUITS (FOUR FRUITS)

- 2.5 gallons Cherry Juice
- 2 gallons fresh Calf's Foot Jelly
- 5 gallons Ratafia de Quatre Fruits (on page 254)

Combine and filter warm.

RASPBERRY SHERBET

- 2.5 gallons Raspberry Juice
- 2 gallons fresh Calf's Foot Jelly
- 5 gallons Ratafia de Framboises (on page 251)(Raspberry)

Combine and filter warm.

RUM SHERBET

- 2.5 gallons Lemon Juice
- 2 gallons fresh Calf's Foot Jelly
- 2 gallons Rum Shrub (on page 292)
- 2 gallons Jamaican Rum
- 24 lbs. Sugar rubbed with the Lemon rinds

Combine and filter warm.

SHRUB

Currant Shrub • Lemon Shrub • Raspberry Shrub • Rum Shrub

SHRUBS ARE CONCENTRATED FRUIT PREPARATIONS SWEETENED WITH SUGAR AND PRESERVED EITHER BY BOILING WITH VINEGAR OR BY MACERATION IN DISTILLED SPIRITS. THIS CHAPTER INCLUDES BOTH VINEGAR-BASED DRINKING VINEGARS AND SPIRIT-INFUSED CORDIALS. TYPICAL RECIPES CALL FOR FRUIT JUICE AND A GENEROUS PROPORTION OF SUGAR (OFTEN BOILED TOGETHER), WITH VINEGAR OR BRANDY ADDED ONCE COOLED— YIELDING A THICK, SHELF-STABLE SYRUP. IN 1860S AMERICA, SHRUBS LIKELY SERVED AS A PRACTICAL WAY TO EXTEND THE SEASONALITY OF SUMMER FRUITS BEFORE REFRIGERATION. WHILE SCHULTZ'S MANUAL DOESN'T SPECIFY SERVING METHODS, IT'S PLAUSIBLE THAT HOUSEHOLDS AND TAVERNS DILUTED SHRUBS OVER ICE OR SODA WATER AS REFRESHING BEVERAGES, AND THAT SPIRIT-BASED VERSIONS DOUBLED AS APERITIFS OR DIGESTIFS IN SOCIAL SETTINGS.

CURRANT SHRUB

- 5 ⅝ gallons Red Currant Juice
- 40 lbs. Sugar
- 1.5 gallons good French Brandy

Boil Sugar and juice for 8-10 minutes. Let it cool, then add the Brandy. Filter.

LEMON SHRUB

- 5.25 gallons Lemon Cordial (on page 193)
- 3.25 gallons Lemon Juice
- 1.5 gallons Plain White Syrup (on page 136)

Combine and filter.

RASPBERRY SHRUB

- 3.5 gallons Raspberry Juice
- 2 gallons Vinegar
- 48 lbs. Sugar
- 1.5 gallons good French Brandy

Combine the juice, Vinegar and Sugar. Boil and skim for 30 minutes. When cold, add the Brandy. Filter.

RUM SHRUB

- 4 gallons Proof Jamaican Rum (50% ABV)
- 15 pints Plain White Syrup (on page 136)
- 3.75 gallons Lemon Juice
- 3 pints water

Combine and filter.

BEVERAGES

Bishop • Delight of the Mandarins • Elephant's Milk • Sighs of Love
Strong Sangaree • Yankee Punch

BISHOP

- 100 grains of ground Nutmeg
- 60 grains ground White Pepper
- 1.25 oz Cardamom seed
- 1.5 oz Mace
- 20 pints of Plain White Syrup (on page 136)
- 60 pints Claret Wine

Combine all the ingredients and then bring to a boil for 1 minute. Filter.

DELIGHT OF THE MANDARINS

- 1 gallon 78-Proof Spirit (39% ABV)
- 4 pints pure soft water
- 4.5 lbs. White Sugar, crushed small
- .5 oz Star Anise, bruised
- .5 oz Ambrette seed, bruised
- .25 oz Safflower

Macerate in a carboy or stone jar capable of holding double the quantity and agitate well every day for 2 weeks.

ELEPHANT'S MILK

- 2 oz Benzoin
- 1 pint of Rectified Spirits of Wine
- 5 cups boiling water
- 1.5 lbs. Sugar

Dissolve the gum into the spirit and add the boiling water. Agitate for 5 minutes in a strong, corked bottle. When cold, strain and add the Sugar.

SIGHS OF LOVE

- 6 lbs. Sugar
- Water sufficient to produce a gallon of syrup
- 1 pint Rose Water
- 7 pints Proof Spirit (50% ABV)
- 1-2 drops Ambergris Essence or Vanilla Essence (optional)

Combine and color pale pink. A drop or two (not more) of the Ambergris Essence or Vanilla Essence improves it. This is a pleasant cordial.

STRONG SANGAREE
Juice Mix:

- 4 oz Candied Lemons, cut small
- 4 oz Candied Oranges, cut small
- 4 gallons Cherry Brandy
- 4 pints Lemon Juice
- 1 gallon Madeira Wine

Spice Mix:

- 8 oz grated Nutmeg
- 8 oz powdered Allspice
- 2 oz pounded Bitter Almonds
- 3.5 gallons Proof Spirit of choice (Arrack, Brandy, Rum, etc)

Place Juice Mix and Spice Mix in separate demijohns. Macerate for 8 days. Strain and press. Mix the two extracts. Filter.

YANKEE PUNCH

- 3 oz Pineapple, sliced
- 6 grains Vanilla
- 1 grain Ambergris, rubbed with a little Sugar
- 1 pint strong pale Brandy
- 1 pint Lemon Juice
- 1 bottle Lemon Syrup (on page 305)
- 1 bottle Claret Wine or Port Wine
- 8 oz Sugar
- 3 cups boiling water

Macerate the Pineapple, Vanilla, and Ambergris in the Brandy for a few hours, being careful to shake it frequently during that time. Strain through a jelly bag, squeezing the bag to get all the liquid. Add the Lemon Juice, Lemon syrup and wine. Dissolve the Sugar into the boiling water and add to the mixture.

NON-ALCOHOLIC / MISCELLANEOUS

*French Mustard • Ginger Beer • Stomachic Beverage • Instantaneous Beer
Lemonade for Bottling • Lemonade Powder, Effervescing
Lemonade Powder, Plain • Orangeade • Raspberry Vinegar • Soda Water
Vanilla Milk*

FRENCH MUSTARD

- 1.5 lbs. ground Black Mustard Seed
- 1.5 lbs. ground Yellow Mustard Seed
- 3 quarts of good strong Cider Vinegar
- 1.5 oz ground Allspice
- .5 oz ground Ginger
- 3 oz Sea-Salt
- 1.5 oz ground Cinnamon
- .5 oz ground Cloves

Bring the Vinegar to a boil. Mix thoroughly with the mustard seeds and let macerate 12 hours. Add remaining spices and mix well. Add more Vinegar as needed to get the required consistency.

GINGER BEER

- 10 gallons boiling water
- 10 oz Cream of Tartar
- 15 oz ground Ginger
- 10 Lemons, sliced
- 15 lbs. Sugar
- 1 pint Yeast

Combine the water, Cream of Tartar, Ginger and Lemons and boil them together. Let stand until nearly cool, then strain and press. Dissolve the Sugar into this mixture. When lukewarm, add the Yeast, then let stand for 14 hours. Skim and filter. Bottle and bind the corks.

STOMACHIC BEVERAGE

- 10 gallons boiling water
- 10 oz Cream of Tartar
- 15 oz ground Ginger
- 10 Lemons, sliced
- 15 lbs. Sugar
- .5 oz Clove Oil
- .5 oz Cinnamon Oil
- 1 pint Yeast

Combine the water, Cream of Tartar, Ginger and Lemons, then let macerate until nearly cold. Strain and press. Rub the clove and Cinnamon oils into the Sugar, then dissolve into the mixture. When nearly lukewarm, add the Yeast. Let it stand for 14 hours. Skim and filter. Bottle, and be careful to bind the corks well.

INSTANTANEOUS BEER

- 9.5 gallons water
- 2 pints Lemon Juice
- 1.5 oz Powdered Ginger
- 10 lbs. Sugar
- 40 drachms Sodium Bicarbonate

Dissolve and mix together the water, juice, Ginger and Sugar. Continue stirring while bottling the mixture into strong bottles. Get corks, mallet and string at hand. For each bottle, add one drachm of Sodium Bicarbonate. Cork and string it quickly.

LEMONADE FOR BOTTLING

- 10 oz Citric Acid, powdered
- 15 lbs. Sugar
- 160 drops Lemon Oil
- 9 gallons water
- 20 drachms Sodium Bicarbonate

Rub the Sugar with the Lemon Oil. Mix in the powdered Citric Acid. Dissolve into the water. Filter and fill it in Soda Water bottles. Add to each bottle .5 drachm of Sodium Bicarbonate in pieces. Cork and string.

LEMONADE POWDER, EFFERVESCING

Mix #1	Mix #2
10 oz powdered Tartaric Acid	10 oz Sodium Bicarbonate
4 lbs. 6 oz Powdered Sugar	4 lbs. 6 oz Powdered Sugar
1 drachm Lemon Oil	1 drachm Lemon Oil

Each mixture should be stored separately and kept dry.

Directions: .5 oz Mix #1 in a tumbler of water. Dissolve .5 oz Mix #2 in another tumbler, then mix the two. Gives a splendid lemonade.

LEMONADE POWDER, PLAIN

- .5 lbs. Tartaric Acid powder
- 16 lbs. Powdered Sugar
- 1.5 drachms Lemon Oil

Rub and mix well.

1 oz of this powder makes 8 ounces of lemonade

ORANGEADE

- 40 Oranges, rinds only
- 10 lbs. Sugar
- 8 gallons water
- 80 Oranges, juice only
- 40 Lemons, juice only

Powder the Orange rinds with the Sugar. Dissolve and mix together with the water in a boiler or tub. Combine the Orange and Lemon juices and add to the first mixture. Filter.

RASPBERRY VINEGAR

- 30 lbs. Raspberries, pulped
- 7.5 gallons Vinegar (Wine or Cider)

Combine and macerate for 8 days. Press and strain.

SODA WATER

- 10 gallons water
- 8.5 oz crystallized Citric Acid
- 8.5 oz Sodium Bicarbonate (lumps or crystals)

Fill a fountain receiver with the water. Add the Citric Acid. Add the Sodium Bicarbonate, then quickly screw on the pipe. Shake to dissolve.

VANILLA MILK

- 12 drops Vanilla Essence
- 1 oz Lump Sugar
- 1 pint new Milk

Pulverize and gradually add the Milk.

FLAVORED SYRUPS

Barberry Syrup (small batch) • *Blackberry Syrup* • *Cinnamon Syrup aka Sirop de Cannelle*
Capillaire (Maidenhair) Syrup • *Capillaire (Maidenhair) Syrup (small batch)*
Cherry Syrup aka Sirop de Cerises • *Morello Cherry Syrup (small batch)* • *Coffee Syrup*
Coffee Syrup (small batch) • *Red Currant Syrup aka Sirop de Groseilles* • *Currant Syrup (small batch)*
Ginger Syrup (small batch) • *Grape Syrup (small batch)* • *Gum Syrup aka Sirop de Gomme*
Lemon Syrup aka Sirop de Limons • *Lemon Syrup (small batch)* • *Marsh-mallow Syrup (small batch)*
Mulberry Syrup (small batch) • *Orange Syrup aka Sirop d'Oranges* • *Orange Syrup (small batch)*
Orange Flower Syrup aka Sirop de Fleurs d'Oranges • *Orgeat Syrup aka Sirop d'Orgeat*
Orgeat Syrup (small batch) • *Pineapple Syrup aka Sirop d'Ananas* • *Pineapple Syrup (small batch)*
Pinks Syrup (small batch) • *Raspberry Syrup* • *Raspberry Syrup (small batch)* • *Raspberry Vinegar Syrup*
Raspberry Vinegar Syrup (small batch) • *Strawberry Syrup* • *Strawberry Syrup (small batch)*
Violet Syrup (small batch) • *Wormwood Syrup (small batch)* • *Tickle my Fancy* • *Usquebaugh*
Verdulino de Turino [D] • *Vespetro [D]*

The best syrups can only be made with the finest qualities of Sugar. Syrup is the juice of fruit, flowers, vegetables or whatever you desire to preserve, mixed with liquid Sugar. The essences or virtues of most fruits, etc., suitable for syrup-making may be extracted by simple infusion. The Sugar should be dissolved in this decoction or infusion, and both placed in a glass or earthenware vessel. Close this vessel down, and place it in a pan on the fire, surrounded with water. Saucepans made of tin, or tinned on the inside, should not be used when making syrups from red fruits, as these act on the tin, and turn the color to a dead blue.

In boiling to the degrees, it is from the "small thread" (on page 131) to the "large Pearl" (on page 132) that syrup is produced. Care should be taken to boil the syrup to the precise point. If not sufficiently boiled, after a time it is apt to become moldy. If boiled too much, it will grain a little, and thus become candied. In some cases, the syrup should not be bottled until quite cold. When ready, cork it securely and stand it in a cool, dry place.

BARBERRY SYRUP (SMALL BATCH)

- 2 pints Barberry Juice
- 4 lbs. Sugar

Mash enough Barberries to yield 2 pints of juice in a colander or sieve, pressing out the juice into a pan or basin. Let the juice stand for a day or two, then strain through a flannel bag until very clear. Boil your clarified Sugar to a "crack". Pour the juice in, in the proportion of one pint juice to 2 lbs. Sugar. Stir it well on the fire with a skimmer and give it one or two boils. If any scum rises, take it off. Let it thoroughly cool, then bottle off, or put in deep jars, and tie down with bladders.

BLACKBERRY SYRUP

- 80 lbs. crushed Sugar
- 5 gallons Blackberry Juice

Combine and boil for 2 minutes. Skim and strain while boiling hot.

CINNAMON SYRUP AKA SIROP DE CANNELLE

- 1 oz Ceylon Cinnamon Oil
- 1 spoonful Carbonate of Magnesia
- 5 gallons water
- 80 lbs. Sugar

Rub the Cinnamon oil into the magnesia and let dry into a powder. Put this into a filter bag and pour 5 gallons of water on it over and over until it runs clear. Dissolve the Sugar into the flavored water, then boil for 2 minutes. Skim and strain.

CAPILLAIRE (MAIDENHAIR) SYRUP

- 1 lb. Maidenhair Fern
- 5.5 gallons boiling water
- 3 Egg whites
- 80 lbs. Sugar
- 8 oz Orange Flower Water

Combine the Maidenhair Fern and boiling water, then macerate until cold. Strain without pressing, to get 5 gallons. Beat the Egg whites to a froth and mix them with the infusion. Keep back a quart of the liquid. Dissolve the Sugar into the remaining liquid and bring to a boil. When the scum rises, put in a little from the quart of cold liquid, and this will make the scum settle. Let it rise and settle 3 times. Then skim and, when perfectly clear, add the Orange Flower Water. Boil once again and strain.

CAPILLAIRE (MAIDENHAIR) SYRUP (SMALL BATCH)

- 4 oz Maidenhair Fern
- 4.5 lbs. Sugar
- Orange Flower Water
- 4 Egg Whites

Cut the Maidenhair Fern (aka Capillaire) into little pieces, then infuse in boiling water, covering the pan over. Add the Sugar and clarify with the whites of 4 Eggs. If you are mixing in the above proportion, boil to a "Pearl". Then pour off through a strainer. When cool, add some Orange Flower Water. Bottle close. Ordinary syrup, with Tincture of Orange Flower in it is often sold for the genuine article.

Christian Shultz: "The best Capillaire is found in America, and grows near ponds or running streams. The leaves are green, and grow double, the stalk long, and the color of ripe Plums. Be careful to obtain the genuine sort, whether foreign or native, whichever kind you require."

CHERRY SYRUP AKA SIROP DE CERISES

- 5 gallons Cherry Juice
- 80 lbs. Sugar

Let juice ferment for a few days. Dissolve the Sugar into the juice, then boil. When clear, skim and strain.

MORELLO CHERRY SYRUP (SMALL BATCH)

- 2 lbs. Morello Cherries
- 4 lbs. Sugar

See that the Cherries are ripe, and having stoned them, mash them in a colander or sieve, pressing out the juice into a pan or basin. Let the juice stand for a day or two, then strain through a flannel bag until very clear. Boil your clarified Sugar to a "crack". Pour the juice in, in the proportion of one pint juice to 2 lbs. Sugar. Stir it well on the fire with a skimmer and give it one or two boils. If any scum rises, take it off. Let it thoroughly cool. Then bottle off, or put in deep jars, and tie down with bladders.

COFFEE SYRUP

- 10 lbs. fresh Java Coffee, fresh roasted and ground
- 6 gallons boiling water
- 80 lbs. Sugar

Combine the Coffee and boiling water, and let it stand, well covered until cool. Strain and press. Dissolve the Sugar into the mix, then boil and skim for 2 minutes. Strain again.

COFFEE SYRUP (SMALL BATCH)

- 1 pint Mocha Coffee
- 2 pints Plain White Syrup (on page 136)

Make a strong decoction of Mocha Coffee, very clear, to the amount of a pint. Take 2 pints of syrup and boil to a "ball". Add the Coffee. Put it again on the fire and boil to a "Pearl". Strain through a cloth. Bottle when cold.

RED CURRANT SYRUP AKA SIROP DE GROSEILLES

- 5 gallons Currant Juice, with the fruits
- 80 lbs. Sugar

Ferment the juice with the fruits for 2 days, then press. Dissolve the Sugar into the juice, then boil. Skim until clear, then strain.

CURRANT SYRUP (SMALL BATCH)

- 2 pints Currant Juice:
- 6 lbs. Currants (white and/or red)
- 1 lb. Raspberries (optional)
- 1 lb. Cherries, pits removed (optional)
- 4 lbs. 4 oz. Powdered Sugar

The use of Cherries and/or Raspberries is optional, and the quantity is to taste. Mix, mash, and ferment the fruit in a warm place for 3 days. While the fruit is fermenting, it is a good plan to cover the pan with a coarse cloth, or anything that will admit the air (which is essential to fermentation) but keep out the dust. Add the Sugar. Place the syrup on the fire, and as it heats, skim it carefully, but don't let it boil. Alternatively, you may mix in a glass vessel or earthenware jar, and place in a pan of water on the fire. This is a very clean way and prevents the sides from crusting and burning. When dissolved to the "little Pearl", take it off and strain through a cloth. Bottle when cold. Cover with tissue paper dipped in Brandy and tie down with a bladder

GINGER SYRUP (SMALL BATCH)

- 2 oz Ginger
- 24 oz water
- 2 lbs. Sugar

Boil together in a pan to the "small thread" and strain through a hair sieve.

GRAPE SYRUP (SMALL BATCH)

- 24 oz water
- 8 oz Sherry
- 4 oz Elderflowers
- 3 lbs. Sugar

Remove the stalks, etc. Boil the water and sherry, then pour on the flowers while hot. Cover and let sit a few hours in a warm place. Pass through a cloth. Add the Sugar, and boil to the "small thread".

GUM SYRUP AKA SIROP DE GOMME

- 20 lbs. best clear white Arabic Gum
- 5 gallons water
- 60 lbs. Sugar

Heat 4 gallons of the water to nearly boiling, then dissolve the gum into it. Melt the Sugar and clarify it with the remaining 1 gallon of water. Add in the gum solution, then boil for 2 minutes.

LEMON SYRUP AKA SIROP DE LIMONS

- 5 gallons Lemon Juice
- 1 oz best Lemon Oil
- 8 oz Alcohol
- 16 Lemon Rinds
- 80 lbs. Sugar

Either dissolve the Lemon oil into the alcohol OR rub the Lemon rinds with the Sugar to extract the oils. Add in the Lemon Juice and dissolve the Sugar. Bring to a boil for 2 minutes. Skim and strain.

LEMON SYRUP (SMALL BATCH)

- 2 lbs. Sugar (or 2 pints syrup)
- 1 pint Lemon Juice

Let the juice settle. Clear off the thin skin, which forms on the top. Strain through a fine sieve or cloth. Boil the syrup to the "little crack", then pour in the Lemon Juice. Place the pan on the fire, and boil to the "Pearl". Stir it well on the fire with a skimmer and give it one or two boils. If any scum rises, take it off. Bottle off when quite cool.

MARSH-MALLOW SYRUP (SMALL BATCH)

- 2 oz Marsh-Mallow Roots, cut into small pieces
- 24 oz water
- 1 lb. Sugar
- 4 Eggs
- Orange Flower Water

Bruise the roots in a mortar. Boil in the water until reduced to a pint. Add the Sugar and clarify with the whites of 4 Eggs. Boil to a "Pearl". Then pour off through a strainer. When cool, add some Orange Flower Water. Bottle close.

MULBERRY SYRUP (SMALL BATCH)

- 2 pints Mulberry Juice
- 2 lbs. 12 oz. Sugar

Mulberries do not require so much Sugar as Raspberries but should be uniformly ripe. Mash the mulberries in a colander or sieve, pressing out the juice into a pan or basin. Let the juice stand for a day or two, then strain through a flannel bag until very clear. Boil your clarified Sugar to a "crack". Pour the juice in, in the proportion of one pint juice to 2 lbs. Sugar. Stir it well on the fire with a skimmer and give it one or two boils. If any scum rises, take it off. Let it thoroughly cool. Then bottle off, or put in deep jars, and tie down with bladders.

ORANGE SYRUP AKA SIROP D'ORANGES

- 5 gallons Orange Juice
- 16 Orange Rinds
- 80 lbs. Sugar

Rub the Orange rinds with Loaf Sugar to extract the essential oil. Dissolve the Sugar into the juice then boil for 2 minutes. Skim and strain.

ORANGE SYRUP (SMALL BATCH)

- 2 lbs. Sugar (or 2 pints syrup)
- 1 pint Orange Juice

Let the juice settle. Clear off the thin skin, which forms on the top. Strain through a fine sieve or cloth. Boil the syrup to the "little crack", then pour in the Orange Juice. Place the pan on the fire, and boil to the "Pearl". Stir it well on the fire with a skimmer and give it one or two boils. If any scum rises, take it off. Bottle off when quite cool.

ORANGE FLOWER SYRUP AKA SIROP DE FLEURS D'ORANGES

- 5 gallons of Orange Flower Water
- 80 lbs. Sugar

Combine, then boil for 2 minutes. Skim and strain.

ORGEAT SYRUP AKA SIROP D'ORGEAT

- 10 lbs. Sweet Almonds
- 4 lbs. Bitter Almonds
- 80 lbs. Sugar
- 1 pint Orange Flower Water

Cover Almonds with boiling hot water. Let them stand until near cold, then peel by pressing through your fingers. Beat them in a stone or brass mortar to a very fine paste with some Sugar, adding water slowly. Press through a linen cloth, to get 5 gallons of liquid resembling rich Milk. Dissolve the Sugar into this liquid. Boil once and add the Orange Flower Water, then strain.

ORGEAT SYRUP (SMALL BATCH)

- 2 lbs. Sweet Almonds
- 3.5 oz Bitter Almonds
- 3 pints fresh water
- 6 - 6.5 lbs. Sugar
- Orange Flower Tincture or Essence of Neroli

Drop Almonds into boiling water. This blanches them, and they are easily skinned. Peel and drop into cold water to wash. When ready, put them into a clean mortar (marble is better than bronze) and mash them. Squeeze in the juice of 2 Lemons or add a little acid. As you pound the Almonds, pour part of a pint of clean water into the mortar. Mash thoroughly, until the mixture looks like thick Milk, and no pieces of Almonds are left. Then add another pint of the spring water. Now squeeze the white mash through a hair cloth, or other good strainer. A common plan is to have a large strainer held by two persons. As they twist the Milk may be caught in a clean basin. Whatever of the Almonds is left in the cloth, put it back into the mortar, and mash it over again, adding a little of the spring water. Then strain it and mix with the former Almond Milk. Boil the clarified Sugar to a "crack". Remove from the fire and add the Almond Milk. When mixed, return the mixture to a boil. Remove the pan from the fire and stir the syrup until cold (this is done to keep it from separating and splitting up after being bottled). Pour in a small portion of Orange Flower Tincture, or the smallest drop of the Essence of Neroli, and pass the mixture again through a cloth. Give the bottles an occasional shake for a few days afterward. It will keep the syrup from parting.

PINEAPPLE SYRUP AKA SIROP D'ANANAS

- 5 gallons Pineapple Juice, with the fruit
- 80 lbs. Sugar

Ferment the juice with the fruit for 2 days. Dissolve the Sugar into the juice, then boil for 2 minutes. Skim and strain.

PINEAPPLE SYRUP (SMALL BATCH)

- 1.5 pints Pineapple Juice
- 2 lbs. Sugar

Cut the outside peel off a Pineapple, then pound the fruit in a mortar. Strain it through a cloth. For every 1.5 pints of juice, add 2 lbs. Sugar. Boil it to the "small thread".

PINKS SYRUP (SMALL BATCH)

- 8 oz Red-Pink Flowers
- 1 lb. Sugar
- 16 oz boiling water

Pick off all the green parts from the pinks. Put the flowers in a mortar and pound them with the boiling water. Strain the decoction through a cloth. Clarify the Sugar, boil it to a "ball" and add it to the decoction. Return it to the fire and boil it to a "Pearl". This syrup may also be made without pounding the flowers, only boiling them with the Sugar. When done, skim it and strain it through a cloth. The dark-red velvety single pink is the best for syrup.

RASPBERRY SYRUP

- 5 gallons Raspberry Juice, with the fruit
- 80 lbs. Sugar

Ferment the juice and fruit for 2 days. Dissolve the Sugar into the juice, then boil for 2 minutes. Skim, strain and filter.

RASPBERRY SYRUP (SMALL BATCH)

- 2 pints filtered Raspberry Juice
- 4 lbs. 4 oz. Powdered Sugar

Select the fruit, either white or red. Having picked them over, mash them in a pan and put in a warm place until fermentation has commenced. Let it stand for about 3 days. All mucilaginous fruits require this, or else they would jelly when bottled. Now filter the juice through a close flannel bag, or blotting paper. Add the Sugar. Place the syrup on the fire, and as it heats, skim it carefully, but don't let it boil. Alternatively, you may mix in a glass vessel or earthenware jar, and place in a pan of water on the fire. This is a very clean way and prevents the sides from crusting and burning. When dissolved to the "little Pearl", take it off. Strain through a cloth. Bottle when cold. Cover with tissue paper dipped in Brandy and tie down with a bladder.

RASPBERRY VINEGAR SYRUP

- 5 gallons Raspberry Vinegar (on page 300)
- 80 lbs. Sugar

Dissolve the Sugar into the Vinegar, then boil for 2 minutes. Skim and strain.

Raspberry Vinegar Syrup (small batch)

- 3.5 lbs. Sugar
- 1 pint Raspberry Juice
- 2 pints White Wine Vinegar

As in making Raspberry syrup, white or red fruit may be used. White Raspberries, however, require the best Loaf Sugar and white wine Vinegar, so as not to discolor the syrup. Clean the Raspberries. Mash them in a pan and put in a warm place for a day or two, until they ferment. Strain them and pour in the Vinegar. Strain again. Add the Sugar, and boil to the "Pearl".

Another plan is to take whole Raspberries (say 2 lbs., 1.5 pints Vinegar and 2 lbs. Sugar) and put them in the Vinegar. Place the jar, well covered, in a shady place for 10 days. At the expiration of this time, filter the mixture. Add the Sugar and place the jar in a pan of hot water and boil gently. This method preserves the finest qualities of the fruit, which are not partially lost by boiling, as in the previous method.

Strawberry Syrup

- Strawberries (enough to produce 5 gallons of juice)
- 80 lbs. Sugar

Mash the Strawberries and ferment the juice with the fruit for 2 days. Dissolve the Sugar into the juice, then boil for 2 minutes. Skim and strain.

Strawberry Syrup (small batch)

- 2 pints filtered Strawberry Juice
- 4 lbs. 4 oz. Powdered Sugar

Select large fruit, either white or red. Having picked them over, mash them in a pan and put in a warm place until fermentation has commenced. Let it stand for about 3 days. All mucilaginous fruits require this, or else they would jelly when bottled. Now filter the juice through a close flannel bag, or blotting paper. Add the Sugar. Place the syrup on the fire, and as it heats, skim it carefully, but don't let it boil. Alternatively, you may mix in a glass vessel or earthenware jar, and place in a pan of water on the fire. This is a very clean way and prevents the sides from crusting and burning. When dissolved to the "little Pearl", take it off. Strain through a cloth. Bottle when cold. Cover with tissue paper dipped in Brandy and tie down with a bladder.

VIOLET SYRUP (SMALL BATCH)

- 1 lb. Violet Flowers
- 1 pints water
- 3.5 lbs. Sugar

Remove the stalks, etc. Boil the water, then pour on the flowers while hot. Cover and let sit for a few hours in a warm place. Pass through a cloth. Add the Sugar, and boil to the "small thread". The violet syrup sold in stores is often adulterated.

WORMWOOD SYRUP (SMALL BATCH)

- 1 oz Wormwood
- 1 lb. Sugar

Make nearly a pint of the infusion of Wormwood. Add the Sugar and clarify it. Boil to a "Pearl". Bottle when cold.

TICKLE MY FANCY

- 2 pints Lemon Juice
- 2 gallons Calf's Foot Jelly
- 8 lbs. stoned Raisins
- 4 lbs. Sugar
- 4 gallons good Cider
- 8 oz ground Cloves
- 8 oz ground Cinnamon
- 16 oz ground Ginger
- 4 oz Lemon Peel, cut
- 4 oz Isinglass
- 2 pints White Wine
- 4 gallons French Brandy 25-Proof (12.5% ABV)

Combine the Lemon Juice, jelly, Raisins, and Sugar. Add enough water to make 2.5 gallons of liquid, then boil. Press and strain. Add the Cider. In a separate container, combine the remaining ingredients and macerate for 24 hours. Combine the two mixtures, then strain, press and filter.

USQUEBAUGH
Tincture #1:

- 20 oz Cinnamon, ground
- 10 oz Cloves, ground
- 10 oz Nutmeg, ground
- 10 oz Ginger, ground
- 10 oz Allspice, ground
- 10 gallons old Irish Whiskey

Tincture #2:

- 2.5oz Spanish Saffron
- 10 oz Isinglass
- 2 pints White Wine

Syrup:

- 8 lbs. Rock Candy
- 4 pints water
- 5 oz Rhubarb Tincture

In two different containers, combine the tincture ingredients and macerate for the same amount of time (8 days). Strain both tinctures. Combine the syrup ingredients until dissolved. Mix all three liquids together. Add the Rhubarb tincture. Filter.

VERDULINO DE TURINO [D]

Distilling	Mixing
1 oz Myrrh	24 lbs. Sugar
4 oz Ceylon Cinnamon	5 gallons water
4 oz Cardamom	
3.5 gallons Neutral Spirits	
4 gallons water	

Combine the distilling ingredients and macerate for 24 hours. Distill from off the water 3.5 gallons of flavored alcohol. Dissolve the Sugar into the mixing water, then add to the flavored alcohol. Color the mixture green, then filter.

VESPETRO [D]

Distilling	Mixing
8 oz Angelica Seed	24 lbs. Sugar
4 oz Ceylon Cinnamon	5 gallons water
1 oz Mace	
40 Lemons, yellow rinds only	
3.5 gallons Neutral Spirits	
4 gallons water	

Combine the distilling ingredients and macerate for 24 hours. Distill from off the water 3.5 gallons of flavored alcohol. Dissolve the Sugar into the mixing water, then add to the flavored alcohol. Filter.

BRANDIED FRUITS

Brandied Apricots • Brandied Angelica • Brandied Cedrats (Citron)
Brandied Cherries • Brandied Grapes • Brandied Melons
Brandied Mirabelles (Plums) • Brandied Oranges • Brandied Peaches
Brandied Pears • Brandied Prunes or Plums • Brandied Quinces

BRANDIED APRICOTS

- Apricots (not yet perfectly ripe)
- Water
- Plain White Syrup (on page 136)
- White Brandy (12.5% ABV)

Take some nice Apricots and rub them slightly with a linen cloth. Prick them with a pin to the stone in different places and lay them in very cold water. At the same time take equal parts of water and syrup, enough to cover the fruit. Boil the syrup mixture in a copper boiler, then throw in the fruit all at once. Use a skimmer to keep the fruit down. When they begin to get soft under pressure of the finger, take them gently out and lay them in a sieve to drip off the syrup. Next, clarify the syrup with the white of an Egg. Arrange the fruit in an earthen dish. Boil the syrup to its regular thickness and throw it boiling hot on the fruit until covered. Let this stand for 24 hours, then take the fruit out of the syrup and put them in glass jars, without squeezing them. Again, clarify the balance of the syrup and mix it with 3 parts of Brandy. Fill up the jars with syrup. Cork and seal.

BRANDIED ANGELICA

- Angelica Stems
- Plain White Syrup (on page 136)
- White Brandy (12.5% ABV)

Take thick, fresh Angelica stems. Cut and free the stems of the leaves. Wipe them clean with a linen cloth. Make pieces of 1 - 1.5 inches in length and put them in fresh water to be washed. Put them in boiling water. Boil up for several times. Let the fire go out. Cover the boiler. Macerate for 1 hour. Take them out with the skimmer and put them in cold water. Take them out again. Press them gently between the linen cloth, so as to get all the water out. Boil them thoroughly in plain syrup and lay them on a sieve to drip off the syrup for 24 hours. Boil the syrup again to its former thickness. Clarify and mix with 2 parts Brandy. Fill up the jars. Cork and seal.

BRANDIED CEDRATS (CITRON)

- Cedrats
- Alum Water
- Plain White Syrup (on page 136)
- White Brandy (12.5% ABV)

Take Cedrats (Citron) with very thin rinds. Cut off with a very sharp knife, the outside part of them, without touching the white. Use some of the rinds to macerate in the Brandy and keep the rest for the use of cordials, etc. Split the white rind in 4 parts, without touching the fruit. Take the rinds off. Put the fruit in Alum Water for a little while (this is done to retain the natural color of the fruit). Boil in plain syrup by a slow fire. When soft enough to take them out with a skimmer, put them in an earthen dish. Cover them with fresh clarified syrup. After 24 hours, take them out of the dish and put them in jars. Mix 2 parts of the infused White Brandy with 1 part of the syrup. Fill up the jars. Cork and seal.

BRANDIED CHERRIES
Fruit Base:

- 6 lbs. Sour Red Cherries with short stems (removed)
- 1 gallon White Brandy (12.5% ABV)
- 4 lbs. Sugar
- 1 pint water

Spice Tincture:

- 1 drachm Cloves, ground
- 4 drachms Coriander Seed, ground
- 4 drachms Star Anise, ground
- 2 drachms Cinnamon, ground
- 36 grains Mace
- 2 pints White Brandy (12.5% ABV)

Start with 2 containers. In the first, combine the Cherries with the gallon of Brandy. In the other container combine the Spice Tincture ingredients. Let both mixtures macerate for 2 weeks. Make a syrup by boiling the Sugar and water. Decant the liquor from the Cherries, add the syrup and skim. Add the Spice Tincture, then filter. Place the Cherries in jars and cover with the mixture. Cork and seal.

BRANDIED GRAPES

- Muscat Grapes
- Plain White Syrup (on page 136)
- White Brandy (12% ABV)

Take some Muscat Grapes. Pick out the soundest and largest fruit. Wash and put them in cold water. Prick each 2 or 3 times with a pin and place them in a sieve to drip off the water. Wipe dry with a linen cloth and arrange them in jars. Cover them with the juice of the smaller fruit, mixed with 2 parts of white quarter-proof Brandy, sweetened with plain syrup to taste, and filtered. Cork and seal.

BRANDIED MELONS

- Musk Melons (or other)
- Lemon Juice
- Plain White Syrup (on page 136)
- White Brandy (12.5% ABV)

Cut the melons in slices. Remove the rinds and inside. Put the melon slices in some water containing a little Lemon Juice and boil them up 2 or 3 times. Take them off the fire and let them stand, covered, for 1 hour. Pour them into another container with cold water containing Lemon Juice and let them cool. Empty the melon slices into a sieve to drip off the water. Boil them gently in plain syrup. When soft, use the skimmer to remove the melon, placing them in an earthen dish and let stand for 24 hours. Clarify the syrup. After 24 hours has passed, bring the syrup to a boil and pour over the melon slices. Remove the melon slices and let the syrup drip off. Arrange the melon slices in jars. Clarify the syrup again. Mix in the Brandy 2:1 with the syrup. Fill the jars with this mixture until the melons are covered. Cork and seal.

BRANDIED MIRABELLES (PLUMS)
Fruit Base:

- 6 lbs. Mirabelle Plums
- 1 gallon White Brandy (12.5% ABV)
- 4 lbs. Sugar
- 1 pint water

Spice Tincture:

- 1 drachm Cloves, ground
- 4 drachms Coriander Seed, ground
- 4 drachms Star Anise, ground
- 2 drachms Cinnamon, ground
- 36 grains Mace
- 2 pints White Brandy (12.5% ABV)

Rub the Plums off with a linen cloth. Prick them on the place of the stem, and on the opposite pole. Place the Plums in a container with the gallon of Brandy. In another container combine the Spice Tincture ingredients. Let both mixtures macerate for 2 weeks. Make a syrup by boiling the Sugar and water. Decant the liquor from the Plums, add the syrup and skim. Add the Spice Tincture, then filter. Place the Plums in jars and cover with the mixture. Cork and seal.

BRANDIED ORANGES

- Oranges (Havana Oranges if possible)
- Plain White Syrup (on page 136)
- White Brandy (12.5% ABV)

Cut off the yellow skins and set aside. Peel off the white pith and throw it away. Prick the fruit with a pin and then lay them in cold water. Pour them at once in boiling water. Boil up twice (about 1 minute). Take off the fire. Let them stand covered for 1 hour. Put them in cold water again, and after the water has dripped off, place them in a heat-safe container. Boil some plain syrup. Cover the oranges with the boiling syrup and let stand for 24 hours. Drip off the syrup and boil it to its regular consistency. Repeat this process twice more. After the 3rd repetition, drip off the syrup and place the oranges in jars. Clarify the syrup with the white of Eggs. Mix it with 2 parts white Quarter-Proof Brandy. Filter. Pour in the jars to cover the oranges. Cork and seal.

BRANDIED PEACHES

- Peaches (not yet perfectly ripe)
- Water
- Plain White Syrup (on page 136)
- White Brandy (12.5% ABV)

Take some nice Peaches and rub them slightly with a linen cloth. Prick them with a pin to the stone in different places and lay them in very cold water. At the same time, take equal parts of water and syrup, enough to cover the fruit. Boil the syrup mixture in a copper boiler, then throw in the fruit all at once. Take them out and lay them on a sieve to drip off the syrup. Next, clarify the syrup with the white of an Egg. Arrange the fruit in an earthen dish. Arrange the fruit in an earthen dish. Boil the syrup to its regular thickness and throw it boiling hot on the fruit until covered. Let this stand for 24 hours then take the fruit out of the syrup and put in glass jars, without squeezing. Again, clarify the balance of the syrup and mix it with 3 parts of Brandy. Fill up the jars with syrup. Cork and seal.

BRANDIED PEARS

- Small Pears (highly fragrant)
- Alum Water
- Boiling Water
- Lemon Juice
- Plain White Syrup (on page 136)
- White Brandy (12.5% ABV)

Bring the syrup to a boil. Skin the Pears, taking care not to damage the stems. Place the skins in a container and pour the boiling syrup over them, and let cool. Cut off the ends of the stems and lay the fruit in iron-free Alum Water for 30 minutes (by this means you retain the natural color of the fruit). Remove the fruit and put in boiling water. As soon as they get soft, take them out and lay them in cold water which contains the juice of a few Lemons. When the water becomes warm, it must be changed with cold. When perfectly cold, arrange them in jars, without breaking the stems. Mix one part of the syrup with 2 parts of Brandy. Mix and filter. Fill the jars. Cork and seal.

BRANDIED PRUNES OR PLUMS

Made precisely the same way as the Peach.

BRANDIED QUINCES

- Quinces
- Alum Water
- Plain White Syrup (on page 136), boiling
- White Brandy (12.5% ABV)

Rub the quinces with a linen cloth and remove the skin very delicately. Macerate the skins in the Brandy. Lay the fruit in cold water. Cut them in 4 parts and take out the hearts. Place in iron-free Alum Water for a few minutes (to retain the natural color of the fruit). Throw them in the boiling syrup until they begin to get soft. Take them out with the skimmer and arrange in an earthen dish. Clarify the syrup and throw it, boiling, over the fruit to cover. After 24 hours standing, drip off the syrup and place the fruit in jars. Clarify the syrup again and add 2 parts Brandy. Filter and fill up the jars. Cork and seal.

APPENDIX

CONTAINING DIFFERENT ARTICLES USUALLY KEPT FOR USE IN LIQUOR STORES

BOTTLE AND BARREL

BOTTLE WAX

- 1 lb. Rosin, white and transparent
- About .5 oz Linseed Oil (varnish), boiled

Melt rosin in a tin dish over a slow fire. Add linseed oil until when a drop is taken out on a cold stone, it loses its brittleness. Stir in coloring agent until all lumps are dissolved.

WAX COLORING AGENTS

- Black = Lamp-Black
- Green = 4 oz Chrome Green
- Yellow = 4 oz Chrome Yellow, finely powdered
- Red = 1 oz Cinnabar (Vermilion)* mixed with 3 oz prepared Chalk
- White = 4 oz Zinc White

NOTE: CINNABAR/VERMILION CONTAINS **TOXIC MERCURY SULFIDE.** USE A MODERN ALTERNATIVE INSTEAD.

WAX PUTTY

- 2 lbs. Spirits of Turpentine
- 4 lbs. Tallow
- 8 lbs. Yellow Wax
- 2 lbs. Solid Turpentine

Used for leaking Casks, Bungs, Corks, etc. The wax and solid turpentine are melted together on a slow fire. Add the tallow. When melted, take it far off from the fire. Then stir in the spirit of turpentine, and let it cool.

BRIMSTONE PAPER

- 1 lb. Brimstone (sulfur)
- 40 - 50 strong ½" x 9" Paper Strips

Melt the sulfur in an iron pan. Draw paper strips through the melted Brimstone and lay aside. When all done, repeat a second and third time to get the thickness of a good-sized pasteboard. Some people take equal parts of ground Coriander Seed, Anise Seed and Fennel Seed, mixed together, which they strew, after the last dipping on the Brimstone paper strips while hot. Pack in 4 oz bundles, with strings on both ends.

Use: Brimstone paper is used for smoking kegs to prevent white wine from getting sour. Take 1 strip for a 60 gallon cask. Light it with a match. Bring it to the bunghole. Put the bung loosely in. Let it burn as long as it can. Let the cask stand untouched for 1 hour. Then take it out, and put in the white wine (red wine would lose its color).

NOTE: CAUTION SHOULD BE TAKEN WHEN MELTING SULFUR. DO NOT PERFORM THIS IF YOU HAVE ASTHMA. SULFUR IS FLAMMABLE AND CAN CREATE A FIRE HAZARD, SO DO YOUR RESEARCH AND LEARN HOW TO DO THIS PROPERLY BEFORE ATTEMPTING IT.

GLOSSARY

DEFINITIONS:

Neutral Spirits

>Spirits distilled from any material at or above 95% ABV (190-proof)

INGREDIENT INFORMATION

The following section contains ingredients listed for use in these two books. I have tried to include some meaningful information, especially for the raw ingredients, which may not be familiar. This information should not be solely relied on in regard to the safety and use of the listed ingredients. I have attempted to identify the correct or most likely type of many plant-based ingredients, but further research may be needed to ensure that the materials used are both correct and safe. There are a few ingredients that I was not able to find in my research.

BASE / RAW

Acajou Nuts (Cashews)

Acetic Acid

>An organic compound also known as ethanoic acid. Acetic Acid is the main component in Vinegar, however the two are not the same. If Vinegar is substituted for food grade Acetic Acid, care should be taken to make sure the acid level is the same. For instance, if 1 teaspoon is equal to approximately 25 drops of liquid, then 1 drop of Acetic Acid can be substituted with 1 teaspoon of 4% acidic Vinegar. This ingredient is deemed generally safe by the FDA. (FDA 21CFR582.1005)

Acetic Ether

>Ethyl Acetate, the most common ester in wine being a product of Acetic Acid and ethyl alcohol produced in fermentation. Among many other uses, Ethyl Acetate aids in bringing a fruity flavor to food products. The FDA states that Ethyl Acetate may

be safely used in food when preparation conditions are met.
(FDA 21CFR173.228)

Agaric

Agaric, also called "gilled mushroom", refers to edible
mushrooms in the Agaricus family. It has been used historically
to strengthen the immune system, fight tumor growth and
perform as an antioxidant.

Alder Flowers

The long slender Male conical flower clusters from Red Alder
tree. High in protein, with a bitter taste.

Allspice

The dried, unripe berry of the Pimento tree.

Almonds

Bitter Almonds

Bitter Almonds contain cyanide and must be cooked or
processed to become safe for consumption. Eating as little as a
half-dozen unprocessed Bitter Almonds can be fatal in humans.
In the United States, Bitter Almonds are not sold in stores.
However, bitter Almond trees can be sold. Although Bitter
Almonds are not sold in stores, the FDA does permit use of
Bitter Almond distillates that are free from prussic acid. (FDA
21CFR182.20)

Sweet Almonds

Sweet Almonds are the nuts found commonly in stores. No
special processing is required for consumption.

Aloe Socotrina

Aloe plant native to Socotra Island in Yemen. Aloe is permitted
by the FDA. *(FDA 21CFR172.510)*

Alum

Alum powder (Potassium aluminum sulfate) is a common
ingredient used in pickling and canning, easily found in grocery
stores.

Ambergris

Ambergris is a waxy, solid substance formed in the digestive
system of Sperm Whales. It is found floating in ocean water and
initially has a strong, unpleasant odor, but over time develops a
sweet, musky fragrance that has been prized for centuries in the

perfume and food industries. Ambergris is extremely rare and expensive, at times being more valuable than gold. Despite Ambergris Tincture being classified as generally recognized as safe by the FDA *(FDA 21CFR182.50)*, it is illegal to possess, trade or use Ambergris in the United States under the Marine Mammal Protection Act of 1972. Some potential substitutes for Ambergris are: Sclareol, Ambroxan or Cetalox.

Ambrette

Ambrette (aka Musk Mallow) is a plant native to the Indian subcontinent. The seeds have a sweet, flowery scent similar to musk. It has been used as an alternative to animal musk. It is traditionally used both medicinally and in vermouths, bitters and other products. The FDA categorizes Ambrette generally recognized as safe. *(FDA 21CFR182.10/20)*

Angelica (Root, Seed, Stem)

Angelica Root (aka Wild Celery or Norwegian Angelica) has been traditionally used to treat digestion, anxiety and circulation issues. Limited lab studies have been done on anti-tumor, antimicrobial properties as well. Angelica is deemed safe for use in food. *(FDA 21CFR582.10)*

Anise Seed

Anise Seed is a common spice, and deemed safe for use in food. *(FDA 21CFR582.10)*

Green Anise Seed

Green Anise Seed (Pimpinella Anisum) is an herbaceous plant native to the Eastern Mediterranean and Southwest Asia regions, used to treat digestive issues.

Star Anise Seed

Star Anise (aka Anisum Chinae) is unrelated to Anise Seed despite the similar name and flavors. It comes from the Chinese tree Illicium Verum, and is known for its antioxidant, antimicrobial and antioxidant properties. Star Anise is deemed safe for use in food. *(FDA 21CFR582.10)*

Apples

Apples are grown worldwide in many varieties. Apples are rich in vitamin C, fiber and antioxidants.

Apple Cider (sweet)

> Apple Cider is made from unsweetened and unfiltered Apples, pressed for their juices.

Apple Juice

> Apple Juice is typically cooked and filtered, then pasteurized.

Apricots

> Apricots are considered native to China, where they have been cultivated for over 4000 years. They are now grown on every continent except Antarctica. Apricots are very nutritious and low in calories. They have many health benefits including promoting eye, skin and gut health.

Apricot Kernels

> An Apricot kernel is a seed found inside the stone of an Apricot fruit. They come in sweet and bitter varieties. Apricot kernels are said to have many culinary and medicinal uses. However, they also contain a chemical called Amygdalin, which the body converts to cyanide. They are generally considered safe for consumption in small amounts.

Basil

> Basil is an aromatic herb in the mint family, native to tropical Asia. The leaves of the Basil plant are used as a culinary herb.

Benzoin

> Benzoin is a sap that comes from the Styrax family of trees. It is used topically for skin ulcers, bed sores and other skin irritations. It is also used in incense, food flavorings and as an expectorant. Benzoin is generally recognized as safe in food. *(FDA 21CFR172.510)*

Bergamot

> Bergamot is a citrus fruit native to Italy. Essential oils and extracts are used to make medicine. It is also used in aromatherapy, and to control high levels of cholesterol or other fats in the blood. Bergamot extracts and distillates are generally recognized as safe in food. *(FDA 21CFR582.20)*

Blessed Thistle

Blessed Thistle is a flowering plant with sharp prickles on the stems and leaves. It was once used to treat Bubonic Plague. It is still used to increase breast Milk production, aid with digestive issues, cough and skin infections. The FDA permits the use of Blessed Thistle in alcoholic beverages only. (FDA 21CFR172.510)

Borage

Borage, also known as starflower, is an herb with bright blue flowers. It is used medicinally and as a salad green.

Brimstone

Brimstone is an archaic term for Sulfur.

Cacao

Cacao is also known as the Cocoa Bean, which is the dried and fermented seed of the Theobroma Cacao tree. Although mostly thought of as the base for chocolate, Cacao has been also used medicinally for centuries.

Cacao Caracas

Venezuelan Cacao

Roasted Cacao

Roasted Cacao loses nutritional value but intensifies the flavor of the Cacao.

Calamus Root

Root from Acorus Calamus, a tall grass-like plant with long scented leaves. Calamus has been used for thousands of years medicinally, but has been prohibited from direct addition or use as human food in the United States since 1968. *(FDA 21CFR189.110)*

Calf's Foot Jelly

Also called Calves' Feet Jelly, is gelatin made from boiling the feet of cows. A sweetened form was popularly used as a dessert in the United States in the 19th century.

Caraway Seed

Caraway seed has been used in European and Asian cuisine for hundreds of years. It is also used in herbal medicine to aid with digestive issues, inflammation and weight maintenance. The

FDA categorizes Caraway generally recognized as safe. (FDA 21CFR182.20)

Cardamom Seeds

Cardamom is a spice from the Ginger family that has been used for centuries in food and medicine. It has many known health benefits. The FDA categorizes Cardamom generally recognized as safe. (FDA 21CFR182.20)

Carob

Carob is also known as Johannesbrot or St. John's Bread. It is often used as a healthier alternative to chocolate and has several health benefits. The FDA categorizes Carob generally recognized as safe. (FDA 21CFR182.20)

Carrot Seed

Carrots are biennial plants. By not harvesting them and letting them grow into their second year, they will produce seeds.

Carrot Flowers

As with Carrot seeds, Carrots will produce flowers in their second year if not harvested.

Cassia

Cassia comes from the bark of a tree in the laurel family and is related to Cinnamon. Commercial ground Cinnamon is actually often Cassia or a mixture of Cassia and real Cinnamon. Cassia does not have the same antioxidant properties as Cinnamon. The FDA categorizes Cassia generally recognized as safe. (FDA 21CFR182.10/20)

Cassia Buds

Dried Cassia buds are used for culinary purposes.

Cassia Flowers

Cassia flowers are yellow and have a mild Cinnamon flavor.

Castoreum

Castoreum is a secretion collected from the castor glands of beavers. It is used as a flavoring agent. It is sometimes used in artificial Vanilla. The FDA allows Castoreum to be listed as "natural flavor" in ingredients. *(FDA 21CFR582.50)*

Catechu

Catechu is the extract of Acacia trees. The FDA categorizes Catechu as safe for use in food. *(FDA 21CFR172.510)*

Cedrats

Cedrats are now referred to as Citron, a thick-skinned citrus fruit from which many other citrus fruits are descendants.

Centaurium

Centaurium, also known as Centaury is an herb often used in medicine and flavoring. The FDA lists Centaurium as a threatened species. *(FDA 50CFR17.12)*

Chamomile

Chamomile is a daisy-like flower often used in herbal Tea. It has been used for thousands of years to calm anxiety and stomach issues. The FDA categorizes Chamomile generally recognized as safe. (FDA 21CFR182.10/20)

German Chamomile Flower

German Chamomile (Matricaria recutita) is a self-seeding annual, used worldwide in medicine.

Cherries

Black Cherries

Black Cherries are common ingredients in many food and drinks. The bark from the tree is also used in medicines, but it should be noted that the bark, leaves and seeds can be poisonous and even fatal if consumed in high doses.

Cherry Kernels

Cherry Kernels can produce cyanide when consumed. I have seen methods such as roasting the kernels to reduce the dangers of cyanide poisoning, but I recommend thorough research before attempting to use these in a recipe.

Sour Red Cherries

Sour Cherries are also sometimes called Tart Cherries. They contain less Sugar then the sweet varieties and are often used in baking.

Cinnamon

Cinnamon is a common spice used for flavoring in food and beverages. The Cinnamon sold in stores is Ceylon (true)

Cinnamon, Cassia, or a mixture of both. The FDA categorizes
Cinnamon generally recognized as safe. (FDA 21CFR182.10/20)

Ceylon Cinnamon

Ceylon Cinnamon (also called "true" Cinnamon) has health
benefits that are not found in Cassia Cinnamon. One way to tell
the two apart is the shape of the stick. Ceylon Cinnamon has a
single roll, where Cassia Cinnamon rolls inward from both edges.

Citric Acid

Citric Acid is a weak acid that occurs normally in citrus fruits. It
is used as a food additive and preservative. Citric Acid can
improve digestions, protect against kidney stones and boost
energy. The FDA categorizes Citric Acid generally recognized as
safe. (FDA 21CFR181B184.1033)

Cloves

Cloves are the flower buds from the Myrtaceae tree family. They
are used as a spice or flavoring, and are rich in antioxidants. The
FDA categorizes Cloves generally recognized as safe. (FDA
21CFR181B184.1257)

Cochineal Powder

Cochineal are small insects that have been used to color food,
clothing and cosmetics for centuries. The FDA lists Cochineal
extract as exempt from certification, but has required
specifications. (FDA 21CFRA73.100)

Cocculus Indicus

Cocculus Indicus, also known as Indian Berry or Fish Berry is
the dried fruit of Cocculus, used in homeopathic medicine for
treating motion sickness. Cocculus Indicus produces picrotoxins,
which can be highly poisonous to humans, producing symptoms
similar to intoxication. Cocculus Indicus was often used in the
19th century by brewers and pub owners to disguise watered-
down alcohol. As a homeopathic medicine, it is not evaluated by
the FDA and appears to be widely available online. I was only
able to find picrotoxins mentioned on the FDA website as an
approved ingredient in Pediculicide (lice treatment). I would not
recommend using this ingredient without further research into
safety of use.

Coffee

Coffee Beans are the seeds from Coffee plants. They are usually roasted and ground to make beverages by the same name.

Java Coffee

Java Coffee is named after the island of Java, where it was first grown. It has a robust, bitter flavor.

Light Brown Coffee

Light Brown Coffee typically comes from Arabica Coffee beans.

Mocha Coffee

Mocha Coffee is a type of Arabica Coffee originating from Yemen.

Conserve of White Roses

A jam (preserves) of rose petals.

Coriander

Coriander is a plant that is commonly used as an herb or a spice. The leaves are commonly called Cilantro, and the seeds are typically called Coriander Seeds. Up to 21% of people have a genetic aversion to Cilantro leaves which, for those affected, will leave an unpleasant soapy taste in the mouth when consuming.

Cream of Tartar

Cream of Tartar, also known as Potassium bitartrate, is a byproduct of wine fermentation. It is high in Potassium, and is often used in baking. Its purposes include anti-caking agent, anti-microbial agent, leavening agent, pH control agent and stabilizer or thickener.

Cubebs

Cubebs are also sometimes called Java Pepper or Tailed Pepper. They are dried unripe fruit from the Cubeb plant, similar in appearance to peppercorns. The FDA lists Cubebs under safe natural flavoring substances. *(FDA 21CFR172.510)*

Cucumber

Cucumbers are a fruit that grow on a creeping vine. They have a mild, slightly sweet flavor and are refreshing to eat.

Cucumber Rind

Cucumber rind may also be called the skin or peel. It has an earthier taste and contains nutrients.

Currants

Currants are berries from the Ribes family of shrubs (gooseberries). They have a sweet and sour flavor, along with acid and pectin. Not to be confused with Zante Currants, which are actually dried, black Corinth Grapes (Raisins).

Black Currants

Black Currants are also known as Cassis. They are high in antioxidants, including vitamin C.

Currant Jelly

Currant Jelly is made from Currants. Because of the high amount of pectin naturally contained in Currants, other gelling agents are not necessary when making jams and jellies.

Red Currants

Red Currants are known as a "superfood" due to their antioxidants.

White Currants

White Currants are a variety of Red Currant. They are different only in color and their flavor, which is sweeter than the Red Currant.

Dates

Dates are the fruit of the Date Palm tree. They are high in fiber, Potassium and antioxidants. Dates are intensely sweet due to high fructose content.

Dill Seed

Dill is an herb in the Celery family with a pungent flavor. Dill seeds are nutritious, providing calcium, iron, magnesium, manganese, phosphorus and Potassium.

d'Ambrettes (drained)

Ambrette may refer to a plant, also called Musk Mallow (see Ambrette on page 329) that is used in vermouth and bitters. However, the recipe in this book calls for "drained" d'Ambrettes, which leads me to believe it may be referring to the other definition I found in dictionaries of being a musky French dessert pear. I have not been able to determine which variety of Pear it may refer to. As this is a distilled recipe, and I am not a distiller, it is unfortunately unlikely that I will ever have the opportunity to try this out to determine which one may be correct.

Egg

Chicken eggs are a common ingredient in many cocktails. They may be called for in whole form, or just the yolk or white portion of the egg. It has been remarked in many of my readings that eggs were much smaller in the 19th century than those that we buy today. Consequently, you should probably use the smallest eggs you can find, or reduce the amount called for in these recipes.

Elderberries

Elderberries come from the Elder tree, which is more like a shrub. There are European and American varieties. Elderberries can be toxic is consumed raw and/or unripe. I have read that either fermenting or cooking the berries will render them safe for consumption, but I encourage readers to do their own research on how to properly process Elderberries. The coloring recipes in this book utilize fermentation for Elderberries, while the drink recipes utilize cooking.

Fennel Seed

Fennel is a flowering plant in the parsely family. Both Fennel and its seeds have a mild Licorice-like flavor and are high in nutrients.

Italian Fennel Seed

Most likely referring to Florence Fennel

Figs

Figs are the teardrop-shaped fruit of the Fig tree (Ficus Carica). They have a mild sweet flavor when raw and are valued for their nutrition and health benefits.

Greengage

Greengage is a type of Plum. When ripe they are described and sweet and succulent. When under ripe, they have the tartness of Rhubarb. Greengages contain a lot of natural pectin, making them good for preserving.

Galangal Root

Galangal Root is native to Southern Asia and is closely related to Ginger and Turmeric. It is a common ingredient in Asian and

Indian cuisine. Galangal Root has been used traditionally in medicine, and modern studies increasingly support this use.

Gentian Root

Gentian Root comes from the herbaceous perennial plant Gentiana Lutea. It is intensely bitter and has a long history of being used in medicine, bitters, liqueurs and brewing. The Gentian plant is widely considered endangered.

Ginger

Ginger is a flowering tropical plant whose root is widely used as a spice, flavoring and in traditional remedies for thousands of years.

Candied Ginger

Candied Ginger is made simply by boiling Ginger and then combining with an equal weight in Sugar along with a little bit of reserved boiling water and heating until the syrup becomes dry and starts to recrystallize.

Ginger Powder

Ginger Powder is easily available in grocery stores. It can also be made by dehydrating Ginger and then processing it in a blender or grinder.

Preserved Ginger

Preserved Ginger may refer to Ginger that has been pickled, fermented, brandied or made into preserves.

Gold Leaf

Gold leaf is used in food for decorative purposes. It is widely available.

Grains of Paradise

Grains of Paradise are a spice native to West Africa, also used medicinally. The plant belongs to the Ginger family, and the seed has a slight spiciness. The FDA categorizes Grains of Paradise generally recognized as safe. (FDA 21CFR182.10)

Green Balm

Green Balm most likely refers to Lemon Balm or one of several other aromatic plants in the Mint family. The FDA categorizes Lemon Balm (Balm) generally recognized as safe. (FDA 21CFR182.10/20)

Green Pine Log

Exactly as it sounds. Almost all pine trees are edible, except for the outer bark. The FDA categorizes Pine generally recognized as safe when used in flavoring. (FDA 21CFR172.510)

Guava Jelly

Guava Jelly is made from the common tropical Guava fruit.

Honey

Honey is a sweet liquid that bees produce from the nectar of flowers. Honey has a myriad of health benefits that have been utilized for thousands of years. If stored properly, Honey has an almost indefinite shelf life.

Hops

Hops are the bitter dried flowers from the Humulus Lupulus plant, and are commonly used in brewing beer. The FDA categorizes Hops generally recognized as safe. (FDA 21CFR182.20)

Indigo Powder

Indigo powder comes from the Indigo plant (Indigofera Tinctoria) and provides rich blues for coloring. The FDA categorizes Indigo as safe in food coloring when standards are met. *(FDA 21CFR74.102 FD&C Blue No. 2)*

Isinglass Gelatin

Isinglass Gelatin is made from the dried bladders of fish. It is used in cooking and also as a fining agent. The FDA approves Isinglass in the clarification of wine. *(FDA 27CFR24.246)*

Ivory-Black

Ivory-Black is made by grinding charred ivory bone. Modern Ivory-Black is almost always Bone Black due to the scarcity of ivory. The FDA categorizes Bone Black use as subject to certification. *(FDA 21CFR74.2053 D&C Black No.3)*

Jasmine Flowers

Jasmine Flowers are a tropical bloom. There are two species of Jasmine: Oleaceae and Loganiaceae. The Loganiaceae varieties are highly toxic. Be certain that you are using the correct type of Jasmine in your recipes. The FDA categorizes Jasmine generally recognized as safe. (FDA 21CFR182.20)

Juniper Berries

> Juniper Berries are not actually berries, but cones. Their spherical shape and purple coloring make them look like berries. They are used in cooking and distilling alcohol. The FDA categorizes Juniper Berries generally recognized as safe. (FDA 21CFR182.20)

Lavender Flowers

> All parts of Lavender are edible. English Lavender is a favorite for culinary purposes. The FDA categorizes Lavender generally recognized as safe. (FDA 21CFR182.10/20)

Lemon

> Lemons are one of the most popular and versatile citrus fruits. They are high in vitamin C and the juice, oil, peel and rind are used extensively in both culinary and non-culinary uses.

Lemon, Candied

> Candied Lemon is easily made by cooking Lemon with Sugar and water.

Lemon Balm

> Lemon Balm is an herbaceous plant in the Mint family. The leaves have a mild Lemon-like scent. It is said to help with stress, relaxation and mood. The FDA categorizes Lemon Balm (Balm) generally recognized as safe. (FDA 21CFR182.10/20)

Licorice Root

> Licorice Root comes from the Licorice plant (Glycyrrhiza Glabra), a member of the legume family. It has been used medically for thousands of years, and is often used as a sweetener, being 50 times sweeter than Sugar. The FDA categorizes Licorice generally recognized as safe, with quantity limitations. (FDA 21CFR184.1408)

Lime

> Limes are small green members of the citrus family. Like many other citrus, Limes are high in antioxidants and Vitamin C, and have many health benefits. There are several different types of Lime citrus, but the most common found in the United States is the Persian Lime.

Linden Flowers

Linden Trees (also known as Tilia, Basswood or Whitewood) are large trees in the Hibiscus or Mallow family. They have fragrant, nectar-producing flowers. The FDA categorizes Linden Flower generally recognized as safe *(FDA 21CFR182.20)*. Note that the FDA categorizes Linden Leaves as approved in alcoholic beverages only. *(FDA 21CFR172.510)*

Mace

Mace is a spice made from the dried lacy outer covering of the Nutmeg fruit. The FDA categorizes Mace generally recognized as safe. (FDA 21CFR182.10)

Maidenhair Fern

Maidenhair Fern (Adiantum Capillus-Veneris), also known as Capillaire Fern, is a fern plant native to temperate and tropical regions. It is used as a flavoring and sometimes as a medicine. The FDA approves Maidenhair Fern for use in alcoholic beverages only. *(FDA 21CFR172.510)*

Malt

Malt is grain that has been partially germinated and then stopped. Barley is the most commonly malted grain. Malted grain is used in making beer, whiskey and as a flavoring in foods. The FDA permits Malt enzymes to be used in foods with no limitations other than good manufacturing practices. *(FDA 21CFR184.1443a)* There are labeling requirements for Malt beverages. *(FDA 27CFR7)*

Pale Malt

Light-roasted malt used in brewing and baking.

Yellow Malt

Medium-roasted malt with a richer taste.

Brown Malt

Dark-roasted malt for a deeper flavor.

Mint

Mint is a series of several herbaceous plants in the Lamiaceae family. It has been used for thousands of years in medicine, cooking, and scents.

Mirabolanti

> Mirabolanti may refer to Cherry Plums, but I have not been able to find a definitive source to confirm this ingredient.

Moldavique Seed

> Moldavique Seed probably refers to Moldavian Dragonhead, and herbaceous plant in the Mint family. More confirmation is needed.

Myrrh

> Myrrh is a resin extracted from trees in the Commiphora genus of trees. Myrrh has been used for centuries in food, medicine and for its scent. The FDA categorizes Myrrh generally recognized as safe in flavorings. *(FDA 21CFR172.510)*

Nutmeg

> Nutmeg is the nut gathered from the fruit of Nutmeg trees. It is one of the oldest cultivated spices. The FDA categorizes Nutmeg generally recognized as safe. *(FDA 21CFR182.10)*

Oak Bark

> Oak Bark usually comes from the inner bark of White Oak trees, native to North America. It has been used topically and orally for centuries. The FDA permits Oak to be used in alcoholic beverages only. *(FDA 21CFR172.510)*

Orange

> Orange Citrus contains several varieties. When called for in recipes, sweet Orange varieties can be assumed unless Bitter Orange is specified.

Bitter Orange

> Bitter Orange is also known as Seville Orange. At the time of this writing, some of the compounds naturally found in Bitter Orange are banned by the NCAA.

Curacao Orange

> Curacao (Curaçao) is also known as Lahara, a Bitter Orange native to the island of Curaçao.

Orange Flowers

> Orange Flowers (blossoms) are the fragrant flower from the Orange tree. It is often used in fragrance and cuisine. The FDA categorizes Orange Flowers generally recognized as safe. *(FDA 21CFR182.20)*

Orange Apples

Orange Apples were common in the 1800's but were considered extinct for some time. In recent years, Orange Apples are believed to have been rediscovered in Colorado and are being cultivated again.

Orris Root

Orris Root also has the common name of Queen Elizabeth Root. It is used in medicine, potpourri, perfumes and Gin. The FDA categorizes Orris Root generally recognized as safe in flavorings. *(FDA 21CFR172.510)*

Peaches

The Peach is thought to have originated in China, but is grown throughout the warmer, temperate climates of both the Northern and Southern hemispheres. This popular fruit has been cultivated for thousands of years.

Peach Kernels

Peach Kernels, or Noyaux, are the Almond-like seeds inside Peach pits. Many food products that you might think are made from Almonds are actually flavored by Peach kernels. Like Bitter Almonds and other stone fruits, Peach kernels contain a compound that can create cyanide, which is poisonous. If processed and used properly, however, Peach kernels can safely be used in food products.

Pearl Barley

Pearl Barley is the most common type of Barley used for human consumption. It is Barley that has had its outer fibrous layer removed, along with some or all of the bran.

Peruvian Bark

The bark of the Cinchona tree. This is the source of Quinine and has a bitter taste. Commonly used in medicinal tonics and bitters.

Peruvian Balsam

Peruvian Balsam is an oily sap derived from scorching the bark of the Myroxylon Balsamum tree. It has a sweet, lasting scent similar to Vanilla. Peruvian Balsam is an allergen, but despite this fact it is used in food and cosmetics. The FDA categorizes Peruvian Balsam generally recognized as safe. *(FDA 21CFR182.20)*

Pimento

Pimento, also known as Pimiento or Cherry Peppers are a sweet pepper with very little heat. Pimento peppers should not be confused with Allspice, which is also called Pimento. They are not related.

Pimpinella Root

Pimpinella is an herb. The root is used in medicine and for flavoring liquors.

Pineapple

Pineapple is an edible tropical fruit indigenous to South America. Pineapples are nutritious and widely used in food and beverages.

Pinks

Pinks is almost certainly referring to Clove Pinks (Dianthus caryophyllus), a type of Carnation which are prized for their spicy, clove-like aroma and often used to infuse spirits.

Polypody

Polypody (Polypodium Vulgare) is a fern. The root is very sweet with lots of tannins, and is used sometimes as an adulterant of Licorice.

Poppies

Wild Poppies (California Poppies) are said to be edible. However, I have also read that all Poppies are toxic. Poppy seeds are edible and used often in cooking. Poppies are called for in only one recipe in this book. Careful research should be performed before using Poppy flowers in a recipe.

Potash

Potash is various mined and manufactured salts that contain Potassium in water soluble form. The FDA regulates Potash sourced from brine lakes. *(FDA 40CFR436.140)*

Potassium Bicarbonate

Potassium Bicarbonate (KO, 2(CO2,)+HO) is an alkaline mineral that can be used to improve the flavor in wine by reducing the acidity. The FDA categorizes Potassium Bicarbonate generally recognized as safe. *(FDA 21CFR184.1613)*

Potassium Carbonate

Potassium Carbonate is a widely used ingredient in the food industry. It comes in the form of a white powder that is soluble in water, but insoluble in ethanol. Other names include Tartar Salt, Pearl Ash, Potash, Potash Carbonate and Wormwood Salt. Among many uses, it can be used to soften water, lower the acidity in wine and other alcoholic beverages and to flavor drinks. The FDA categorizes Potassium Carbonate generally recognized as safe. *(FDA 21CFR184.1619)*

Prince Pine

Prince Pine is an evergreen plant in the wintergreen family (Chimaphila Umbellata). It has been used in traditional herbal medicine. The FDA categorizes Prince Pine generally recognized as safe. *(FDA 21CFR182.20)*

Prunes

Prunes are dried Plums. They are high in fiber.

Prune Kernels

Prune Kernels, like all the other stone fruits mentioned in this book, have a compound that can convert to cyanide which is toxic. With proper preparation and usage, stone fruit kernels can be used in recipes. Please do careful research before using.

Quassia Wood

Quassia is a plant. The wood is used in medicine and as a bitter flavoring. The FDA categorizes Quassia generally recognized as safe in flavorings. *(FDA 21CFR172.510)*

Quince

Quince fruit is a hard bright yellow fruit similar in shape to a Pear. The fruit is nutritious and tart. The blossoms are also used in culinary applications.

Raisins

Raisins are dried Grapes. They come in several varieties, seeded and seedless. Sun-dried Raisins are also called Bloom Raisins.

Raspberries

>   Raspberries are the edible fruit from the Raspberry plant in the rose family. The berries are both sweet and tart. They come in many varieties, but red Raspberries are the most common.

Ravenzara Nuts

>   I was unable to determine what Ravenzara Nuts are. The term Ravenzara or Ravintsara refers to essential oils from Cinnamomum Camphora trees in Madagascar. Allspice can be used as an alternative ingredient.

Red Saunders Wood

>   Red Saunders Wood, also known as Red Sandalwood, has been used in traditional medicines. The FDA categorizes Red Saunders Wood generally recognized as safe in alcoholic beverages only. *(FDA 21CFR172.510)*

Red-Pink Flowers

>   See Pinks. Clove Pinks naturally come in various shades of color. Red-Pinks is likely to be referring specifically to red-blooming Clove Pinks.

Reseda Flowers

>   Reseda is a fragrant, herbaceous plant. I could not find a reliable source on whether the flowers are safe for use in distilled products.

Rock Candy

>   Rock Candy is made by letting Sugar crystalize on a suitable surface from an extra heavy syrup (3:1 Sugar to water) for about a week.

Rosemary Flowers

>   Rosemary is a fragrant herb used widely in cooking. The plant produces blue flowers that are said to be more intense in flavor than the leaves.

Rue

>   Rue (or Ruta) is also known as Herb of Grace. It is a bitter aromatic herb that has been used historically in medicinal, culinary and spiritual applications. The FDA categorizes Rue generally recognized as safe (FDA 21CFR184.1698)

Saffron

Saffron is a spice that comes from the flowers of the Saffron crocus plant. It is one of the world's most expensive spices. Saffron has uses in both medicine and food.

American Saffron

I am unsure what the original author was referring to with American Saffron. I have read one reference that says American Saffron is actually Safflower.

Seltzer Water

Seltzer Water is carbonated water. The name comes from the German town of Niederselters, where natural carbonated water was bottled and sold worldwide in the 18th century. In the 1860's there were over 100 plants manufacturing soft drink water in the United states.

German Seltzer Water

German Seltzer Water refers to naturally carbonated water imported from Germany.

Sloe Berries

Sloe Berries, also called Blackthorn, are small dark berries full of nutrients and antioxidants. They are bitter when eaten raw.

Smallage

Smallage is the strongly scented wild version of Celery.

Snakeroot

Canadian Snakeroot (Asarum canadense), also known as Wild Ginger, has a history of being used as a poultice to treat wounds. Medical studies have identified two antibiotic compounds in the plant, confirming their validity in historical use.
Virginia Snakeroot (Aristolochia serpentaria) is native to the Eastern United States. While Virginia Snakeroot has been used in medicine, it is also known to be toxic. It can permanently damage kidneys and is carcinogenic. The FDA categorizes both of these types of Snakeroot as safe to use in flavorings, but limits Virginia Snakeroot to use in alcoholic beverages only. *(FDA 21CFR172.510)*

Sodium Carbonate

Sodium Carbonate, also known as DiSodium Carbonate or Soda Ash is white odorless water-soluble salts used as a food additive. The FDA categorizes Sodium Carbonate generally recognized as safe. *(FDA 21CFR184.1742)*

Sodium Bicarbonate

Sodium Bicarbonate is widely known as Baking Soda. It has many uses in cooking, cleaning, disinfecting, agriculture and medical purposes. The FDA categorizes Sodium Bicarbonate generally recognized as safe. *(FDA 21CFR184.1736)*

Spearmint

A type of Mint. See Mint on page 341

Strawberry

Strawberries are a member of the rose family. The are widely cultivated worldwide for their fruit.

Styrax Calamitus

Styrax Calamitus (Liquidambar Orientalis) is also known as Storax Balsam, Black Storax or Oriental Sweet Gum. It has been used since ancient times in Mesopotamia and Egypt. The FDA categorizes Styrax generally recognized as safe. *(FDA 21CFR172.510)*

Sugar

Sugar, or Sucrose, is equal parts glucose and fructose. It is usually made from sugarcane or Sugar Beets.

Sugar, Brown

Refined Brown Sugar is White Sugar that has had Molasses added back into it. Unrefined Brown Sugar is Sugar that has been allowed to retain some Molasses when processed.

Sugar, Double Refined

Double Refined Sugar is Sugar that has gone through the refining process twice to remove more molasses and create smaller crystals. Today's table Sugar is typically Double Refined Sugar. Single refined Sugar would be closer to "raw" or Turbinado Sugar found in stores.

Sugar, Loaf

> Loaf Sugar is conical with a round top. This was how Sugar was typically sold until the late 1800's. Sugar Nips would be used to break off pieces of the Sugar.

Sugar, Lump

> Lump Sugar was invented in the mid 1800's. However, it was not popularized until around 1870. Lump Sugar in this book was probably Sugar loaf that was cut by hand into manageable pieces. A Sugar lump today is about 1 teaspoon of Sugar compressed into a cube.

Sugar, Powdered

> Powdered Sugar, also called Confectioner's Sugar, is regular Sugar that has been ground into a fine powdered state.

Sugar, White

> White Sugar is Sugar that has been refined and filtered to remove the Molasses content and produce smaller crystals.

Sulphuric Acid

> Sulphuric (Sulfuric) Acid is a very strong acid used in the manufacture of fertilizers, pigments, dyes, drugs, and other uses. The FDA categorizes Sulfuric Acid as safe to use in foods within specified limits of good manufacturing practice. *(FDA 21CFR184.1095)*

Tansy

> Tansy is an herbaceous flowering plant in the aster family. The FDA allows Tansy (Thujone free) in alcoholic beverages only. *(FDA 21CFR172.510)*

Tartaric Acid

> See Cream of Tartar on page 335

Tea

> Tea is a beverage made from steeping young leaves and leaf buds from Tea plants (Camellia Sinensis) in boiled water. Tea can also be cold brewed by infusing the Tea for a longer time in cold water. Oolong, yellow, white, green and Black Tea all come from Camellia Sinensis plants.

Gunpowder Tea

> Gunpowder Tea is Tea leaves that have been rolled into small round pellets. Most often, Gunpowder Tea is made from Green or Oolong Tea.

Hyson Tea

> Hyson Tea, sometimes called Lucky Dragon Tea, is a Chinese Green Tea from the Anhui province. It is picked early in the season and is rolled into a long twisted appearance that unfurls when brewed.

Souchong Tea

> Souchong Tea is an oxidized Black Tea that is smoke dried over a fire.

Thyme

> Thyme is an aromatic herb belonging to the Mint family. It is widely used in cooking worldwide. It also has medicinal properties.

Toasted Cracker

> Toasted Crackers can be found in many varieties in stores, or can be homemade.

Trefoil

> Trefoil, sometimes called Bird's Foot Trefoil, is a small plant in the pea family with yellow flowers and clover-like leaves. Trefoil does have toxins, but it is generally considered non-poisonous to humans as the level of toxins is low.

Truffles

> Truffles are a subterranean mushroom prized for their flavor and aroma. They are considered a delicacy and are expensive.

Turkish Rhubarb

> Turkish Rhubarb is an herb whose root has been used medicinally for thousands of years. The stalks of Rhubarb are tart and used in food, but the leaves are considered toxic. The FDA categorizes Turkish Rhubarb generally recognized as safe in conjunction with flavoring. *(FDA 21CFR172.510)*

Turmeric

> Turmeric is a spice that comes from the Turmeric plant. It has anti-inflammatory properties and antioxidants. Turmeric is also used as a coloring agent. The FDA categorizes Turmeric

generally recognized as safe, but does not allow it to be used in salad dressing or standardized mayonnaise. *(FDA 21CFR182.20)*

Turpentine

Turpentine is a volatile oil distilled from the resin of Pine Trees. When used properly, the FDA categorizes Turpentine generally recognized as safe in conjunction with flavoring. (FDA 21CFR172.510)

Valerian Root

Valerian is a flowering plant native to Europe and Asia. The root has a long history of medicinal use. The FDA categorizes Valerian Root generally recognized as safe in conjunction with flavoring. *(FDA 21CFR172.510)*

Vanilla Bean

Vanilla Bean is a spice obtained from the pod of the orchid genus Vanilla, which grows in tropical climates. Vanilla extract and other products made from Vanilla Beans are popular flavoring agents.

Vanilla Powder

Vanilla Powder has a more intense flavoring than Vanilla extract. It is made from finely ground dried Vanilla pods.

Venetian Theriac

Theriac is an ancient concoction which was originally used for curing bites from snakes, mad dogs and wild beasts. It later became known as a "cure-all" for all known poisons. The most famous Theriac from the Middle Ages until it fell out of use in the late 1800s was Venetian Theriac, or Venice Treacle. Theriac is no longer produced, and trying to recreate it or the recipes that call for it is, in my opinion, impractical at best.

Verbena

Verbena, also known as Vervain is an herb native to Europe and Asia. It is used worldwide as an herbal remedy. The FDA categorizes Verbena generally recognized as safe in alcoholic beverages only. *(FDA 21CFR172.510)*

Vinegar

Vinegar can be made from any liquid that can be fermented and produces Acetic Acid. The result is a sour tasting liquid with a flavor profile that depends on the source material.

Walnuts, Unripe

Walnuts are a tree nut from the Walnut tree. The FDA categorizes green Walnuts generally recognized as safe in conjunction with flavoring. *(FDA 21CFR172.510)*

White Pepper

White Pepper comes from the same berry as Black Pepper. Fully ripe berries are fermented, and their skins are removed in the process of producing White Pepper. The FDA categorizes White Pepper generally recognized as safe. *(FDA 21CFR182.10/20)*

Wine Must

Wine Must is freshly pressed juice that contains the skin, seeds and stem of the fruit.

Wormwood

Wormwood is an herb with a bitter aromatic taste, used in making Absinthe and Vermouth. In its natural form, Wormwood contains Thujone, which is a toxin. The FDA permits Wormwood to be used as long as the finished product is free of Thujone. *(FDA 21CFR172.510)*

Pontic Wormwood

Pontic Wormwood, also known as Roman Wormwood (Artimisia Pontica) is smaller in stature than other types of Wormwood.

Yeast

Yeast is a microscopic fungus that is capable of converting Sugar into alcohol and carbon dioxide.

Brewers' Yeast

Brewers' Yeast is a type of Yeast used in the production of beer and Bread.

Zedoary Root

Zedoary is a plant in the Ginger family. It is used as a condiment and also to produce flavorings and bitters. The FDA categorizes Zedoary Root generally recognized as safe. *(FDA 21CFR182.20)*

SYRUPS, OILS AND EXTRACTS

Bitters

Bogart's Bitters

Bogart's Bitters is believed to be a misspelling of Boker's Bitters. The exact recipe for this particular bitters is unknown, but the Bitter Truth company was able to acquire an intact bottle that was produced around 1900. They believe they have reverse engineered as close as we're ever likely to get to the original bitters.

Oil of Portugal

Oil of Portugal is an old term referring to Bitter Orange Oil extracted from the peel of Seville Oranges.

SPIRITS

Hock Wine

German White Wine

Hockheimer Wine

German White Wine, specifically from Hochheim.

INDEX BY RECIPE

C

F

G

H

M

N

O

U

V

W

Y

INDEX BY INGREDIENT

D

M

N

O

P

Q

R

Y

Z

www.ingramcontent.com/pod-product-compliance
Lightning Source LLC
Chambersburg PA
CBHW060052150626

46556CB00017BA/21